Tim Hilton has bee...
pendent on Sunday ...
Raphaelitism and Pi...
described as 'one o...
(Geoffrey Wheatcroft, *Daily Mail*). He has been a dedicated cyclist for over forty years.

For automatic updates on Tim Hilton visit
harperperennial.co.uk and register for AuthorTracker.

'An exhilarating work . . . just the book for anyone who, shooting past a traffic jam on the way to work, imagines himself wearing the winner's yellow jersey at the head of the Tour de France pack'   *Independent*

'Remarkably infectious and richly atmospheric; so much so that the effect is like being hoisted up on to his handlebars and swept along for the ride. His enthusiasm drives everything forward at an exhilarating lick'   *Sunday Telegraph*

'A hugely engaging history of the sport'
SIMON O'HAGAN, Books of the Year, *Independent on Sunday*

'A charmingly eccentric account of his love of cycling, mixed in with a history of the sport'
JOHN PRESTON, Books of the Year, *Sunday Telegraph*

'This strange, funny and moving memoir is irresistible. A quirky, oblique elegy'   *Financial Times*

'A deeply affectionate mental scrapbook . . . Hilton has the skill as a writer to make the subject of cycling fresh and compelling again. Fascinating . . . Exuberant'
MATT SEATON, *Guardian*

'Hilton is a brilliantly quirky, inventive writer . . . A wonderful testament to a life in the saddle'   *Daily Telegraph*

ONE MORE KILOMETRE AND WE'RE IN THE SHOWERS

Memoirs of a Cyclist

TIM HILTON

HARPER PERENNIAL
London, New York, Toronto and Sydney

Harper Perennial
An imprint of HarperCollins*Publishers*
77–85 Fulham Palace Road,
Hammersmith
London W6 8JB

www.harperperennial.co.uk

This edition published by Harper Perennial 2005

1

First published by HarperCollins*Publishers* 2004

Copyright © Tim Hilton 2004

Tim Hilton asserts the moral right to
be identified as the author of this work

A catalogue record for this book is
available from the British Library

ISBN 0 00 653228 4

Set in PostScript Linotype Galliard with
Erbar Light Condensed display by
Rowland Phototypesetting Ltd,
Bury St Edmunds, Suffolk

Printed and bound in Great Britain by
Clays Ltd, St Ives plc

For Daniel

INTRODUCTION

This is a book about cycling and my enthusiasm for cycle sport. Its title was provided, in five seconds, by my son Daniel Hilton – a super invention by a boy who was then in his twelfth year of life. I had complained that cycling books often have conventional titles, such as Reg Harris's *Two Wheels to the Top* (1976), Russell Mockridge's *My World on Wheels* (1960) or Eileen Sheridan's enchanting *Wonder Wheels* (1956). I enjoy these books. They remind me of the days when I grew up and first became a cyclist. That was some time ago. I have been cycling for half a century, so feel ready to contribute to the literature on 'wheelfolk', as we used to call ourselves. Like the poet he subsequently became, Daniel could not say how he devised his name for my book. 'It just arrived in my mind.' Was it by any chance a metaphor, words spoken by defeated riders at the end of a long, hot race, just as elderly people might think of death? 'No, Dad.'

Ours is a father-to-son sport and parents who are cyclists love to tell stories of the road to their children. I include some personal comment and passages of autobiography, and why not? Other people can describe the sport in a more measured way. I am not a sports historian, just a veteran club cyclist with a typewriter. None the less I have academic interests, of an undisciplined nature. My bound books on cycling are on shelves, more or less in order. The lists, Road Time Trials Council hand-books, pathetic training diaries, newspaper clippings, start sheets, photographs (some signed 'yours in sport' or *fraternelle-ment*), programmes, poems, Holdsworth's Aids, gear tables, plus lovely maps of the high Pyrenees in the mid-1950s, are in cardboard boxes which I keep in the attic space above the library. I might hammer a bat box to the side of the building.

It is a curious fact that maps lose their beauty when framed and hung on the wall. They are beautiful because they want to be books rather than pictures. I wish that magazines could be regenerated as books. Other boxes and black bags, also roughly piled in the attic at the bottom of the garden, hold thousands of old cycling magazines, mostly English, many French, some Italian. All too few are the journals in Flemish: I must get some more next spring and work at the language. Modern-day cyclists ought to be linguists. Basque magazines would be interesting, though I do find the tongue daunting and am more at home in Belgium than *en el Pais Vasco*.

American cycling magazines mean little to me. I want old Flemish mags because – like so many racing cyclists of my generation – I feel increasing love for cycle racing in Flanders and wish that, when young, I had taken the boat to Ostend as often as to Calais. *Wielersport* is so old-fashioned and full of local patriotism. Like Flemish art, it is provincial in an admirable way. I mean *old* Flemish art – a preference which indicates my antique view of the world. But the Ronde van Flaanderen, the Het Volk and similar events (let us include Paris–Roubaix, though that race traverses French soil) are marvellously and essentially traditional. If they were to change with the times, all would be lost.

Paris–Roubaix is criticised by some competitors, led by no less a man than Bernard Hinault, as absurd and having no place in the contemporary world. Hinault (the winner of the 79th edition, in 1981) speaks with feeling about its 'nonsense'. My view is that of the thousands of fans who do not have to ride over those hideous roads to the north-east of Le Cateau-Cambrésis. We attend the Roubaix epic and the Ronde van Flaanderen because these races – the Classics, the 'monuments' of cycling – take us back to grimy but glorious years in the past.

Is the Tour de France a 'monument'? Unquestionably,

because of its long and magnificent history. It is always an epic. Yet I join the whispers of discontent. The managers of the Tour always seem to be looking for extra revenues, new territories to conquer, a more contemporary style. I believe that the greatest years of the Tour came after the 1939–45 war, and before the *mondialisation* that was an objective in the mid-1980s. Younger people will no doubt have a different perspective. After all, the Tour is now more than 100 years old. Many lovers of *la grande boucle* prefer the race as it was in the 1920s and 1930s. To me, that's prehistory. I am a war baby, will be a war baby until death and associate cycle sport with the new European life after 1945.

My view of the Tour de France was formed in the 1950s. I can just glimpse that it was a period when, for the peoples of southern Europe, cycle racing provided a vague metaphor for the human condition. Those times have gone, but have left a legacy in the quasi-religious admiration of Fausto Coppi. We sense rather than define the end of European folk religion. But it is certain that the fortunes of dozens of riders tell us about the changes from peasant subsistence to life under industrialisation. Cycle sport also touches many other concerns of the twentieth century. First and maybe foremost, the freedom to go where one wills. Then, the development of technology; the attractions of positive leisure; commerce and advertising; the despoliation of the countryside; and the values of sport and popular culture.

* * *

In Paris in my teenage years I saw Fausto Coppi in action – and took a photograph of him! Not a good one. At the same period I observed the rituals of English club runs and rode every spring to the cyclists' annual gathering at the church at Meriden in Warwickshire. These dissimilar experiences were part of my novitiate, and the present book is concerned with differences between British and continental cycle sport.

A declining number of people know about the Meriden service. I doubt whether there is anyone who is not an old British cyclist who would recognise a Frank Patterson drawing, or salute the long history of the Clarion clubs, or give renewed applause to Ray Booty's 100 or Eileen Sheridan's End-to-End. I've written about such matters because they ought to be placed in a book. Our native cycling has long traditions that will soon be lost. Many cycling bodies are now about a century old. My own allegiances are of more recent times. They are owed to a network of clubs and individuals who came together in the later years of the last war, the British League of Racing Cyclists. Great rebels! Up the League! The BLRC was not merely about racing. It was a social movement. The League was made up of men (they were almost always men) who felt little respect for their elders and wished to have some experience of French and Italian life, if only from afar. They liked the thought of money but expected that their jobs would always be of an ordinary sort. Leaguers had had a strong sense of style and enjoyed glamour almost as much as they relished their disputes. They had no political agenda but would not be told what to do. And they have not gone away.

It is now difficult to trace the history of the British League of Racing Cyclists. The confusion is part of the League's anarchist legacy. Half a century on, its veterans often revisit old battles. Are these twinkling-eyed, grizzled men stirring the embers of memory? No. Their purpose is to pour paraffin into the fireplace. Many of them are still racing, though now in their seventies. That's a part of cycling, a sport in a world of its own. Old wheelers continue in our youthful ways and do so until we drop from the tree. As the motto puts it, 'We're all young on the bike'.

ACKNOWLEDGEMENTS
AND A NOTE ON SOURCES

My first thanks go to hundreds of fellow cyclists who, over the years, on the road or in the cafe, have talked to me about our shared interests. Such conversations are always genial and seldom precise. A favourite topic is the past and present doings of other cyclists, whether they be potterers or champions and whether we know them or not. We also speak of dead comrades. The life of cycling has its own ways of commemoration. There is a specialised magazine devoted to such matters. The quarterly *Fellowship News* (founded in 1965) is the shared property of the members of the Fellowship of Cycling Old-Timers.

There are generally around 1,000 members of the Fellowship. Each year new veterans join, after they have reached the age of 50 years, and others die. Members include former Tour de France riders as well as local clubmen who have scarcely ever raced. The democratic magazine records all opinions. Its illustrations are mostly by Frank Patterson. There are no formal articles in *Fellowship News*, only short or long letters to the general membership. All members write whatever they wish, at any length. We are kept in order by our publisher, Derek Roberts, whom I now thank for his work.

Most of my cycling poems and songs come from *Fellowship News*. Some have been sent to me privately or first appeared in club magazines. John Leeson's 'The Veteran's Song' is distributed in cyclostyled form by Derek Roberts. Many other publications by old wheelmen are hard to find. I lament that I have never seen a copy of *The Clarion Song Book* so am all the more grateful to Denis Pye for his *Fellowship is Life* (Bolton, 1995), which is the centenary history of the Clarion movement.

The most complete records of British cycling are in the files of two magazines that have been published since the end of the nineteenth century. The recreational aspects of cycling life are well covered by contributors to the *CTC Gazette* (now retitled as *Cycle*), which is the official journal of the Cyclists Touring Club. *Cycling* (now retitled as *Cycling Weekly*, but always known to us as 'the *Cycling*' or 'the comic') is – despite everything – our indispensable weekly newssheet. A.C. Armstrong's *From Bouverie Street to Bowling Green Lane* is a sound company history of the Temple Press, the original publishers of *Cycling*, and also describes the birth of the BAR competition.

Most British and continental cycling magazines now have 'retro' sections. Their pages respond to the widespread and sometimes fanatical (but who am I to say?) interest in the history of the sport. Such magazines entice but do not always satisfy historians and librarians. I am keen on *Vélo Légende: le Magazine de l'Epopée Cycliste*, which is published from Marignane, near Marseilles. I find that most of its back numbers are *épuisés*. Similarly desirable, and difficult to find, are the French-language Belgian pamphlets published *hors série* by the magazine *Coups de Pédale* (Neupre, generally n.d.). I am indebted to the Italian correspondent of *Coups de Pédale*, Stefano Fiori, for his statistical analyses of the shared careers of Gino Bartali and Fausto Coppi.

I mention these fugitive publications both to acknowledge them and also to illustrate the problems to be solved by future historians. There ought to be a European cycling archive, perhaps based in Ghent. Its curator would have an enviable job. Here in the English countryside I have relied on weighty books compiled by French and Belgian journalists and statisticians, so now salute Guy Crasset, Hervé Dauchy and Pascal Sergent. Fer Schroeders' *Les Classiques du 20e Siècle* (Eeklo, 1999) is the best account of the great one-day races. Pascal Sergent, who is a native of Roubaix, is the author of the invaluable *A Century of Paris–Roubaix* (Eeklo, 1997). The English translation is by Richard Yates, whose writings on French cycling I have long admired.

There are now many video records of important races. I am grateful to David Bromley of Bromley Television International for supplying me, and many others, with tapes. Richard Allchin and Mick Clark of Sport and Publicity have been helpful. Ray Pascoe (Old Kent CC) was among the first British cyclists to realise how much of our sport could be preserved on film. I thank him for interesting conversations and of course for his filmed accounts of Percy Stallard and of Tom Simpson. Chris Sidwells, who is Simpson's nephew, kindly gave me the manuscript of his biography *Mr Tom* (Norwich, 2000).

Chas Messenger's *Ride and be Damned* (Harpenden, 1998) is an exciting, slightly unbalanced history of the British League of Racing Cyclists. He is also the author of *Cycling Crazy* (1970), an account of early forays by British riders into the world of continental racing. John Turner (Midland C and AC) shared his memories of Wilson's Cycles and the unique atmosphere of Isle of Man week. Another Birmingham friend, the painter John Walker, talked with me about his childhood in Balsall Heath. I have had many discussions about childhood as a communist with the late Fanny Hill, Caryn Nuttall and Alan Simon. We have never known how much to forget. Lynda Fairbairn, my tandem stoker, has taken me on nostalgic visits to the Manor Abbey stadium at Halesowen – once her local track – and has helped me write this book.

The late Richard Cobb, during many a *déjeuner allongé*, told me both about his love for the Roubaix region – which he first knew in the last days of Hitler's war – and about his sympathy with French working-class communism. He had less fellow feeling for communist intellectuals. Like a good Frenchman, he could speculate for hours about the probable, or alleged, characteristics of Tour de France riders. My preferred books about the Tour are by journalists with real personal knowledge of racing cyclists. David Walsh's *Inside the Tour de France* (1994), for instance, is a humane study of riders who suffer more than they triumph.

Walsh has wise and forthright comments about drugs and pseudo-medicines in cycle racing. Paul Kimmage's *A Rough Ride* (1990) speaks frankly about drugs, so is to be applauded. Dope use and detection is the most saddening part of cycle sport. The problem seems ineradicable. A useful though now somewhat dated survey of drug use is in Les Woodland's *Dope* (1980), which looks at cycling among many other sports.

I am grateful to that fine cycling journalist, the late Dennis Donovan. He told me things that he did not commit to print. The late Peter Carter's interest in cycling history has been an inspiration to me. Charlie Woods and Adrian Bell have encouraged my own attempts to explain a love of the racing bicycle. Everyone who lives on the bike has the support of clubmates. I am grateful to John Loker, who began in the Aire Valley Road Club in the early 1950s, to Mario Moscardini – of an immigrant Tuscan family, and who grew up in the hard school of the Glasgow Wheelers – and to Nicky Hamlyn of the Artists CC. Many members of my own club, the Godric CC, have been kind about my writing. I give handshakes to Jim Caplin, Geoff Mayne and John Pugh – John who rode the first of his many 24s in 1956, at the age of 19. Long and active life to us all.

INTRODUCTION TO THE
PAPERBACK EDITION

The paperback edition of this book allows me to thank fellow cyclists whose help I forgot to acknowledge in the previous introduction. First among them is Eric Auty. Years ago he gave me his *'Shake', the Monckton Boys and the Hercules Professionals* (Cheltenham, n.d.), which describes 1930s cycle racing in the East Midlands coalfields. His book also gives an account of riders who, like Shake Earnshaw, were the first to join the 'paid ranks', to use the old journalists' expression. Not that there have ever been large numbers of British professionals. For good or ill, our sport is predominantly amateur. But we all admire the band of lonely cyclists who left their British clubs for an uncertain professional life on the Continent. I should have acknowledged Rupert Guinness's *The Foreign Legion* (Huddersfield, 1993), the classic history of their pioneering adventures.

The first sentence of my own book has turned out to have been an invitation to friends old and new. To my delight, nearly one hundred people have sent me their life stories, photographs, poems, programmes and club magazines. Their letters show that cyclists – of the older generation, for they are the best cyclists – are generous historians. Something about cycling life encourages reminiscence. We all wish to pass on the lore of cycling tradition. Lore is nothing if it is not shared, as my correspondence proves. So, in this second introduction, I give thanks to people who have augmented my brief snatches of history and have, gently, questioned the evidence for various prejudices.

Some memories take us back through many years, happy days and wars. Ethel Brambleby (Aldershot Wheelers), for instance, is the daughter of an Edwardian who discovered cycling in 1902. She began racing in 1934. A little later, Ethel tells me, she made herself a teatime guest at Pear Tree Farm. She must be the last of the few visitors at Frank Patterson's strange home. But was the farm as unusual as I have imagined? There may have been dozens of Englishmen who built such castles around their yeoman dreams. I am not hostile to Patterson's art, which is a genuine part of our national life, and hope not to have upset his devotees.

In *One More Kilometre* ... I did not write enough about women racing cyclists of former years. The records are lacking, though somewhere they must exist. I still have no definite information about the Rosslyn Ladies. Harridans or heroines? Surely the files are with a daughter of the club. I know – this is to counter one of the myths about them – that some of the Ladies had husbands. It's still true that young women cyclists became independent when they ceased to be tandem stokers, especially at the time of Hitler's war. They were, and remain, spirited people. Connie Charlton, *née* Stubbs (Priory Wheelers), has excellent recollections of North London and Hertfordshire cycling. And she writes: 'I must be the only woman to catch Alfie Engers. I was riding up Hornsey Rise when I drew level with a very young lad. He told me his name, said he worked in a bakery and was thinking of joining a cycling club . . .'

Connie Charlton advised him, so was at the birth of a marvellous career. Connie also recalls the especial friendship between the Priory Wheelers and the Coventry Road Club. Every year they had a Warwickshire reunion. Stalwarts of the Coventry RC, as I have mentioned, were Ron and the late Edie Atkins. I thank Ron for the gift of some of his memorabilia and urge readers to look at his wife's end-to-end bike. Its frame is by R. O. Harrison. The machine is now preserved in the Coventry British Transport Museum. Snowy Woodhall (Addiscombe CC, formerly Redhill Clarion CC) recalls, as does Ron Atkins, tyro cyclists who were also in the Young Communist League. He questions my brusque statement that there were no cyclists in the navy. He knew a number of them in the Portsmouth area. Thanks, Snowy. We agree that it's better to be on a bike than in a boat.

Mike Daniell (Stevenage CC) has joined with me in adding to our lists of cyclists who are artists. He could write a fine book on this affecting topic.

I wrote that there was a mystery about Reg Harris's training methods. Now I can add information from Trevor Fenwick.

> One winter (1953) I was his sole training companion for six weeks . . . every morning winter and summer he rode 36 miles. I would call at his house . . . this was the first time I had seen fitted carpets outside a cinema.
>
> We would ride 20 miles at a brisk pace . . . then stop for a coffee at Knutsford . . . after coffee we would do 6 miles flat out bit and bit to Holmes Chapel . . . When I first went out with him he rode 74" fixed.
>
> One day I drew level with his bottom bracket in the final sprint at Holmes Chapel and he asked me what gear I had sprinted in (88"). He did not comment . . . Next day his bike had gears, and after that he always used gears training on the road . . .

This is an extract from a much longer letter. I say again that more cyclists should write books. Trevor Fenwick, who these days goes out with a 'gentleman group' in Wessex, shone in the first four Tours of Britain (1952–5) and competed as a professional in France and Belgium. Other memories of League days have come from Dave Orford (The League International), John Scott (Twickenham CC) and Terry Thornton (Sheffield Phoenix RC), who loves the spirit of the 1950s, so much allied – he and I believe – to social change. Terry, who in the early 1960s ran all the new Sheffield modern jazz clubs, says of his teenage life: 'What a thrill to strut into a tea room to hear the whispers of "It's the League" and no-one would leave until we had left . . .' Today's young people do not realise that some of the battles of the British League of Racing Cyclists were fought (or their lines were drawn) over cakes and teapots in rural cafes. But so it was.

Such Leaguers – who love their reunions and publish an excellent quarterly, *The Veteran Leaguer* – have put me right about details of old events and their riders. I have corrected my slips, silently. My greatest debt is owed to a French scholar, Eric Stables, now in his seventy-fourth year, who was an active cyclist in South Yorkshire in the 1940s. With much courtesy and understanding, he has made a list of my errors. On one matter we disagree. Mr Stables is sure that many of the miners he rode with were coal-face workers. I persist in my view that racing cyclists from the collieries were mainly employed at the pit head, though they would not have had desk jobs. Perhaps there is not much difference between us, and we should both ask for advice from Eric Auty.

T. H., Uggeshall, 2005

I

Bohemian communists:
the author's parents in an Oxford pub.

Everyone has their story of the way they became a cyclist, and this is mine.

I was an only child. My parents were communists. They had joined the Party – the Communist Party of Great Britain, that is, but known to us simply as the Party – when they were Oxford undergraduates in the 1930s. My father had won a splendid scholarship from Manchester Grammar School. He was the son of a weaver, John James Hilton of Middleton, who later became the manager of the local co-operative society. Nowadays a suburb of Manchester, Middleton was in John James's time an independent village with customs and traditions of its own, some of them still rural, others connected to the weaving trade. By 'John James's time' I mean long ago, at the beginning of the twentieth century. My father never knew his father. A motor car had run over him as he was cycling from work to his home.

My father's mother was also a weaver. She was sent to the mill at the age of twelve. I remember her Lancashire accents describing how, at mid-morning, she and other girls were allowed to leave their places at the looms to run down to the nearby fast-flowing river 'to play'. Those little wage-earners were still children when they were made to work. In later life my father, Rodney, was her youngest and favourite child. She wished that he would never leave her.

I refer to my father as 'Rodney' because I was never allowed to call him 'Dad'. This was one of the conventions of the intellectual wing of the Communist Party. Children spoke to, and of, their parents by using their first names. I do not know what anyone hoped to gain from this practice. It certainly did not promote family love and intimacy. Probably the idea was that children should consider themselves as part of a larger family, or something bigger and better than any family could be – the Party.

My parents were mismatched and had grown apart in the years when Rodney was fighting in the north African desert. I remember them mainly as hosts to other Party members. Our Birmingham home was the centre of a quite large community of local Marxists. The local Party branch had a strength of about twenty comrades. Their meetings were held every Thursday evening at our house, 90 Bristol Road, near the corner of Speedwell Road, from 1948 to 1956. My task was to pour beer for the comrades after they had finished their business. At a quite early age I was allowed ('compelled' might be a better word) to take part in the discussions. Little wonder that, ever afterwards, I have done my best not to attend meetings of any kind. I don't even go to the AGM of my own cycling club.

Our Party branch, which was based in the University of Birmingham, had quite a good run. There were eight years of regular meetings and other activities – demonstrations, summer schools, pamphlet distribution, and so on – before the collapse of British communism in 1956. This was the world of my childhood. It made me into a cyclist. Cycling is not a middle-class sport and in the 1950s was certainly not practised by university people. But I wanted the life of the bicycle. I became a cyclist because I was brought up as a communist, which made me classless. I am also devoted to the bike because it represents freedom. And, as I was soon to find, cyclists had a generosity that did not exist among the crazed Stalinists of my early days.

Before I got a bike it was already obvious to me that there was a life of friendship and pleasure beyond the four walls of the Party branch meeting. From my chair near the door (comrades always sat in the same places, week after week) I could gaze through the window and dream while some paper on culture or industrial strategy was being read. *During the past half century capitalism has ceased to be a progressive force; the bourgeoisie has ceased to be a progressive class; and so bourgeois culture, including poetry, is losing its vitality.* Through the window I could see the pear tree and thought of its fruit. *Our contemporary poetry is not the work of the ruling class* – I wonder how long this talk will last *what does big business care about poetry? – but of a small and isolated section of the community,* I wish I had more mates at school *the middle-class intelligentsia* I can see to the very top of that pear tree *spurned by the ruling class* when he shuts up I can go to the kitchen to get the beer *but still hesitating to join hands with the masses of the people* now that the cloud has come over by the Pershore Road the pear-tree leaves look silvery, not green *the proletariat, who alone have the strength* why doesn't my mother play the piano any longer? *to break through the iron ring of monopoly capitalism!*

It was characteristic of these talks that, just when a boy thought that a conclusion had been reached, the comrade coughed, lit another cigarette and started up again, like a car revving up after a breakdown. *And so bourgeois poetry has lost touch with the underlying forces of social change.* I wonder if I could be a poet. *It is no longer the work of a people, or even of a class, but of a coterie.* Hasn't he said that before? *Unless the bourgeois poet can learn to reorientate his art, he will soon have no one to sing to but himself . . .* – And my present-day reader will understand that, as soon as I had a bicycle, I could indeed sing to myself. The bike was my escape from the dullness and conformity, and I would even say the ugliness, of a communist household.

*   *   *

When I was eleven Rodney and Margaret, trying to maintain or revivify their marriage, went to France and Italy without me. I was to stay with Margaret's parents in their big house in Raynes Park, which is at the further side of Wimbledon. (Raynes Park is notable as a catchment area for the Redmon Cycling Club, whose name is an anagram of Morden.) My grandparents were gentle people, old, each of them absorbed in their own thoughts. Early on the morning of my parents' departure I went and hid in a creosoted shed in the garden and then in the Raynes Park church. I thought that Rodney and Margaret would not dream of searching the church, and I was right. And I reckoned that they had to catch their boat train or all would be lost to them. So it was. Off they went without saying goodbye, which is what I wanted.

I received a couple of postcards in the next few days. They must have meant a lot to me, for I kept them and have them still, after forty years and more. This was Margaret: 'Dear Tim, where oh where were you when we wanted to say goodbye this morning? We are on deck on this boat now and it is very cold and blowy. We shall be in Paris at suppertime.' *Bon appétit*, comrades everywhere. The next week my father writes from Italy – Florence actually, now I look at the postmark. 'Dear Tim, we had a very jolly ride in a bus today. In every village the people were having feasts in the open air to celebrate the paper which is the Italian Daily Worker. Lots of Love Rodney.'

I resented these messages, since I liked being in France and thought that I should not have been left in Raynes Park. My grandparents did not know what to do with me. By good fortune, they had a library in their house, a real library with fitted bookshelves. Within this room I dreamt of becoming a writer. Its windows opened on to a large garden. There was a veranda, a workshop, a garage, lawns, a tennis court, the orchard, the kitchen garden and then the chicken runs. One day in that summer of 1951, bored, lonely and not a happy boy, I wandered into the garage. My grandfather had a Bentley but scarcely ever drove it, preferring to potter among his redcurrant bushes. So the garage was not much used. I pushed open the door and saw a bicycle behind the Bentley. And that is how I began.

II

On the ASP at Aunt Tess's Cottage near Hay-on-Wye,
and just off to Birmingham.

Most boys or girls need to be taught how to ride a bicycle. In my case no tuition was needed. I was a natural. Just as some young animals swim as soon as they are thrown into the water, I was immediately balanced, fast and athletic. The machine from the garage was too big and I perched between the saddle and the top tube. None the less I managed. Within half an hour the bike and its rider were on the road, down Grand Drive towards the Kingston by-pass, whose concrete blocks and expansion gaps I recalled in many a later time-trialling effort.

My first days as a cyclist were magical. Never in my short life had I felt anything like the aerial liberation the bicycle granted me. Yet the Raynes Park bike was nothing special. Later on, I had another crucial physical experience. That was when I first rode a light racing machine. Suddenly I was a bird: uncatchable, self-contained, soaring and zooming towards the horizon, free from human worry and therefore happy. Cycling is about physical pleasure and happiness. I know that the bike can also make you weep, especially when you're a teenager and don't understand your body. Pleasure is none the less our goal and daily bread; and at some point in a good ride – as any time triallist will tell you, but will not be able to explain – pleasure and suffering are one and the same thing.

After long pleading with the ruling class of 90 Bristol Road I was finally granted my own bike. It was not to be a new machine. Some puritanical ukase of the communist ethos forbad expenditure on goods that were easily advertised. For years, I'm amazed to recall, my family didn't even have a radio. However, from the cycling point of view I was fortunate that my first bike was patched together. It was built by an old metalworker who produced cheap machines as a hobby. Bikes of his sort were known as ASPs, the initials standing for All Spare Parts. Superficially, my ASP had the look of a racing machine. It had dropped bars, a bottle cage and Benelux gears. In reality the ASP was cumbersome and went dead on the hills. But it taught me to appreciate good equipment. Nowadays one of my spacious garden sheds contains twelve good bicycles, all in use at various times of the year. I have never been a motorist and have never owned a car.

The man who assembled my ASP was a club cyclist. By this term I mean someone who is dedicated to the culture of the bike, as well as being a member of a club. He showed me his own best machine, which was of great beauty and had the *céleste* colour of Bianchi frames from Italy. Perhaps it was indeed a Bianchi? Or had he somehow, in 1951–2, realised that this was the colour of Fausto Coppi's frame? He said that his son, who was then entering an apprenticeship and for a couple of years had been a member of his father's club, would not be allowed such a bicycle until he was much older. Father and son lived alone together, the boy's mother having died, and the son was no doubt taught that cycling is a serious business. I never met this boy and didn't really like his father. I guessed he thought it correct that the experience of bereavement should be a part of growing up.

*   *   *

Cyclists of my generation were usually brought up within local divisions of the Cyclists Touring Club and then joined more specialised clubs when they began to race. This was my experience. I had the good fortune to have a mentor in Albert Burman, a family man who was active in both the Birmingham CTC and the Warwickshire Road Club. Many people who did not know him will recall Albert with affection for the cartoons he contributed to our weekly paper, *Cycling*. A collection of his draw-ings, *Laugh with Burman*, is a treasured possession. Albert and his wife Gwen died long ago. Their daughter, my adored Joan, went away to somewhere in Canada, her lovely, liquid brown eyes a legacy from her father.

In the 1950s Albert Burman was still a useful time triallist, especially at the classic 25-mile distance, but was taking it easy when I, as a boy, became his clubmate. Not too easy. A club run when Albert was captain would have a fast pace. He had also been a pioneer of cyclo-cross and off-road riding. So his routes were always difficult, with forays on unmetalled roads, across fields, along canal banks and through the tracks of the Forest of Arden or Yarningale Common. Albert also insisted that the lunch break should be taken in the garden of some country pub. One of his favourites was to the west of Bewdley, on the hill towards the Wyre Forest. I always sat next to Joan. Her father would settle himself opposite us, take the first sip from his pint of mild and then produce a folded copy of that day's *Reynolds News*, his preferred Sunday reading, for Albert was a co-operator and a trade unionist.

So also were many of the adult cyclists whose company I joined. At that period cycling still had many links, or at least a general friendship, with the labour movement. The ethos – still with us – was of egalitarianism and hands clasped in fraternity. We do not always live up to this ideal, but it is accepted that cyclists always talk to each other, and mostly as equals, whether they are boys or men, the racing members of an elite club or the most leisurely of tourists. Beside this camaraderie there is no political agenda among cyclists, which is one reason why I found them much more agreeable people than communists; and I still believe that the 'fellowship of the road', or whatever similar phrase was used, reflected a great social reality.

Cyclists thought themselves set apart from the rest of the world, as they were and are; but in the 1950s it was gladdening that we were so numerous. There were hundreds of cycling clubs throughout the land and as many as sixty people might join the Sunday club run, especially if the club was in a city. Club runs were often organised so that racing members – whose events had been held much earlier on Sunday mornings – could be joined by their clubmates at the elevenses halt, maybe 20 miles or so from the 'meet', which for us was a point on one of the roads leading south from Birmingham: the Maypole on the Alcester Road, the Robin Hood roundabout on the Stratford Road, the Barley Mow in Solihull, which was on the way to Warwick, or the Northfield Baths on the road that led to the Lickey Hills and Worcester.

Practically everybody raced occasionally, even if they didn't race every week. Cycling as recreation was mingled with cycling as sport. Then as now, people talked about 'going out training' when they were simply leaving the house for a ride. Racing members of a club also took part in social activities that had none of the dash and excitement of competition. There were many camping weekends, map-reading competitions and panto-mimes. 'Rabbit pie suppers' could be good. They were begun in the days of austerity and rationing. Many were the whispers about the poacher-cyclists who provided the rabbits. I thought it strange that fit young men were prepared to attend the lantern-slide lectures that were held not only by sections of the CTC but also by clubs whose first concern was with racing. But cyclists did go to such events; and these are some of the talks they might have heard:

How to use your camera
Blue skies and good companions
The infinite variety of cycling
Their abiding splendour
Where the mountains blush
The quest

Over the Welsh hills with a cycle and a camera
British railways
The Cotswolds
France: its customs and characteristics
Peeps through the microscope
Scotland through the lens in colour
Hill tracks and valleys in central Wales
The hillside figures of Britain
Holidays with cycle and camera

These lectures were free, but sometimes a souvenir programme was offered, its price usually 1s. 6d. The lecturers themselves had some renown within the cycling community and their discourses were heard in more than one place. A large wooden box containing lantern slides would be put on a train and would precede the lecturer, who of course went from one venue to the next by bicycle.

Don't the lectures sound dull? But they served a purpose and supplied a need, or there would not have been so many of them. The reason for their popularity must have been that people simply did not know other parts of their own country and were eager to explore the land on two wheels. This curiosity and desire for travel was not confined to cyclists with little holiday time. Passion for research has led me to the 1950s file of a magazine issued by the Civil Servants' Motoring Association. It would be hard to imagine a more bourgeois society. Yet the CSMA magazine carried touring articles that were very like the cyclists' lectures and journalism – except that the motorists were recommended inns rather than cafes, hotels rather than youth hostels or bed and breakfast places.

Touring articles, often written by the same men who gave the lectures, continued in *Cycling* until the mid-1970s. Reports of the Tour de France alternated with reminiscences of gentle rambles through the Berwyns or the villages of the Isle of Wight. The accompanying photographs were often of a high standard. My lecture titles suggest that 1950s cyclists were often preoccupied with the camera. Articles and advertisements in the *CTC Gazette* describe quite new, even racy, pieces of photographic equipment. The cameras concerned were often quite expensive, adventurous purchases by cyclists who were seldom affluent and on the whole had conservative tastes. I can illustrate this conservatism by describing the cycling seasons.

III

Late 1950s cycling club.
Young Tom Simpson is back row, right.

The cycling year had its own feast days or observances and a racing man's calendar was almost a matter of routine. In the twenty-eight Sundays between March and September many races had an allotted and unchanging slot, whether they were important events – the Bath Road 100, the Anfield 24 Hours, the Solihull Invitation 25 – or less significant local time trials. Massed-start road races did not have these definite dates, firstly because there were so few of them and secondly because road-men did not have a firm and long-established governing body. However, bunched road racing was always celebrated in the 'Isle of Man Week' at the end of every June.

Trackmen also knew when and where they were going to compete. They would go to meetings held at regular intervals in the summer months, generally in the evening. For trackmen who raced on grass there were many 'sports days'. Agricultural sports days were often part of a country show and were held on Saturdays. Urban sports days, organised by a factory, a colliery or a local police force, took place on Wednesday or Thursday afternoons, depending on the early closing day. These after-noons were shared with athletics. The runners often wondered at the feats of men on wheels, so cycling made some converts. It looked so specialised and brawny. Good grassmen were indeed among the sporting mighty and their muscular prowess over slippery, uneven ground also served them well in hill climbs – the peculiar races that end the cycling year.

Hill climbs are organised by cycling clubs in later October and November. In essence, they are time trials from a low to a high point. On the continent there are some extremely taxing mountain time trials, notably on the roads above Nice and on the Puy de Dôme. These are sometimes part of a stage race. They were introduced to the Tour de France in 1939. British hill climbs became popular in the 1920s and have a quite different character. They are festive and look forward to Christmas. But they are also hard. You need legs that are filled with months of racing – though we have known climbs to be won by the agility of delightful, underweight teenagers. They get special applause.

Depending on your part of the country, the climbs are long or short, but never very long. They are either 'technical' or straightforward. Some demand guile, others brute strength. Famous longer hills, like the Horseshoe Pass or Nick O'Pendle, are in the Peak District or North Wales. They are used by Manchester and Merseyside clubs. Birmingham clubs use hills in Mid Wales or the valley of the Teme. Londoners go to the North Downs or the Chilterns. In flat East Anglia clubs use what they can find. Hill climbs in Suffolk, for instance, are sometimes ridden in only forty seconds. Welsh climbs, however, can occupy a competitor for ten minutes.

Not longer, or the drama of the race would be lost. Hill climbers need a clapping audience. The climbs attract much larger crowds than other events against the clock. They are also held later in the morning, so as to race in light but also to attract knowledgeable spectators. The people who devise the hilly courses want to make their races into theatre. They look for a narrow road, preferably a lane with poor surfaces, stretches of *faux-plat* and – exquisite touch – a cattle grid at the hardest corner. If there is a pub near the hill, so much the better.

Some purists believe in hills that can be ridden on a fixed wheel. Others like varying gradients that demand the use of gears. Either way, the spectators are connoisseurs of a ritualistic race. The crowd will be on either side of the lane, all the way to the top, crying 'Up! up! up!' to each panting rider. At the summit are 'catchers' to grasp and hold the cyclists who, totally spent after the extreme effort of the brief climb, fall with their machines. The finishers are warmed in blankets, or sometimes by a brazier. Steam and smoke mingle with the cold air.

Next, beer and mince pies. Racing is over until the following year. Now the 'social season' begins. Miscellaneous entertainments, club runs and other gatherings reach a climax with the club dinner. Like so much else in the cycling world, these dinners have a standard pattern. They are held in late January and early February. On these occasions the club's prizes and trophies will be awarded by an honoured guest, most often a well-known racing cyclist from another club. At the dinner there is a mixture of formality and licence. A three-course meal is served by waiters. Men wear suits, ladies wear gowns. At the end of the dinner there is a series of toasts, to 'The Club', 'The Visitors', 'The Ladies', sometimes 'The Road' and finally 'The Queen'.

After the Loyal Toast – still observed by a surprisingly large number of clubs – cross-toasting is permitted. Anyone can bang on the table, jump to his feet and say, 'I wish to take wine with . . .' and then name some person or group of people with a jesting or semi-private reference. Then another person will say, 'I wish to take wine with . . .'. This can go on for some time, and with hilarious or disappointing results. The custom of cross-toasting is an old one, and perhaps now belongs only to cycling clubs; I know of no other organisations which follow the ritual. Its cycling origins are in the convivial dinners held by clubs in the 1890s and Edwardian times, the golden age of bohemian dining.

Bohemianism never wins the day. The turn of the last century was also the period when respectable working men first dined together with their wives as members of voluntary societies. To this day, cycling club dinners are properly managed. Hotels are preferred to pubs. The tables have a *placement*. The top table is occupied by the club's committee members and local dignitaries, often including a mayor or local councillor and a representative of the county police force (it is politic to be on terms with the police: we need their permission to race on the public highway). So club dinners have a social dimension, expressed in various ways. There is no cross-toasting between those seated at the top table and other diners. It is not done. In this way cycling club etiquette obeys a quite ancient taboo. English has a technical term for drinking with a person of a different class. It is called 'hob-nobbing'.

The new cycling year begins after the club dinners. The 'social season' was too long for many keen racing men, who – after the mid-1950s – took up the new winter sport of cyclo-cross. Some people considered the 'mud pluggers' a little raffish. That was because, in the early days of cyclo-cross, courses were improvised and the racing unregulated. One or two clubs offered short time trials on the mornings of Christmas Day and New Year's Day. The best known of these yuletide events, in which competitors often wear fancy dress, is organised by the Chesterfield Spire Road Club. In February we find 'reliability trials', fast training rides open to all comers. Then come the first time trials of the year, often on restricted gears, and two-up events, the riders competing in two-man teams. Serious competitive riding begins with the North Road Hardriders 25 on the last Sunday in February. This superbly uncomfortable race is on the Hertfordshire lanes north of Potters Bar and is often ridden in snow or on icy roads. That's why tricyclists like it.

The next high point in the cycling calendar was the movable feast of Easter. On Good Friday all trackmen and their fans would be at Herne Hill for the meeting organised by the Southern Counties Cycling Union. This is among the oldest of cycling traditions, for track riders have made their way to Burbage Road, SE24, every Good Friday since 1903. An even more ancient Easter event is the annual rally of the Clarion clubs, generally held in Sheffield and consisting of a 25 championship followed by a great picnic. The Easter weekend offered a full programme of racing everywhere in the country. For some reason it was also regarded as the best time for family touring, though the paschal weather is often cold.

There were regional differences in the repeated festivities of the club cycling year and many local celebrations. I have been told tough stories about the way that Scottish cyclists rode to the Gordon Arms for their Burns Night reunion, passing the night in a large shed-cum-dormitory behind the famed hostelry before the dawn ride back to Glasgow or Edinburgh. There were other reunions and rallies at Cumnock in Ayrshire, Chigwell in Essex, Matlock in Derbyshire, Harrogate in Yorkshire and Mildenhall in Suffolk. These gatherings often take place on the weekend of August bank holiday. The biggest reunion is the York Rally, which occupies a weekend in June and was first held in 1945. Five hundred people were expected. Five thousand turned up. This event marked the beginning of the post-war cycling boom. The York Rally is still held every year, and many are the quarrels about its organisation and purpose.

*   *   *

In the mid-1950s I had begun to learn about such matters, and am still learning. Nobody gave me direct instruction about the culture of British cycling: I picked up my knowledge here and there. It was none the less good knowledge. I realised that it was important to know what cyclists valued. The lore of wheelmen was more interesting than the things that schoolteachers thought important. Difficult teenager that I was, I rejected many of the old ways and wanted change. Yet love for the bike encouraged me to listen to all sorts of tales that, on first hearing, seemed inconsequential or tedious. As, for instance, when dedicated cyclists spoke – with growing enthusiasm as spring turned to summer – of their future expeditions

18

to the Isle of Man, where they would spend the week that includes the year's longest day.

Why go every year to this small island in the middle of the Irish Sea? Here is my short version of the Isle of Man story. It takes us from the grass roots of British leisure riding to the heights of racing cycling; for on Mona we will meet Fausto Coppi, to this day the vital symbol of the sport; Louison Bobet, three times winner of the Tour de France; and Tom Simpson, who in 1967 would ride himself to death on the Ventoux mountain in Provence. One late June day in 1959 all three men were in Douglas, the Isle of Man's unremarkable capital. And so were thousands of other cyclists. Here is an odd corner of our collective history, but an instructive one.

The Isle of Man has always been a cycling island, thanks I suppose to a certain backwardness and a tardy adoption of the motor car. There are 500 miles of lanes for the tourist. At least three clubs have looked after the native wheelmen. Racing was always popular and in former days there was a macadam track in Douglas's Oucham Park. The person who made his native place into an international centre of cycling was a journalist, Curwen Clague. When he wasn't on the bike Clague worked for the *Isle of Man Examiner*. Since he was a competent editor he was on terms with the island's right-wing but eccentric government. Clague also knew the leaders of local industry. There wasn't much money in fishing, nor in agriculture, so that industry was mainly tourism.

In the 1920s and 1930s there had already been contacts between the clubs in Man and their counterparts in Ireland and the British mainland. Merseysiders went to Man for holidays. Manx cyclists put their bikes on the ferries to compete in Cheshire and Lancashire. Curwen Clague saw how these cycling habits could be expanded. His idea was to promote a road race within the series of events that, since 1907, had given the Isle of Man its position in the world of motorcycle sport.

A harmless and maybe profitable venture, said the Tynwald,

the Manx parliament. The island's elders also offered to close the roads to other traffic on the day of the cycle race, which would never have happened on the mainland. Furthermore, massed-start racing was opposed, even forbidden, by the governing bodies of British cycling. Fortunately, the men of the House of Keys had no interest in the policies of the National Cyclists Union or the Road Time Trials Council. They would govern their own island as they wished. So, in 1936, the first of the Manx international road races was held on a course that had already been established by motorcyclists. A 37¾ mile circuit took riders from sea level at Douglas, first to Ramsey and then up a 5-mile climb to a point at 1,384 feet on the mountain of Snaefell. There was a thrilling descent before a return to the finish at Douglas. The winner of the race was a Birmingham man, Charlie Holland of the Midland Cycling and Athletic Club. In later years competitors have ridden this circuit three times, covering 113¾ miles.

*   *   *

From the height of Snaefell on a clear day it is possible to see the mountains of Mourne in County Down, more mountains in Galloway, yet more mountains in the Lake District and the peaks of Snowdonia in Wales. There is a theory that the Isle of Man has a share of four countries and possesses some of the character of each of them. It is hard to define such a mixed character. What data might we use for evidence? The names of the boarding houses that formerly gave a welcome to cyclists must tell us something. For the modern essence of Man is not in its agriculture or religion (Methodist), nor in anything preserved by the National Trust, since nothing at all on Man has attracted that Trust. It is rather in the wealth of small houses, terrace after terrace of them, that were lodgings for holidaymakers.

An abbreviation of my master list of their names goes as follows.

Ballasalla
Rosegarth
The Oban
The Winston
South View
Greg-Malin
Thiseldo
Stoneleigh
Woodside
Mannin
Annandale
Hollyrood (sic)
Ellesmere
Palatine
Wavecrest

A bit of mainland patriotism here, some Scottishness, a more pronounced hint of Ulster than of the Republic of Ireland, one or two remnants of the ancient Celtic tongue of the Manxmen. Palatine is an obscurely boastful name for a boarding house. These places of lodging have masculine-sounding names, with the exception of Thiseldo, which I think must be a contraction of 'this will do'.

Also masculine and gritty are the indigenous family names of Man. Here were born the Caines, Cregeens, Crellins, Kermodes, Kewleys, Killips and Quayles. Once they worked the land and scratched for its sparse mineral deposits. Some went to sea in the herring boats. Then they entered the lodging-house business or were employed in catering, amusement arcades, dance halls and the adventurous network of electric railways.

After the war the pattern changed again. Agriculture and fisheries went into further decline. The native population decreased. Young people were the most likely to leave. The older people of Man were joined by retired couples from the surrounding four countries, who often supplemented their pensions by opening guest houses. Old British club cyclists were among this influx. They had enjoyed their Manx holidays and preferred to live in Douglas than in Liverpool. There is also an Italian community on the island. Most Manx Italians were in Douglas because they were interned there during the war. Then they saw no reason to return to mainland Britain, especially if they were in the catering businesses. Some of the Italians, like the Signorio family of the Mannin guest house, were cycling fans and took block bookings from clubs.

The British interned Italians; and the Germans kept Curwen Clague in a prisoner-of-war camp for the duration of the conflict. Back home and back on the bike, Clague used his demobilisation period to make plans for the future of cycling. The Manx holiday calendar worked by the week rather than by day trips. Clague saw the opportunity for six consecutive days of varied cycling events and realised his vision in the Manx Cycling Festival, which was to grow until the early 1960s. In the 1950s thousands of cyclists regularly packed into the steamers for their holiday in Douglas, Ramsey or Peel. By day they raced or toured. Each night they went to the dance halls or the pubs (which had notably long opening hours). Clague was certain that his festival should occupy the same week of every June. He was right. Under his direction 'Isle of Man Week' became cycling's equivalent of the Lancashire Wakes Week or the Birmingham Industrial Fortnight, when so many factories were closed or operated at half strength.

Clague's programme included time trials, team time trials, the long mountain time trial around the Snaefell circuit, kermesses, Britain's only summertime hill climb, various holiday games and contests ('Miss Bicycle Belle') and of course the international road race. In 1946 it had a French winner, Jean Baldessari, who went on to a professional career and rode the Tour de France in 1950–1. A more notable winner at Douglas would be Ercole Baldini. He won in his last year as an amateur, 1956, and a couple of months later, even before he had signed professional forms, took the hour record on the Vel Vigorelli. In 1958

Baldini was the world professional road champion and also came first in the Giro d'Italia.

By 1959 there were continental professionals at the Isle of Man Week, with entries from France, Italy and Spain. The pros included Jacques Anquetil, Federico Bahamontes, Louison Bobet, Fausto Coppi, André Darrigade and Raphael Geminiani. The top men of the day, they arrived in state at the little airport at Castletown. They didn't race hard, but at least they had come to the Isle of Man. Their presence pleased everyone, especially no doubt Jim Hinds of the Southern Roads CC, who won the international race in front of these legendary champions.

So, in the unlikely venue of the Isle of Man, some of us could feel that British and continental cyclists were becoming closer. But we were still British, in our old ways and modest aspirations. I remember 1959. It was my year of dreams. Bahamontes won the Tour. Alf Engers, of the Barnet CC at that time, reduced the British 25 record to 55.11. I was shaving my legs and doing 300 miles a week, fantasising about going to spend a week on the Isle of Man. What a steamer journey from Fleetwood to Douglas, chugging across the wide straits of Colwyn Bay . . . I imagined a place where tailless cats chased red squirrels, where I might meet a Bicycle Belle and perhaps ride in the lesser races. Fun and glory in the land of kippers and fairy lights! The plan came to nothing, like most of my cycling projects at that date and ever since.

* * *

On a bike you can go anywhere – and in my own book, if I wish, I can go on and on about the Isle of Man. Curwen Clague died in 1981, but his enterprise continues to this day. For some time the cycling festival has been directed by Desmond Clague and the annual 'Curwen's Race' is ridden in his father's memory. Long may it continue.

But now I return to the 1950s. My list of lodging houses

tells me that the price of bed and breakfast on the Isle of Man was generally between 8*s*. 6*d*. and 12*s*. 6*d*. The steamer fare from Fleetwood to Douglas was 17*s*. The ferry would take your bike for an exorbitant 6*s*. Tandems cost an even more exorbitant 9*s*.

The prices I mention are part of our cycling story. Nearly everyone had to make prudent calculations in shillings and pence, either to race at any level or to go on holiday. Ours has been a sport for people who had to count money saved from their wages. Unlike some sports – athletics, rugby, rowing, tennis, cricket, boxing – competitive cycling never had any wealthy adherents. There were gentlemen amateurs during the short fashionable craze for cycling in the 1890s, but none thereafter. A handful of people made money from racing but there was no professional class. In the 1950s British cyclists were almost always employed in sound and unglamorous ways. I will describe their jobs in a moment. My point now is that they never had any spare money, cash that they could spend in a careless way.

All the same, there were signs that quite big money was almost within reach – money and glamour too. The Manx international race had such prestige. So many people wanted to see it that Curwen Clague used grandstands at the race finish on Douglas promenade. He was able to charge £6 for grandstand seats. That was about the cost of a week's lodging in a Douglas boarding house – a pretty high price – but the stands were none the less filled. The fans were no doubt prepared to pay more to be near the continental stars, especially if they could mingle with them after the race, as often happened.

My fellow Brummie John Turner (Moseley Road Junior Art School and then of the Midland C & AC) has a telling story about the end of the international road event in 1959.

> I had a short talk with Louison Bobet and André Darri-
> gade at the end of a pro race in the IOM one year . . .

Bobet was polite, immaculate, not a hair out of place, apologised that he needed to sponge himself down with Eau de Cologne before talking on the wall by the grandstand. Darrigade joined us looking very fierce and all I could see were his massive thighs and lower legs totally criss-crossed with varicose veins that stood out like ropes on his muscular limbs. Simpson came along . . . just out of sympathy I said . . . 'remember what Bobet has been through' (a major op to remove masses of pus from his back, taking seven hours of surgery). Without a change of expression Simo looked straight at me and said 'Who cares a **** about Bobet?'

I can annotate John Turner's reminiscence. By the time of Isle of Man week in late June of 1959 Tom Simpson had gone to France (with £100 in his pocket) and had been offered a professional contract. He was not in Douglas to compete in any of the races. Probably he just wanted to look at his future opposition. He was by nature a quick learner, had surveyed the continental scene and was not overawed. Simpson knew that Bobet's career was over, or in its twilight. And this young man was competitive. Hence his uncouth remark to John Turner. There is another possible interpretation. Simpson may have been thinking of his hero Fausto Coppi, who was also on the Isle of Man. Here was a person whose racing days should have been concluded a couple of years before. But his prestige was immense. Although he had done nothing at all in the Man race the other riders rose to clap as Coppi entered the dining room of the Douglas Bay Hotel.

IV

A typical club run.

Before this summer of 1959 Tom Simpson had been a draughtsman, which is a typical job for a cyclist. It had not always been so. For a few brief years at the end of the nineteenth century cycling was an upper-class fad. Ladies rode in Rotten Row. Gentlemen with cheroots chatted about the new pneumatic tyres. Then the rich gave up their enthusiasm for the bicycle: it was becoming common. There was still quite an amount of genteel cycling, and 'collar and tie' clubs lingered until the late 1920s. Their members were generally clerks, low-ranking civil servants or the employees of the great London department stores.

On the whole, however, the cycling sport and pastime has belonged to a lower social class. I have no name for this stratum, but refer to a class that is modest, mostly respectable, city-dwelling, waged rather than salaried, whose members generally work with their hands, who may well have gone through an apprenticeship and are very rarely educated beyond secondary school level. No statistics or analyses of cyclists' professions are known to me, so my comments on employment are simply a report of personal observations.

Over the years since the 1950s I have known or have met cyclists who were printers, fitters, turners or other lathe opera-tors, railwaymen, compositors, mechanics and electricians. I also think of a cobbler, a glazier, a washing-machine repairer, a man who installs cash machines and a lampshade maker. Large numbers of cyclists, particularly in the Midlands, are engaged in the metalworking industries. It is characteristic of them that they prefer small-scale engineering shops over factories. There is a marked connection between cycling and the photographic and film industries, whose employees also work in small and neat units, 'flatted factories' as they used to be called.

Builders and decorators are found in cycling clubs, as are cabinet makers and carpenters. Labourers are not common. In general, cyclists avoid heavier manual work, though there are exceptions. I used to train around the Eastway track with a dustman. He specialised in those big round containers you see behind hospitals and other public buildings, and said that the job was good for top-of-the-body fitness. In the afternoons he did thirty or forty fast laps before going in search of women. The Eastway circuit is a hilly mile, and this is one of the tracks where there are showers. 'I have three showers a day,' said the refuse collector.

I have ridden quite often, on different roads, with two male hairdressers (one ladies', one gents'). Alf Engers was a pastry-cook. Eddie Adkins, Alf's successor as 25-mile champion, is a motor mechanic. Frank Edwards, who rode the Tour of Britain in 1953, was the proprietor of the Woodbine Cafe near the Lowestoft fish docks. Then he had a fish and chip shop. There are a number of policemen in cycle sport and dozens of firemen. Some cyclists spend their working life in the army and many, many more are attached to the RAF. There are few cyclists in the navy. We have a scattering – no more – of shopkeepers, far too many schoolteachers (who often are their clubs' secretaries) and some lab technicians. In the old days there were miners, especially in the East Midlands and Yorkshire. I suspect that their jobs were usually at the colliery's surface.

A number of cyclists, especially women, work in market gardening or park maintenance. That great champion Beryl Burton was in the rhubarb-forcing business. The Land's End–John O'Groats record breaker Andy Wilkinson and the former Tour de France rider Sean Yates are both landscape gardeners. Some women cyclists work as jobbing gardeners or in general duties in garden centres, for they are not expert horticulturalists. Other women are nurses. They are never, ever, secretaries.

In Hertfordshire one morning I passed a young man who was late for work and asked to get on my wheel. We did bit-and-bit towards outer London. It turned out that he drove a tube train for his living. He clocked on at Cockfosters, went to and from Heathrow on the Piccadilly Line, then returned to his bike and rode home to Ware. This dull employment was worth a bit of chat. 'Everyone asks me that question,' he said. 'They give you counselling. If you don't want to drive again you're shifted to a platform job. Personally I'd just leave altogether.' Thus spoke the underground driver. Quite apart from the problem of suicides, it seemed odd to me that a cyclist should voluntarily spend so much time in a distant tunnel. Were there not other things to do, nearer home? My new friend explained that the tube gave him time for training. In the summer months he could combine the Piccadilly Line with 60 miles a day, fast on the old Cambridge road, hard and hilly near Essendon.

Saturday was a day off. He raced on Sundays. Therefore his working life helped him towards the rational goal of speed and power on the bike. Cyclists often choose their jobs so that they can cover numerous 'work miles'. They seek employment 20 or 30 miles from their homes; or they make sure that they knock off in the middle of the day. Here is the first and most obvious reason for the large number of racing cyclists who are postmen, or have some other role within the old General Post Office, once the country's biggest employer. There are other reasons. Postmen are early risers. So are cyclists. Postmen are wary of dogs. So are cyclists. Postmen like coarse fishing. That enthusiasm is shared by cyclists. The postman's functional walk corresponds to the cyclist's daily routine of training over familiar roads. Postmen usually know that they are in their job for life. Cyclists also sign up for all time. There is not much of a hierarchical structure within the postal service: you don't expect to rise within the GPO. Cyclists also avoid hierarchies. Postmen are often the sons of postmen. Cycling is essentially a sport in which sons are taught by their fathers.

We will hear more about postmen. Now I turn to a social group that is particularly difficult to explain, even to describe. Many racing cyclists are or have been artists. By the term 'artist' I mean someone who once went to a college of art. This is the only sensible way to differentiate between an amateur artist – who might be anyone and might be personally rich – and a professional artist, whose profession often brings no financial reward. Cycling artists begin at art school. And, to this day, one can walk round the studios of many an art college to find the iconic photograph of Fausto Coppi pinned up in a student's personal enclave, surrounded by other tokens, favourite images and gallery postcards – forty years after Fausto's death.

Why are so many art students and artists committed to cycling? As with other groups, it comes down to their background. The great majority of art students come from the same social band that produces racing cyclists. And, as I have described, that band is the skilled working class. To these people, art meant work. In Birmingham and other places, notably Sheffield, boys might go to art school at the age of twelve. They were not encouraged to be creative: they learnt how to draw designs for manufacture. This helps to explain the numerous cyclists nowadays who are graphic designers. A mystery remains. How do we account for the cyclists who practise the fine rather than the applied arts? That is, the painters and sculptors?

*   *   *

I imagine a boy – an adolescent, hardly yet a young man – with the bright eyes of youth and eagerness for life, who likes looking at things and gets on well with his friends; and yet is not sociable all the time, for there is some loneliness in his character, perhaps born of a frustration he cannot comprehend. He quite often roams after school and in lessons he does not do well, because of a reading difficulty. His parents and teachers know that he is gifted. They do not understand dyslexia. So all parties agree that Adam, as we may call him, shows precocious talent in drawing and might find his right place in the local art school.

Art school would be fine, Adam thinks. No more maths, no more book-learning. There is a painting in the municipal gallery he has always gone to look at when he gets off the tram in Navigation Street. And so Adam goes to college, where he finds that he can make friends with older people. One of his tutors in the printmaking department is a cyclist. It happens that Adam enjoys riding a bike, sometimes taking expeditions into the country. And he has seen the brilliant machines belonging to racing cyclists who live quite near his home. One way or another Adam finds the money to buy a racing bike. A man in the specialist shop advises him and gives him the address of the secretary of the local club. Adam joins club runs. He goes out training. Soon he rides his first time trial. At last he is fulfilled: another cyclist who went to art school.

For some of us, to be an art student and a young racing cyclist represented the height of happiness, a height within reach. My vision of Adam is not a fantasy. I grew up with boys of his sort and met more of them when teaching in art schools. That was in the 1970s and early 1980s, when art education was still a pleasure for all concerned. Students kept finding things within themselves, which is a reason why they were so highly motivated. There were still a number of problems for the cycling art students. Growing cyclists need to coordinate body and mind. They learn about themselves by training. And then, often, their efforts on the bike take the edge off their creativity in the studio. I am not talking about tiredness but about the deep contentment one experiences after a good 50-mile training ride. That particular glow is unhelpful for a young artist needing to live on his nerves.

*   *   *

Our young Adam, like so many people with their first bikes, may have got his real education in the world when he joined his cycling club. To learn about the club would take him a couple of years. To learn about all the other cycling clubs – as we should – is the task of a lifetime.

Some of them are as ancient as oaks. Today there might be a couple of dozen clubs that were founded in the nineteenth century. Hundreds more have lived and died. There are around 500 in existence in the United Kingdom at the time of writing (2003). They are local or regional, mainly local. They take their names from some town or suburb, as in the case of the Finsbury Park Cycling Club (always known as 'The Park' to its members), the Ipswich Bicycle Club (which is one with a nineteenth-century foundation date) or the Cardigan Wheelers. When you meet another cyclist it's not long before you enquire about his club. Then you know a wheelman's home base and can also guess who his mates are. 'So you're in the Saracen. Then you must know Johnny Roberts!' Other bits of this kind of conversation, mainly jocular, include 'Never heard of them' – when of course you have – or 'So you're one of those, are you?', which is an invitation to debate.

The Cyclists Touring Club, founded in 1878 (motto: 'This Great Club of Ours'), was often the parent organisation for smaller local clubs. The CTC was concerned with leisure riding and cyclists' rights. If younger CTC members were more interested in racing than touring they would band together to call themselves a 'road club'. Thus we have the Warwickshire Road Club, already mentioned, the Corsham Road Club, the Oxford City Road Club, the Yorkshire Road Club, and so on. If the word 'path' appears in any title it means that the club also specialises in track racing. Hence the name of the Redditch Road and Path CC. Older cyclists still use the word 'path' when they are talking about a cycle racing track.

How many people make a cycling club? About half a dozen, at the lowest count. And the maximum is about 100. The history of British cycling tells us that defections will occur, or a formal split, if this number is exceeded. A sociologist, perhaps aided by a psychiatrist, might be able to explain why it's best if a club has sixty to seventy members. There are or have been much larger clubs, but they are seldom tied to a locality. The RAF CC once had more members than any other club (maybe it still has) but really was an umbrella fellowship organisation. Other fellowships include the Army Cycling Union, the National Clarion CC and the Tricycle Association, whose members are spread throughout the land.

Do cycling clubs differ in their nature? Some people say that all clubs are the same; others maintain that there are vital differences between one club and the next. The truth probably lies somewhere between these two claims. Individual clubs do have their own traditions and personalities, but these resist description and are difficult for an outsider to grasp. So we rely on rumours and odd remarks that we have heard on the road.

Here is a list of some clubs past and present in more or less alphabetical order, but occasionally straying from the A–Z.

A5 Rangers. Still in existence? I believe so. Their base was somewhere in the Rugby–Nuneaton area. They used to follow the straight and determined route of the A5 to Shrewsbury and thither into Wales. Other names of clubs announce their usual runs and destinations. The Kentish Wheelers, for instance, rode into Kent: but the club's home was in Brixton in south London. Do not be misled by the name of the Rutland CC: its members lived around Rutland Road in Sheffield. Other club names indicate peripatetic habits. There was the Wanderers CC, based I know not where, the Tyneside Vagabonds CC, the Colchester Rovers CC, the Bedouin CC, from Croydon, the Thirty-Fourth Nomads CC and the Nomads (Hitchin), who for some reason like to have this parenthesis in their name. I have an enemy in the Nomads so I hate the lot of them. He says that I cut him up in a race. It's just that I was faster.

The Buckshee Wheelers is a fellowship club. By reason of its constitution the club is in terminal decline. The members of the Buckshee were in north Africa in the last days of Hitler's war and somehow managed to organise bike races in the desert. Their motto, one Buckshee Wheeler told me, was 'Growing and Growing and Growing'. Shouldn't that be 'Dying and Dying and Dying?' I pertly said. 'Tim, the *roll of honour* is growing and growing.' Though not rebuked, I felt chastened. The Buckshees allowed some post-war national servicemen to join their ranks, with a cut-off date of 1953. The youngest Buckshee Wheeler is said to be the fine roadman Brian Haskell, who is now seventy-four. It is understood that the very last member of the Buckshee Wheelers will bequeath all the club records to the Imperial War Museum.

My father should have been a Buckshee, just as he should have ridden with the Clarion. The opening lines of one of his favourite songs were learnt, I believe, in Alexandria in 1943 or 1944. If any Buckshee Wheeler reads this book I hope he will now smile. Lil is a stripper in an Alexandria brothel.

> Oh her name was Lil, she was a beauty,
> She lived in a house of ill reputy,
> She drank whisky, she drank rum,
> She smoked hashish and o-pi-um . . .

Also under B there's the Bon Amis CC (thus spelt), which calls to mind other British clubs with French names. Among them we should applaud the San Fairy Ann CC (they live in Kent), reputedly flourishing as never before, the Compagnons du Petit Braquet, the Vélo Club Pierre (who come from Stone in Staffordshire) and the Vélo Club Lanterne Rouge – a bunch of north London veterans who may be encountered at the Halfway House on the Cambridge Road just to the east of Enfield.

The Barrow Spartans CC doesn't sound a convivial club. I've ridden from Barrow-in-Furness, a depressed industrial town, once the home of shipbuilding and nuclear submarines, into the Lake District. That morning I nearly died from cold and lancing rain. A lovely lady at Grange-over-Sands gave me shelter in her off-licence. We drank two miniatures of brandy, so as not to be too spartan, while the downpour washed her windows. No doubt this comfort was illegal. If you're wet through on the bike a good plan is to head for a launderette, strip off and put all your clothes in the dryer. Good fun on a club run, if the local housewives don't call the police.

CCCP are the initials on the all-red road jerseys of the Comical Cycling Club of Penshurst. They don't seem like communists to me. I know from experience that at least two of them are very fast and fit. The Curnow CC represents cycle racing in Cornwall. (The Vectis CC does the same for the Isle of Wight, as do the Manx Viking Wheelers in the Isle of Man.) The Chesterfield Cycling and Athletic Club has now gone, though other clubs that once united cycling with athletics are still in existence, notably the Halesowen A & CC and the Midland C & AC.

Letter D. The Dartford Wheelers were in great rivalry with the Medway Wheelers. The De Laune CC is a south-of-the-river London club. The Derby Mercury CC, the Dudley Castle CC and the Dursley CC speak for themselves, as far as their origins are concerned.

The Elizabethan CC (defunct) and the Festival Road Club (still going well) remind us of the birth of so many clubs in the early 1950s. The Festival RC still uses the logo of the 1951 Festival of Britain. On the subject of logos (club signs which you drew when registering at a youth hostel, or in correspondence), that of the Unity CC is of two hands clasped in fellowship. Unfortunately, fellowship sometimes collapses. The names of the Kettering Amateur CC and the Kettering Friendly CC record a split between the cyclists of a quite small town. I do not recall the details of their dispute but know that it was a tremendous business.

On now to the Lancashire Road Club, always to be thanked for their promotion of twelve- and twenty-four-hour time trials,

the Liverpool Co-operative CC and the Ladies Cycling Fellowship. Members of the Liverpool Century Road Club probably
had to prove their worth with a 100-mile ride. The League
International exists to promote massed-start events for veterans.
The London Italian RCC was a forerunner of the Soho CC,
which had a brief glory in the late 1980s. Its members were
Italian waiters or were concerned in other ways with the catering
trades.

Montague Burton's Cycling Club must have been composed
of the store's employees. The Monckton CC took its name
from the colliery in which so many of its members earned their
living. The Monckton was a very strong club in the 1930s, with
little to fear from their neighbours in the North Nottinghamshire Road Club.

The Out-of-Work Wheelers belonged to a time of high
unemployment during the premiership of Margaret Thatcher,
while the Pickwick Bicycle Club is a century older, founded in
the late 1880s. Nowadays it is mainly a social club with membership by invitation. It keeps to the original rule that a prospective
member must show knowledge of *The Pickwick Papers*.

Speaking of which book, nowhere in Dickens's pages is it
explained why his various characters came together to form their
Pickwick Club. Thus the novelist gives us a clue to the pointless
affability of so many voluntary societies, which exist solely to
promote the pleasure each member finds in other members'
company. Within cycling (as elsewhere) advanced age and a
liking for carousal are characteristic of such clubs. I point to the
Potterers CC, whose members must be old and retired. There
is one notorious club for old men in the West Country, known
as the Scrumpy Wheelers.

The Sunset CC, now long gone, also had elderly people on its
club runs, while the Stourbridge CC, the Stockport Wheelers,
the Shaftesbury Wheelers and the Sydenham Wheelers all have
well-deserved reputations for looking after fast young racing men.

Letter T. Nowadays, most people who ride 'twicers' are at

the other end of life, and they may belong to the Tandem Club. If you want to buy a tandem, look at the small ads in their well-produced magazine. Upper Holloway CC, the Unicorn CC, the Uxbridge Wheelers, all gone; and now we arrive at the letter V. Who are the members of the Valkyries CC? The name of the Vegetarian C & AC – which flourished until the late 1950s – takes us back to the early days of this kind of idealism. The Vegetarian Road Club was probably an offshoot whose members were devoted to hardriding and racing.

Under V I also note the Vancouver Bicycle Club, the Vancouver Cycling Club and the Vancouver Cycle Touring Club. These clubs probably register an affiliation with British governing bodies because they were founded by emigrants from the British Isles. There were quite a number of these cycling emigrants, often from Scotland. They went to Vancouver because it's the best area in Canada for cycling. The best known British cyclist in Canada is Tony Hoar, formerly of the Emsworth CC in Portsmouth. He was the popular *lanterne rouge* of the 1955 Tour de France, then came back to England, got fed up and sailed away.

The Wandsworth and District Cycling Club was originally titled the Wandsworth and Balham Co-operative Society Cycling Club. The Waverley CC is of course a Scottish foundation, while the Welwyn Wheelers and the Stevenage CC were formed by people who moved out of London at the time of the 'new towns movement'.

Continuing with letter W, the Westminster Wheelers is long gone. It was probably a collar-and-tie club for civil servants in the days before the Kaiser's war. The Wobbly Wheelers exists only as a widespread joke, made up I believe by Johnny Helms, cycling's favourite cartoonist, who must have been guest of honour at more club dinners than anyone else in the sport. The Wolverhampton RCC is famous among us because it was the cradle of the British League of Racing Cyclists. I recently met one of its former members, and asked him what Percy Stallard, founder of the BLRC, was like. 'He was okay when he was drunk!' This particular Wolverhampton RCC member hails from Kinver, the last place in Britain where people lived in caves – as lately as the twentieth century. They burrowed into the cliffs of the soft red local sandstone. No doubt there were many people who thought that Stallard had emerged from a cave. I'll come to him later.

The Yorkshire Road Club is so distinguished (and pompous) that it even has a hardcover club history that can be bought in bookshops. Most club histories, if they exist, are in the form of enlarged pamphlets and have no circulation beyond the club's members. West Yorkshire has a complex network of cycling clubs, currently numbering two dozen and formerly even more. Perhaps the number of small and distinct towns explains why there are so many cycling clubs in the West Riding, along with the splits and breakaways caused by cycling politics. The Bradford RCC, for instance, took many of its members from the conservative Yorkshire RC; and that was because the Yorkshire RC was so opposed to the British League of Racing Cyclists.

V

Robert Blatchford:
a visionary's gaze and a lecher's moustache.

A sign of my age, apart from riding in the small chainwheel most of the day, is a wish to find the records of old clubs, preferably modest ones. I also make pilgrimages to cycle sport's 'sacred' places: Pangbourne Lane, or the further Savernake turn of the Bath Road 100, or Tanners Hatch. These destinations are seldom grand, but they appeal to my interest in early council estates, seaside housing development, piers, canals, ports, maltings, early factories and small town halls. I dislike parish churches, consider most British castles ugly (besides being the strongholds of injustice) and don't believe cathedrals and abbeys can be appreciated when you're cycling. I've had these prejudices since childhood.

*   *   *

First thing one Sunday morning, when I was grown up and indeed a father, I left the Arundel youth hostel for an awkward ride along the south coast. The plan was to give a wave to the Isle of Wight, soldier through Southampton, and then I wanted to pass through the New Forest before spending the night at the hostel in Winchester. The outing was a little delayed almost as soon as it had begun. I paused in Chichester, a place new to me. On the north side of the cathedral, still in the saddle, right foot in the toe clip, left foot on the pavement, I dutifully looked at the flying buttresses and gothic windows.

All was quiet. An early service of Holy Communion had just ended. Towards me walked a man in long black canonical garments. He was good at whistling. Through his shrivelled lips came the thin but accurate strains of a canticle. I supposed that he was one of the cathedral's clergy. Still whistling holy music, this man approached me. A look of contempt came into his eyes. Perhaps the bright cycling clothing had annoyed him. He cleared his throat and spat into the gutter at my feet, then walked on his way. *His spittle might have landed on my bike!* I was so astonished that I could not reply to the affront, rode off and have never visited Chichester again.

Speaking as a cyclist, I have never had much truck with English ecclesiastical buildings. Perhaps because I come from Birmingham, I prefer late nineteenth-century municipal architecture, if possible in red brick. About ten years ago, curiosity about that sort of building led me to make a discovery at Wrentham in Suffolk. Wrentham is on the A12, 10 miles south of Lowestoft. My hope was that the Eagle might still be in business. I wanted to raise a glass to a Victorian chambermaid – a girl who ought to be celebrated by all cyclists. More of her in a moment.

Sadly, the Eagle had closed down. A few yards down the road was an unattractive brick place called Wrentham Hall, recently converted into flats and an antiques emporium. Placing the bike against its façade (gear side next to the wall, as always) I made my inspection from the other side of the road. Surely the building was too large for a village hall, and of the wrong date? Perhaps it had once been a school. There was a tower for a bell and a circular hole for a clock. This nondescript edifice had a mouldering tablet which read:

This tablet was erected
[illeg.] people of Wrentham to mark [illeg.]
the many improvements which have been made by
Sir Alfred Shirlock Gooch, Bart.
in this building and especially with the clock,
which has been altered at his sole expense
to commemorate the diamond jubilee of H.M. Queen Victoria.
June 22 1897.

Something puzzled me about this testimonial from the people of Wrentham. It recorded an event of little interest, but there was a distant familiarity in its wording. Suddenly, memory took me to the sooty buildings of central Birmingham. In Balsall Heath there had been an Alfred Street, a Wrentham Street, a Gooch Street and a Shirlock Street. My map showed a Benacre Hall next to Wrentham. That must have been the baronet's home. And there had been a Benacre Street in Balsall Heath.

Empty, melancholy lanes skirt the grounds of Benacre Hall. You can't see the house from these roads, only parkland, woods and a home farm. My communist upbringing gave me a feeling of political anger about the Benacre estate. Years ago, I had been given much childhood instruction on the evils of *rentier* capitalism. My guess (an accurate one: I later checked it in the library) was that there were people who lived at their ease in Suffolk because they took their money from the poor of my home city.

Shirlock Street, Gooch Street, Benacre Street were once well known to me. My mates lived there. We were friends because we went to Bristol Street Primary School. We sat together at shared desks, where we learnt nothing, then played dangerous games on the bomb sites, where we learnt how to make bonfires. On Saturday mornings I returned to Balsall Heath, for there I sold the *Daily Worker*.

It was an easy job because I had a round with regular customers. They didn't buy the *Worker* in the week but on Saturdays the paper carried an extra page, i.e. six instead of four, and offered the tips of 'Cayton', its incomparable racing correspondent. Most of my regulars lived in houses built on the close-court system, with no back doors or back windows. They had water and electricity but no bathrooms or lavatories. Each court was entered through a 'snicket', an arched and enclosed brick alley. The courts themselves were rectangular, with eight dwellings on each side. In the middle of each court was a block of privies.

42

*   *   *

Now I return to Wrentham in 1990 and the nature of my pilgrimage to the Eagle. Wrentham was a place of good fortune for Robert Blatchford. Though he is largely forgotten today, Blatchford had an enormous effect on British cycling. Paradoxically, he wasn't really a cyclist himself. He did ride a bike occasionally, but not often. And it seems that he had no contact with all the cycling clubs that were formed in alliance with his weekly paper, *The Clarion*.

That splendid periodical belonged to the 1890s. Blatchford was himself a happy-go-lucky adventurer of the nineteenth century. He reminds me of the Victorian motto 'A clean shirt, a merry heart and a guinea', the point of which was that with these three requirements you could get through the day and have a good time. Blatchford was a child of Bohemia who never knew his father. His mother, an Italian singer and actress, probably didn't know Blatchford senior for very long. In her young widowhood (that was her cover story) she toured the country, mostly in the north, her son on the back of the cart among stage props, costumes and a few personal belongings.

Blatchford did not say how he lost touch with his mother. I know that he ran away from an apprenticeship and, at the age of twenty, found himself in Yarmouth, Norfolk. With five shillings in his pocket, he decided to go to London. In 1871 the best way to reach London from Yarmouth was by boat, but Blatchford decided to walk to the capital. Twenty miles down the road, in Wrentham, he came to an exhausted halt. He asked for shelter at the Eagle, too grand a place for such a lad. But the chambermaid I have mentioned took a fancy to him and smuggled him to her room upstairs. In the morning she sent him off from the back door with a farewell kiss and a sandwich – and he still had the five shillings.

Next, like many another runaway apprentice, Blatchford took the Queen's shilling. He was a soldier until 1880, then started on the road that was to make him a social campaigner by doing 'press work', as he called it, soon earning good pay on the *Sunday Chronicle*. A journalistic assignment in the slums of Manchester converted him to socialism. The former vagabond had previously thought that poverty was a natural fact of life, but Manchester housing convinced him that something had to be done.

Blatchford began to read political treatises, the most influential of which was H. M. Hyndman's and William Morris's *What is Socialism?* 'Directly I grasped the collective idea I saw that it was what I wanted.' In 1892 he began a weekly newspaper, *The Clarion*, which expressed the 'collective idea'. By the next year it was a national success and carried the first text of Blatchford's William Morris-inspired *Merrie England*. This appeared in book form in 1894 and is said to have sold 700,000 copies in a few months.

Now a strange thing happened. Without intending to do so, Blatchford's paper gave birth to cycling clubs rather than a political movement. *The Clarion* was all the more popular a paper because it was not in the least doctrinaire. Its politics were those of its founder: an independent, pleasure-loving man who believed in equality, preferred his native land to any other place, still had some fond feelings for the classlessness he had found in the army and took his lead from William Morris's dictum 'Fellowship is life. Lack of fellowship is death'.

It is clear that Blatchford's unscientific form of socialism was suited to cyclists. In a short period following the launch of *The Clarion*, seventy cycling clubs were founded with 'Clarion' in their names. They used the paper's masthead logo (winged young goddess blowing a trumpet) and repeated, time and again, that 'fellowship' was their bond. Thus a tradition was created. Even in the twenty-first century, 'fellowship' and 'fraternity' are the watchwords of British cycling associations of all sorts.

A number of the original Clarion clubs are still in existence, though many more have been disbanded. The first Clarion Cycling Club was founded in Birmingham in 1894. Later in that year more Clarion clubs were formed in Hanley, Liverpool, Bradford and Barnsley. In 1895 there were further foundations in Nottingham, Newcastle, Leeds, Rochdale, Blackburn, Wigan, Hyde and Nelson. Clearly, there was a northern bias, although there were Clarion clubs in London and other places in the south of England, notably Bristol and Portsmouth. The pattern probably reflects the circulation of the newspaper that was the clubs' inspiration.

The Clarion phenomenon may be called a truly popular movement because the clubs were unregimented, non-hierarchical and had no specific political goal. The more political a Clarion club, the greater the danger that its spirit would be lost. A movement based on fellowship found it difficult to tolerate leaders or to develop committee structures. At the same time there had to be a certain amount of organisation. Someone had to look after the lists of members, send out comradely addresses, receive subscriptions and promote the inter-club time trials. Volunteers could always be found to perform these functions. Divisions arose in the Clarion clubs only when some members grew too keen on running things, or tried to make clubs more active within the formal labour movement.

In these ways the Clarion clubs have given us two leading characteristics of British cycling. First, cycling is not a political sport, but it does belong to the leftward side of humanity. Second, cyclists do not on the whole wish to be governed and are often unable to govern each other. The administration of cycling, from the smallest clubs to the largest, has often been a shambles. That's the way most of us like it.

In the early Clarion movement, Blatchford sensed the coming dangers and showed himself to be on the side of disorder. It was well known that Clarion committees simply re-elected themselves in the warmth of the pub before getting back on their bikes. Some people disapproved of this easy-going wisdom, but not Blatchford. He thought that the Clarion clubs' annual Shef-field conference ought to be a merry lunch and that speeches should be banned, except for toasts. He repeated the message in many *Clarion* editorials: 'No leaders, no rules, no delegates, no machinery!'

Writing much later, in 1932, Blatchford remembered his editorial cry. He then lamented:

> All went merrily for some years and then a number of earnest young men joined up, and there arose a demand for 'organisation'. I pointed out at the time that the Fellowship was a genial crowd of congenial spirits and that it was impossible to organise friendship. But the Fellowship was organised and its glamour slowly faded. The old Fellowship gave us something precious which no organisation had to offer, the organised Fellowship could only go a little better than any other party organisation. And now the clouds began to gather . . .

That reference is to the onset of the First World War. The Clarion movement was at its height – at least in terms of membership – in 1913, with around 7,000 members. A pretty good figure, and one reason why the movement survived the Kaiser's war. Many clubs then died, but there were enough people to keep up the cause of Clarion fellowship. A casualty of the war was *The Clarion* itself, which ceased publication in 1916. But the cyclists were not extinguished, and they are still up the road. If one cyclist says of another 'He's an old Clarion man' or 'She's got a Clarion background', we know that we are talking of someone with an especial pedigree.

Another reason for the longevity of the Clarion clubs is that they always included women. Cycling girls married fellow members and started Clarion families. At the last published count, on the occasion of the National Clarion Centenary in 1995, there were eighteen separate Clarion clubs with a combined membership of around 800 people. So life goes on as the wheels go round, and a number of celebrated veteran cyclists owe their lives to the Clarion movement. The most famous of them is Barry Hoban, multiple stage winner in the Tour de France in the 1960s and 1970s. Barry is the son of old Joe Hoban of the Calder Clarion CC, who on the occasion of the 1995 centenary was still riding his bike at the age of eighty-four and was one of the members who could reminisce about the half-century reunion fifty years before.

VI

The young Percy Stallard
in a rare road race.

Although I love the thought of the Clarion movement the British League of Racing Cyclists gives me more exciting memories.

The story of the BLRC is one of protracted warfare with other cycling bodies. Internecine disputes lasted for sixteen years before a sort of truce was signed. The hostilities are not yet concluded. Much has been lost in futile bitterness. In the 1950s previously happy clubs were torn apart, and cyclists and potential sponsors left the sport. On the whole, though, the League was successful. It made British cycling modern and international. Furthermore, the BLRC represented a glorious rebellion. In what other sport, of any type, do we find the rank and file gathering together to overthrow their officials and governing bodies?

The civil war might not have been necessary if those rulers of cycling had not been so hidebound. Here, in brief, is their political history.

The Bicycle Union was founded in 1878 as an alliance of a few London clubs. By 1893 it was much enlarged, had absorbed members from outside the capital and decided to change its name to the National Cyclists Union. In the new century more and more clubs sought affiliation. As they did so, the leadership of the NCU appears to have become more conservative and autocratic. The NCU believed in cycle touring – as did everyone – but not in much else. In particular, it was wary of competitive cycling and held that all racing should be on cycle tracks.

The NCU opposed, indeed forbade, road racing. But what about record breaking in solo rides from one place to another?

This kind of competition was already popular in the 1890s, but the NCU was hostile. Consequently, another body was formed, the Road Records Association, and in 1937 the Road Time Trials Council was founded to supervise the fast-growing sport of time trialling: that is, events in which the contestants start at intervals and ride alone. Both the NCU and the RTTC were united in opposition to road racing: that is, 'massed-start' events in which the riders start together, *en ligne* in the French expression.

This was the situation until the war years. Now enters a hero of the British bike game, Percy Stallard of the Wolverhampton RCC. He was a natural roadman and had a good record in domestic and international sport. Stallard represented Britain in the world amateur road championships at Monthléry in 1933, Leipzig in 1934 and Copenhagen in 1937. It is astonishing to note that when he went to Monthléry Stallard had ridden in only one massed-start event, at Donington Park, which was a motor racing circuit. So the race was not on open roads and could not contravene NCU regulations. Massed-start races had also been held at the Brooklands motor racing track and on the Isle of Man. But there had been few such events when Percy Stallard began his campaign in 1942.

It was nearly a decade since Percy had ridden in his first world championship, and he had never had enough racing to satisfy him. He was a man of physical prowess, sometimes shown in unconventional ways. In Wolverhampton pubs he won pint after pint by jumping from a squatting position onto table tops. Percy was a rough leader of men – the kind you can imagine in command of an army unit – and was frustrated at not fighting in the war. He remained in Wolverhampton in a reserved capacity as a cycle mechanic. Percy was also a frame builder. May I tell connoisseurs that I have ridden a Percy Stallard frame. It was lovely. The owner wouldn't sell it to me.

Stallard's qualities were unrecognised in the Doughty Street headquarters of the NCU. He was provincial, had a lowly social status and was without skill when it came to writing letters. I think that the NCU officials may have been deceived by Percy's Wolverhampton accent, which gave a note of wonderment to his voice, as though he could not fully believe in the existence of a quite simple fact that he himself was describing. This accent, combined with his unlovely features, gave some people the impression that he was one of society's and nature's underlings.

That was wrong. Percy Stallard was as revolutionary as Wat Tyler, an opponent of the hierarchy (any hierarchy) who would never give up and never admit defeat. And all he wanted to do, in the spring of 1942, was to organise a cycle road race along the lines of the continental racing he had briefly tasted. Letter after letter in Percy's uneducated hand went to the NCU, asking for co-operation or at least permission. Always the answer was no, just no.

*   *   *

Percy Stallard would not obey. He decided to go ahead with a race. The birthplace of his plan, and therefore of the League, was a remote farmhouse at Little Stretton in Shropshire. This village is 30–40 miles west of Wolverhampton, in a river valley before the land rises sharply towards the Welsh border. There ought to be a commemorative plaque on the farm. I have made a pilgrimage but could not locate the building. Veterans such as myself can recall the nature of such places. It was one of those homes recommended by the Cyclists Touring Club ('appointed', in CTC language) where cyclists could find a cheap place of rest and, with luck, some food. They slept in makeshift dormitories and washed under the farmyard tap.

Racing men were gathered at this farm during Easter of 1942 because they were to compete in the Wolverhampton RCC's hill climb. There was a course of a mile and three-quarters on the unmetalled Burway Hill, which goes up the Long Mynd. A nice little event, but all the riders wanted more. In the farmhouse

51

kitchen Stallard led the future agitation. It was ridiculous that their races should be in remote places and held in secret. There were massed-start events in continental countries, applauded by spectators, even in wartime. Why not in Britain?

Repeated applications to the NCU were rejected. What explains their mindset, the lack of sympathy and indeed the folly of their prohibition? I imagine that they liked being in charge, feared a vulgarisation of cycling, didn't like Percy Stallard, and wished to put down the Black Country bighead. The enemies of 'Stallard's race', as they called it, referred to its contravention of the genteel spirit of their pastime. They had only one argument that made sense: that if massed-start racing were to be seen on public roads, then the government would be inclined to ban all cycle sport.

Stallard had foreseen this argument. His proposed race was to cover the 59 miles between Llangollen and Wolverhampton. He secured the co-operation of the chief constables of both Shropshire and Staffordshire, having assured them that the forty riders were experienced racing men who would obey the rules of the road. Any profits from the race would go to a police-force charitable fund. Stallard also provided a programme, a press car and publicity via the Wolverhampton *Express and Star*.

The race took place on 7 June 1942, animated by the same men who had banded together in the Shropshire farmhouse. There were no incidents. An exciting sprint finish in Wolverhampton's Park Road was cheered by a crowd of 2,000 people. Two local riders were first and second, Albert Price of the Wolverhampton RCC crossing the line in front of Chris Anslow of the Wolverhampton Wheelers. The event had been a success in every way.

The NCU's response was to suspend, *sine die*, Stallard, all the riders in the race and all the officials named in the programme: three dozen of the best wheelmen in the country were forbidden to race again. People immediately resigned from the NCU in protest. Some Midlands clubs formed a new organisation, the Midland League of Racing Cyclists. Further leagues were formed in the north and in London, later amalgamating to form the BLRC. In November the NCU, now joined by the RTTC, issued the following warning: 'As from today's date, any person or club associating itself with the British League of Racing Cyclists or any of its constituent parts will be suspended.'

The committee of the NCU simply did not understand the wishes of its membership. The same went for the RTTC. Neither body attempted diplomacy, and therefore could not stem the flow of defections. By 1943 about 450 people had joined the League in defiance of the NCU's threat of suspension and in scorn of the editorials in *Cycling*, in which they were regularly condemned. If their own club had taken the NCU side they resigned, often to form new clubs. The BLRC gained further and further strength. Eighteen months after 'Stallard's race' it had five regional sections and thirty affiliated clubs.

The sudden rise of the BLRC has something in common with the speedy formation of the Clarion clubs in the 1890s. A spirit was everywhere, but dormant. All that was needed for revolution was a catalyst or pioneer, whether in the form of Blatchford's newspaper or in the person of the obstinate Percy Stallard.

A difference between the Clarion movement and the rise of the BLRC is that the first led to fellowship, the second to division. After the summer of 1942 there was schism in club after club. Old friends were no longer friends. People who had never met regarded each other as enemies. Sons of cyclists were told by their fathers to avoid certain other cyclists. A height of the wrangling was reached when servicemen came home after 1945. Let us imagine two cases. A young man returns from fighting and is not inclined to obey the edicts of old non-combatants in the NCU. So he becomes a Leaguer. Another war veteran returns to civilian life and finds that his beloved club has been torn to pieces by Leaguers. So he resents them, especially since they – like the NCU committees – had also not been combatants. He joins another club or loses interest altogether.

*   *   *

From 1945 to 1946 the League wished to send its members to race on the continent and – yes please! – to accept any invitation to enter a British team in European stage races. The problem for racing cyclists, who were neither linguists nor diplomats, was to get on to terms with the world's governing body, the *Union cycliste internationale*. The UCI recognised the NCU as cycling's governing body in Great Britain. How then was the BLRC to proceed?

Help came from the Belgian-born sister of Alec Taylor (2nd, Tour of Britain 1951, National Amateur Champion 1947). Miss Taylor went to Brussels at her own expense, for the League had no funds, to put the BLRC case. More assistance was given by Victor Berlemont, the landlord of the York Minster in Dean Street, Soho, always known as 'the French pub'. This small bohemian bar had been the unofficial headquarters of the Free French during the war. Berlemont had an interest in cycle sport and was the UCI's London consul. Victor's son Gaston (who as a young man can be seen in Willi Ronis's famous photograph of the pub, part of his record of the life of French people in England) inherited the York Minster after his father's death in 1951.

Victor advised the BLRC. Gaston, like his father, did a bit of commissaire work for road racing until late in his life. The Berlemont family have all gone now, but there is an annual Victor Berlemont Memorial Road Race, organised by the Surrey League. The French pub still has a connection with our sport, a place of rendezvous for racing cyclists as well as bohemians. Photographs of old champions are on the walls, where they always have been. That handsome woman in the middle of the display is Lilian Dredge.

If we lived in Belgium we would know dozens of bars of this sort. But we are British. In the 1950s, when you could buy *Miroir-Sprint* from the foreign-language newsagent Solosy, Leaguers from the London area would go to Soho on Saturday mornings. They would sit in the French pub in winter, and in summer they would ride to race on the circuit that goes round the perimeter of Finsbury Park. Its surface was bumpy, there was no proper hill, kids and prams and footballs were all over the road, people took illegitimate laps out, since there were no real commissaires – but it was urban bike racing of a kind never seen before, nor scarcely since.

Looking back on Gaston Berlemont, I feel that he ran his Soho bar in much the same way that a commissaire controls the riders in a continental bike race. Even the maddest of us had respect for him. Gaston could stop fights in a few seconds, and was never angry. If you were barred from the French he would reinstate you the next day. When in need he would lend you money. And always there was the same calm, the twinkle in the eye, the same ample stomach and enormous gallic moustache.

There were many famous people in the French pub. Gaston gave them no more deference tham he would accord to any art student. He was like a commissaire in the Tour de France who listens to the *domestiques* as well as the champions. In person and demeanour Gaston resembled the greatest of modern commissaires, Jean-Marie LeBlanc, who has directed the Tour de France since 1994 after previous careers as a professional cyclist and a journalist. Gaston, like LeBlanc, was a linguist of sorts. He could make his decisions clear to anyone from any country, usually in simple French. An essential skill in Soho, and also in the man who supervises the affairs of the peloton.

*   *   *

The League needed a *patron* in the Berlemont mould. There was no single person who could unite so many difficult racing cyclists. Members of the BLRC fought with each other as well as with the NCU. They even managed to suspend Percy Stallard, the man to whom the League's very existence was owed. In some areas there were totalitarian demands that records of errant members be excluded from the minutes and account books. But minutes were not often kept and finances were always in disarray. Meetings were inefficiently chaired and the arguments went on for twelve hours or more.

The indiscipline was a caricature of democracy and the political process. The wonder is that the Leaguers were able to put on so many good bike races and to assemble international teams of high quality. But so they did, and furthermore were usually victorious when it came to outwitting the NCU. This was the work of many remarkable characters, generally the more experienced Leaguers, among whom I single out Jimmy Kain.

Jimmy, a shoe repairer from Enfield, was probably the oldest of the rebels. In his sixties when he took a hand in the League's affairs, Jimmy had fought in the First World War and claimed that, in its darkest days, he and his comrades had been issued with guns that were 'ex-Crimea carbines' that 'must have come from condemned stores'. If so, this modern racing cyclist had been in a war carrying a gun that had been manufactured in the 1850s. He was an ancient patriot, was Jimmy Kain, and he ended his days in uniform as a Chelsea Pensioner.

From his hand came the most ludicrous triumph of the BLRC over its enemies in the NCU. He devised and wrote the 'Loyal Address' to King George VI on the occasion of the League's chaotic (and, according to the NCU, illegal) 1945 stage race between Brighton and Glasgow. A precious photograph of this document shows its elaborate penmanship. I wonder whether Jimmy's shoemaking trade helped him to find a source of parchment? Anyway, the address begins

Most Gracious Sovereign,

> We, the Chairman, Members of the National Executive
> Committee, Honorary Secretaries and Members of the
> British League of Racing Cyclists, your Majesty's loyal
> and dutiful subjects, on the occasion of a 'Victory Race'
> being held by its members . . .

and ends many paragraphs later with the hope that, with the
end of European hostilities,

> all Sports, including the sport of Cycling with which we,
> your Majesty's loyal and dutiful subjects are particularly
> concerned, may be resumed and long continued so that
> the objects of our League, namely, the development of
> healthy competition and friendly rivalry in Cycling
> Events may proceed unhampered.

> James Kain, 24 Disraeli Road, Ealing, in the County of
> Middlesex.

The address was delivered to Buckingham Palace by four
Leaguers (Alex Hendry, Ernie Clements, Alan Colebrook and
'Acker' Smith) on their bikes and in racing gear. Only a day
later Jimmy got a reply from the Palace in which he read, 'The
King will be grateful if you will convey to the members of the
League his sincere thanks . . . etc. etc.'. How could the NCU
compete with such a propaganda coup? The sovereign himself
seemed to have become an ally of the rebels.

Back at 24 Disraeli Road Jimmy Kain faced a crisis in his
cycling life. The names of two local clubs indicate a schism that
was partly of his making. The Ealing CC and the Ealing Paragon
CC were once one body, but split because of a local war between
Leaguers and non-Leaguers. Which side was to inherit the original club's records, its bank account and its precious silver
trophies, many of which had been donated by the cycling parents
of the club's present members? How many people were on the
NCU side? They could be counted. How many people were

on the League side? Did the League keep an accurate list of its members, and had subscriptions been paid and properly accounted? (Very often the answer was no.)

The problems in Ealing were repeated all over the country. It was a hard time for clubmen – and for their wives. They had joined the Wobbly Wheelers through simple love of the bike. Now they had to make decisions that would brand them as conservatives or partisans. Stallard always said that there could be no compromise. 'You were either with us or against us.' He also claimed, untruly, that within the League 'we were one big happy family'. It is hard to explain the mixture of high spirits and nihilism in the collective League mind. Jimmy Kain's rare pamphlet *Britain's Cycling Frankenstein: A Disunited Colossus* (n.d. but 1953) takes as its motto a quotation from *The Rubáiyát of Omar Khayyám*:

> To grasp this sorry State of Things entire
> . . . Shatter it to bits . . . and then,
> Re-mould it nearer to the heart's desire . . .

I wonder whether the quotation represents one kind of post-war attitude, the frustrated feeling that everything had to be torn down before we could begin anew. Those years, we know, saw the largest recruitment to the company of British anarchism and 'libertarianism'. Jimmy Kain, however, was a monarchist. He sometimes sent long telegrams to Clement Attlee threatening to report him to the King, like this one about possible Home Office objections to road racing:

REPRESENTING THOUSANDS LAW ABIDING MEMBERS BITTERLY RESENT LETTER ZV STOP STROKE 22 JULY AND DISCRIMINATION EXPRESSED WHILE YOU STOP TRAFFIC FACILITATING SURGING CROWDS ATTEND SPEEDWAY AND DOG RACING STOP SPEEDWAY RACING BREEDS SPEED CRAZED PILLION RIDERS OF GRISLY RECORD STOP THUS KEEPING DEATH ON THE ROADS

STOP REPEAT DEATH ON THE ROADS WILL TAKE THIS
MATTER TO HIS MAJESTY THE KING IN EFFORT TO
OPPOSE YOUR DISCRIMINATION . . .

As for the spirit of the League – perhaps it depended on your
generation. Jimmy Kain sent his angry telegrams to a prime
minister who was younger than himself. His objections to dog
tracks and speedway sound like those of an old man. Percy
Stallard, the original rebel, had begun racing in 1927, and was
a family man. The other pioneers from the Little Stretton farmhouse were also grown up. A number of them worked in the
Sunbeam body shop, a reserved occupation because they might
be needed to build military vehicles. They knew the boredom
of wartime. It was folly to deny them a cycle race.

Then comes a later generation, typified by another Wolverhampton man. In 1945 Bob Thom came back from war service,
signed up with the BLRC and rode the Brighton–Glasgow. He
was BLRC champion in 1948 and in that year became a small-
time professional for Viking Cycles. Team mechanic for the
BLRC team in the 1952 Warsaw–Berlin–Prague, he was also
mechanic for the British team in the 1955 Tour de France and
managed British teams abroad until the mid-1970s. He and his
wife Jeannie still ride their bikes, always in the colours of the
Wolverhampton Wheelers.

The third generation, younger than Bob Thom by a decade
or more, were those racing men who joined cycling in the early
1950s, at the end of austerity and rationing but before mass
motoring had begun. These adherents to the BLRC displayed
a new working-class sense of modishness and were sometimes
said to be the Teddy Boys of sport. I never saw any cycling
Teds, but there was certainly a smart and disobedient look. In
the 1950s you could identify a Leaguer by his roadman's position on the bike, his continental equipment, his preference for
derailleur gears, Campag if possible, a flashy Italian road jersey
and dark glasses. Unlike more traditional cyclists, a Leaguer was

likely to be a (modern) jazz fan, would frequent coffee bars, might go out with a girl from the local art school, was a snappy dresser on and off the bike and had no respect for the culture of touring and youth hostelling.

*   *   *

Something else made a difference between the Leaguers and traditional cyclists. They were so good! They trained harder, rode harder, had high ambitions and studied the sport with Europe in mind. The League was inspired by France and Italy, countries with a mass following for the bike game. Leaguers always wanted to ride on equal terms with the continentals, and soon they did.

The BLRC alone introduced road racing to Britain, gave us stage races on the continental pattern and looked for sponsorship and publicity from newspapers and other interested parties. The first Tour of Britain was held in 1951, under the banner of the *Daily Express* and with much help from Butlin's holiday camps (which often gave hospitality and shelter to the caravan of a British stage race). Quite soon, however, the *Daily Express* pulled out of cycle sport, fed up with the feuds between the BLRC and the NCU. The League's Dave Orford approached the Milk Marketing Board, and the Tour of Britain was reborn with a different name, by which it is still fondly remembered: 'the Milk Race'.

The Tour of Britain and The Milk Race invited foreign competitors, and British teams went abroad. There was friendliness between the League and the sporting bosses of the Warsaw Pact countries, probably because the communist nation-states saw no need to obey the dictates of the *Union cycliste internationale*, which was always suspicious of the BLRC. So a major triumph was Ian Steel's victory in the tough 1952 Warsaw–Berlin–Prague, the 'Peace Race', in which Leaguers from Great Britain also won the team prize.

The BLRC also developed a British professional or semi-professional class. Apart from Ovaltine and BSA, the sponsors of the new professionals were usually small bike firms – i.e. shops that also made frames – or importers of Italian accessories. I like to remember the pioneering racing men who wore the colours of such marques and lament that, today, we don't have the events that made them famous. Here are some of them, in no particular order – for who can impose order on the League?

Dave Orford (Belper), Ovaltine/Langsett Cycles, Ist BLRC Junior Road Race Championship, 1948, Ist Circuit des Grimpeurs, 1955; Bev Wood (Preston), Viking Cycles, Ist London–Dover, 1950; Ken Russell (Bradford), Ellis Briggs Cycles, Ist Tour of Britain, 1952; Peter Proctor (Skipton), BSA Cycles, King of the Mountains, Tour of Britain, 1952; Alec Taylor (Marlborough), Gnutti Accessories, 2nd Tour of Britain, 1951; Les Wade (London), Frejus Cycles, Ist Nottingham–Butlin's Holiday Camp, Skegness, 1950; John Perks (Birmingham), Falcon Cycles, Ist Tour of Wessex three-day, 1954; John Bennett (Derby), Mottram Cycles, Ist Battle of Britain Road Race, 1954, Ist Birmingham Road Race, 1959; Phil Ingram (London), Dayton Cycles, 2nd London BLRC Time Trial Championship, 1944.

All the British riders who were good enough to ride the Tour de France in the years after 1955 came from a BLRC background. Let's remember one person who didn't ride the Tour but was present at its worst moment, Tommy Simpson's death in 1967. This was the British team's mechanic, Harry Hall (Manchester), Harry Hall Cycles, Ist Three Shires Road Race, 1952, Veteran World Road Champion, 1989. He tended to Simpson on the Ventoux mountain before the stricken rider died and heard his friend's last words. 'The straps, Harry! The straps!'

VII

Poster for '*le petit tour*', 1946.

Just a boy and a teenager in the 1950s, I had no part to play in the BLRC disputes, though it was easy to know which side to join. Up the League! Veteran cyclists still greet each other with the slogan and use other phrases we learnt many years ago. We shout 'Ally ally ally' as encouragement in races – and not everyone realises that this old League chant is an innocent corruption of the French *Allez!*

I am a child of the League and of communism, a powerful and ineradicable mixture. The League formed my adolescence, while I had been drinking the red milk of communism since birth. My real first name is Timoshenko, after the renowned marshal of the Red Army. I doubt whether my parents' politics inclined me towards the League, which attracted everyone who wished to flex the muscles of youth. But its internationalism and pariah reputation suited a person with my background.

I first visited France in 1948, when my communist father drove his small family to the Midi in my maternal grandfather's Bentley. Little boy though I was, I could master books like a journalist. A box at the back of the car held my reading matter. There were books about Robin Hood, Geoffrey Trease's *Bows against the Barons* (1934) and such Soviet works as *Timur and his Comrades*, a children's story about a young member of the Komsomol and his work in building a new socialist state (a book which I secretly dismissed in about twenty minutes). On the journey I was content to look at France through the windows of the Bentley: long avenues of trees, rivers, castles, vineyards, towns which seemed partly to have fallen down. My diary is in existence, but memory serves better to recall the wine I tasted, the strange, wonderful food eaten out of doors at twilight. The weather was hot. What was that noise of crickets? Then it became cold and windy, and my father drove to high Alpine villages whose people were goitred. Their swollen faces were brown with filth, they dressed in rags and lived in *taudis*, hovels, with their animals.

A few years later, when I became a cyclist, thoughts of that 1948 expedition increased my wish to understand the Tour de France. Cycling is not merely about physical pleasure. It is also about knowledge and living memory: the memories we can share with those who are still alive.

The Tour is now a hundred years old. Every year it is an epic; and every year there are stages of the race that are epics in themselves, containing dozens of human stories of heroism, toil and suffering. The Tour is both theatre and poetry. It reflects all the history of France, and indeed Europe, in the last century. The ideal historian of the Tour would also know about social geography, international relations and folk religion; together with the nature of immigration, the use of drugs, television, money, political power and advertising. This historian should also be a linguist, French, and a racing cyclist with a feeling for the tragedy of the twentieth century.

Such a writer has never been born, so we must look elsewhere. No need to waste time with, for instance, the vile scribes of *Les Temps modernes*, except to say that French intellectuals have missed a wonderful subject that lay right before their eyes. Personally I prefer French journalists. They have more relish for life than academics. The vast majority of people who have added to our knowledge of the Tour have been from the press; but, alas, their accounts and interviews are mainly hidden in the archives of newspaper libraries. Many general books recount the history of the Tour, generally beginning with its origins in the press.

*　　*　　*

The Tour de France was founded in 1903 by Henri Desgrange, a racing cyclist (the first *recordman de l'heure*, with 35.325 kms) who was also a journalist. Desgrange had the idea of a very long race as a publicity vehicle for his paper *L'Auto*. It was in rivalry with *Le Vélo*, which organised the two longest cycling events of the time, Bordeaux–Paris and Paris–Brest–Paris. A race all the way around France, Desgrange thought, would give *L'Auto* an advantage over the other publication. The pattern of the Tour was established very early in its life. First, it was to be a circuit of the country. Second, there were to be long stages between different towns and cities. Third, the difficulty of the Tour would be augmented by climbs in the Alps and the Pyrenees. Mountain stages were an essential part of the race from 1910. The winner of the Tour – the person who rode back to Paris with the shortest aggregate time in a race that lasted for three weeks or more – would need to be a climber.

The development of the Tour de France was interrupted by the two world wars but enjoyed a 'renaissance period' between 1947 and 1953, the year of its golden jubilee. It is difficult to say when the 'modern' Tour de France began. Was it formed by commerce, or by publicity, or by globalisation, *mondialisation*? Did it begin with the rise of trade teams rather than regional or national teams, after 1961? Or with television coverage, which began in 1955 and was first transmitted *en direct* in 1957, and with the help of helicopters after 1975? Or with the failure of French cyclists in their own national event, for a Frenchman has not won since Bernard Hinault in 1985?

On another view, the 'modern period' belongs to riders who have won the Tour three times or more. There had been multiple winners before Hitler's war, notably the Belgian Sylvère Maes (in 1936 and 1939), but the tendency to win again and again began in 1953. Here is a list of the dominating multiple winners:

Louison Bobet, 1953, 1954, 1955.
Jacques Anquetil, 1957, 1961, 1962, 1963, 1964.
Eddy Merckx, 1969, 1970, 1971, 1972, 1974.
Bernard Hinault, 1978, 1979, 1981, 1982, 1985.
Greg Lemond, 1986, 1989, 1990.
Miguel Indurain, 1991, 1992, 1993, 1994, 1995.
Lance Armstrong, 1999, 2000, 2001, 2002, 2003.

These seven men have achieved thirty-one victories between them.

In the years when the multiple champions did not take the Tour there were some equally memorable victors. On rare occasions they won because their team leader had crashed or had been taken ill. In 1966, for instance, Jacques Anquetil – suffering from bronchitis and, at the age of thirty-two, exhausted by a career that had begun in his teens – climbed off when there were only six stages left before Paris, having first ensured that the Tour would be gained by a modest teammate. Lucien Aimar saw his opportunity and took it, riding into the Parc des Princes in yellow, but without a single stage win to his credit.

Let no one imagine that Aimar was a cyclist of the second rank. It is true that he regarded Anquetil as a revered elder brother. Although they shared rooms for five years Aimar always addressed his team leader as *vous*. But Aimar was a vital presence and a potential winner in any race. In 1968 he won a stunning victory in the French national championship, beating Roger Pingeon, who had outdistanced him in that year's Tour de France. Pingeon, like Aimar, could have won the Tour more than once. Both men had their victories and failures in the political team tactics of the Tour in the 1960s. Pingeon was the more calculating of the two. Aimar often said that he had the relaxed attitude of his homeland, the Côte d'azur, while Pingeon was reserved (he would not share a room with anyone) and a perfectionist. After 1968 his career and his spirits were destroyed by the rise of Eddy Merckx.

The most surprising winner of the Tour has been Roger Walkowiak, a miner's son from the Polish enclave in Alsace. He rode the 1956 Tour as an unnoticed member of the Nord-Est-Centre regional team. When he finished in yellow there were no extended plaudits, though the Tour had been run at a record overall speed of 36.268 kph. Walkowiak gave his winnings to his old dad, raced intermittently for three more seasons and then went back home to a job in a factory. It is said that 'Walko' was a stupid man who lacked the will to dominate. In 1956 he was certainly directed by his team manager to get into the right breaks and then to take it easy. Would it have been better if he had gone for senseless adventures off the front of the bunch, and then lost the race?

Another unexpected winner was Joop Zoetemelk, who wore the yellow jersey on the Champs-Elysées in 1980. As a competitor, he was the superior of Aimar or Walkowiak. The reasons why people were surprised that he won were, first, because he was Dutch; second, because he was old (thirty-four); and, third, because they were used to him failing to win. Zoetemelk's *palmarès* is in some ways unmatched. He started and finished no fewer than sixteen Tours and was second on six occasions. His long and admirable career was concluded when he won the world professional road race title in 1985, at the age of thirty-eight. On the Giavera di Montello circuit he used finesse and then sheer speed to defeat Greg Lemond and Moreno Argentin.

That may well have been Zoetemelk's favourite victory. 'There are those who win the Tour once and then no longer speak about it,' says Zoetemelk. 'I was one of them.' The Dutchman is also one of the sizeable number of former Tour heroes who become reclusive in later life. Some of them are very odd and anti-social. We hear of them living on a farm in a remote part of their native region, or in a forest, not much liking human contact, a gun-dog their preferred companion. Others, by contrast, make their living from former sporting renown. Old Belgian champions often own bars. The more renowned a cyclist, the more likely that he will enter the public relations business. French Tour veterans contribute to the vast, and still growing, hospitality industry that accompanies cycle sport. Or they drive team cars and supporting vehicles. Retired cyclists are better at this task than rally drivers or other professional motorists.

A select number of Tour winners become team managers. One of them is Bjarne Riis, the Dane who put an end to Miguel Indurain's reign when he dominated him on an Alpine stage in 1996. I would rather not call him a great man of the Tour de France. The same applies to Marco Pantani. In 1998, a year in which he had already won the Giro d'Italia, Pantani flew up the roads of the Alps and the Pyrenees to become only the third man (after Fausto Coppi and Stephen Roche) to win both the Italian and French tours in the space of only a few months.

1998 was the year of the Festina drugs scandal, when it became clear that EPO was used throughout the peloton. Whatever the illegal fuel that helped him ride, Pantani was a climber in the grand tradition. After one day in the mountains he sprinted to the heights of Les Deux Alpes nine minutes clear of his nearest rival. He was never again to ride so well.

Like most long-time lovers of the Tour, I mull over the years in which *la grande boucle* was won by a specialised climber.

Now follows a list that gives a different slant to the history of the post-war Tour. On page 66 I gave a list of the multiple winners, cyclists with three or more wins. Here are the Tour winners *excluding* the multiple victors.

1947 Jean Robic, France
1948 Gino Bartali, Italy
1949 Fausto Coppi, Italy
1950 Ferdi Kubler, Switzerland
1951 Hugo Koblet, Switzerland
1952 Fausto Coppi, Italy
1956 Roger Walkowiak, France

1958 Charly Gaul, Luxembourg
1959 Federico Bahamontes, Spain
1960 Gastone Nencini, Italy
1965 Felice Gimondi, Italy
1966 Lucien Aimar, France
1967 Roger Pingeon, France
1968 Jan Janssen, Netherlands
1973 Luis Ocaña, Spain
1975 Bernard Thévenet, France
1976 Lucien van Impe, Belgium
1977 Bernard Thévenet, France
1980 Joop Zoetemelk, Netherlands
1983 Laurent Fignon, France
1984 Laurent Fignon, France
1987 Stephen Roche, Ireland
1988 Pedro Delgado, Spain
1996 Bjarne Riis, Denmark
1997 Jan Ullrich, Germany
1998 Marco Pantani, Italy

Let readers imagine that we are in a cafe, bar or *buvette* in rural France. It is the late morning of a warm day in mid-July. The television is switched on and it is following the Tour de France from, shall we say, Figeac to Superbesse, a distance of 221 kilometres. The village is quiet and so is the cafe. Fewer than a dozen customers, all male, are sitting with their morning drinks, wine mostly, maybe a Suze, in my case a Ricard, '*un peu de soleil dans une bouteille*', as its inventor, the Marseillais genius Paul Ricard, liked to say.

We have newspapers which give reports of yesterday's events on the road and a page of the Tour's General Classification, from the *maillot jaune* to the *lanterne rouge*. There are flies on the ceiling. The television grinds on. Nothing much happening in this early part of a transitional stage. Some of the men smoke Gauloises, others Caporals. I am making marks in biro against the *Classement général*. In an hour or so lunch will be offered, probably hors-d'oeuvre, chicken, fruit, cheese. From my place at a formica table I can see the village priest walking up and down the street. What big black boots in this summer weather. Time for another Ricard. Some children run in and out of the cafe. The television says that there has been a breakaway, not an energetic one, and after 80 kilometres of racing the peloton has come together. The TV commentator talks of the old days.

'*Messieurs!*' I might cry to other men in the bar. 'I am myself a former racing cyclist, from Birmingham near Wolverhampton, of little merit, it is true, but I am a true lover of the *vélo*. I have with me a list of all the winners in the Tour de France in the last fifty years which excludes every rider who has won the Tour more than three times. Tell me, my friends, tell me this, were not those Tours more interesting, more *émouvant*, than those in which we saw the repeated triumphs of the greatest champions in the race which has occupied us for all of our lives?'

Try this conversation in a provincial French cafe before lunch and you will still be in fierce or genial debate all afternoon, and until the dinner plates are cleared. This is the way that the Tour is – or used to be – discussed. I wish I had spent more time in such cafes. Perhaps it is not too late. A few months ago I had a café-cognac *sur le zinc* in a Parisian bar before the next day's Paris–Roubaix, and the drink was with my son. So there may be a future for us all – though I can never rid myself of hankering for the old days of English poetry about club runs, which I shall now describe.

VIII

Post war pastoralism:
Tintern Abbey from the *CTC Gazette*, 1945.

The first British cyclist to ride the Tour de France was Charlie Holland, a hero from Birmingham. A member of the Midland C & AC, he spent most of his life as a newsagent but had a short professional career before the war. In 1937 (the year Roger Lapébie won) he survived the Tour until its eleventh stage. He could have gone further, but was eliminated as a result of one of Henri Desgrange's most absurd regulations. The father of the Tour had decreed that riders could not carry more than two spare tubulars. Holland suffered from punctures during the stage between Perpignan and Luchon, so was ruined.

It had been a brave contribution to the Tour. Charlie Holland had never even seen a bigger mountain than Snaefell on the Isle of Man, so the Galibier – the fearsome, snow-capped col that rises above Briançon, the highest town in Europe – was a challenge beyond his experience or imagination. That year the riders had to struggle through thick mud from melted Alpine snow. On his dogged way to the summit of the Galibier Charlie passed Maurice Archambaud, sobbing by the wayside, unable to continue. And Archambaud was a champion, the holder (like Desgrange before him) of the hour record *sur piste*, an experienced man of the Tour who was willed on by thousands of French fans. Holland had no one at all to support him. As far as the bosses of British cycling were concerned, he might have been riding on the moon.

Charlie Holland's pioneering ride in 1937 was a high point in British cycling. High, and also remote. Eighteen years would pass before, in 1955, there was again a British presence in the Tour de France. To this day (2003) only fifty-one British cyclists have ridden the Tour and only twenty-one of them have completed the race. This is a modest number. But let us be grateful to the BLRC. If it were not for the League there would have been even fewer British riders on the continent. All of the earlier British riders in the Tour were brought up in the BLRC. Tom Simpson – the dead king of British cycling – was an utterly characteristic Leaguer whose early career was formed by BLRC attitudes.

Why have there not been more British cyclists in the Tour de France? Dozens of our boys had legs for the job. Alas, they were not encouraged by our official bodies. The professional class was weak and big cycle companies like Hercules and Raleigh retreated from sponsorship. We were all absorbed in the domestic sport of time trialling. And always in the background was the innate pastoralism of our cycling culture. This attachment to rural rambles and the gentle pleasures of the countryside is most obviously seen, I think, in cycling poetry.

The Britons who raced on the continent are a different breed from those who wrote poetry after riding their bikes in the English countryside, but there is some common ground. The racing men and the poets understand each other, for they come from the same background in British cycling club life.

*   *   *

Poetry!? By racing cyclists!? Yes, though mainly by recreational cyclists. Hundreds of people, maybe thousands, have become poets with no other reason for writing poetry, or writing at all, than their devotion to the bicycle. On my shelves is a collection of their verses. It is a small anthology in proportion to the huge total number of cycling poems written since the 1890s. The tradition continues and flourishes, not quite in secret but in privacy, for the poems are published in club magazines and nowhere else.

The themes of cycling poetry are quietly stated and the verse is not obscure. Cycling poets write in conventional ways. They

73

describe the weather and the alternation of the seasons, matters that everyone can understand. Time trialling is a common subject. Our poets are also inclined to discuss age and death, for the further ends of life are a cycling preoccupation. Yet they don't treat death as a drama. Oddly enough, I have never come across a poem about the death of Tom Simpson. Perhaps they don't get published. I wouldn't be surprised if Simpson poems exist or once existed. They would be sealed in a feeding bottle and then buried under the stones at the horrible monument on Mont Ventoux. People take *anything* to this shrine.

Passionate love poetry is rare. Cyclists do of course write about attractive women. The most favoured women are barmaids. Next most popular are the owners of traditional cafes and teashops. In third place, some way behind, are other cyclists. Here is the author of 'Lines written after a chance encounter with a charming member of the Merseyside Ladies' Cycling Association':

> A presence brought enchantment to the ride
> A presence, riding with me, by my side . . .

There are also many poems which address a favourite bicycle as though it were a good old wife:

> We've had some pretty good times together
> Awandering up and down the hills and dales . . .

Other categories of cycling verse include the very important rolling-road poems, with their tales of memorable rides:

> At the witching hour one winter's night, snow
>   thick upon the ground
> Some Clarion lads from Manchester left Handforth
>   homeward bound . . .

And there are many good-cheer poems:

> There's an inn down in Surrey that's known far and wide
> For the welcome extended to all those who ride . . .

At one time it was also common for clubs to sing as they went along the road together. The club run, especially after it turned for the homeward ride, but before the final 'blind', became a wheeled choir. If the run was well attended there had to be a choirmaster in the middle of the bunch to coordinate the tempo and remind clubmates of the words of songs. The effect was probably ragged, but a singing club run must have been an impressive thing, astonishing to a bystander.

Some songs – I write of days long gone by – were from the music hall or were well-known ditties such as

> Summer rain brings the roses again
> After the clouds roll by . . .

Less often, clubs sang the classics of choral music. Beethoven's 'Ode to Joy' was a favourite, though no one knew the German words and there has never been a translation into English. Ignorance of the words of songs led cyclists towards mockery. 'The Soldiers' Chorus', for instance, was sung as 'Beer, boys, and bugger the Band of Hope', probably as the Sunday club run passed some nonconformist chapel.

Some clubs had their own poet who wrote songs and coached other members. The Catford CC was one of them. This song comes from the Catford:

> We're boys of every sort, in all the branches of the sport,
> The road and track boys, the lady-back boys,
> Our object is good sportsmanship, our racing is good fun,
> Our motto is Good Fellowship, for each and ev'ry one . . .

A 'lady-back boy' is the owner of a tandem who has a girlfriend. This Catford song probably has an early date, since the singing club runs were most popular in the 1920s and 1930s. The last report I have of a club wheeling through the lanes in song (a CTC section: it would be, wouldn't it?) comes from the mid-1950s. I never myself experienced a singing club run though I know some people, rather older than me, who recall the phenomenon. One of them points out that only cyclists would have joined in such a practice. 'Other people aren't crazy enough.'

The songs, recitations and poems began with the first Clarion 'smokers' and the birth of club magazines. Some of them relate to a minor development in English literature. In the 1890s there was a vogue for rolling-road poems from the pens of such official writers as Hilaire Belloc, G. K. Chesterton and John Masefield. They made an addition to English nature poetry simply by writing so much about roads. Many of their sentiments were transferred to verses by cyclists. The same official writers often give us descriptions of gypsies. And, sure enough, a preoccupation with the wandering people of the countryside also has a place in the literature of cycling. For what is a cyclist, if he is not a postman who dreams of becoming a gypsy?

The Romany is weather-beaten, misunderstood, ungovernable and free. So he entered the lore of cycling as soon as the sport became truly popular and became an alternative way of life for the low paid. Many of the clubs founded in those days – plenty of them still in existence – have the words 'nomads', 'wanderers' or 'vagabonds' in their names. It had been easy for the young spirits who founded such clubs to make an association with the gypsy. Cyclists went their own way through the lanes or across the heath, as the wind or fancy took them. They carried few possessions, wore bright clothing, were refused entry to the more genteel pubs, tinkered with their mounts at the side of the road, took their meals behind hedges and slept in haystacks.

*　　*　　*

I am old enough to remember the haystacks and still think it was a good way to spend Saturday night. Today, veteran cyclists bore their sons and teenage clubmates with tales of rough nights when they burrowed into barns and ricks, fearful of the farmer even after the pint or two they had probably drunk. How scratchy the haystacks were, how rural they smelt, how a lad longed for a lass to be with him in his hayhole!

Haystacks were useful to us for quite practical reasons. They provided cost-free lodgings close to the start of time-trial courses. You could spend Saturday night in a haystack and be there and ready to race on Sunday morning. Many time triallists camped before an event, but there was more than a touch of respectability about their Bukta or Blacks-of-Greenock tents, their shaven faces and wifely wives. A racing man from a haystack was a more dangerous sort of cyclist.

Haystack nights disappeared in the 1960s, when people had more money and looked for a different style. The old prestige accorded to haystackers came from their vagabond or wild-man demeanour. Cycling lore contains many stories about strangers who appear in the night or who join the road from a woodland path. A lone cyclist enters a remote country pub. He asks for a pint and an empty smaller glass, then produces half a dozen duck eggs from a brown paper bag. The mysterious wheelman pours a little beer from his pint into the smaller glass, cracks an egg into it and drinks the mixture. He does this five more times. Then he finishes his beer and leaves the hostelry, away on his bike to who knows where.

All stories signify something beyond themselves. What does this story mean? Perhaps the cyclist is really a fox. Are there parallels in the folk legends of, for instance, Belgium, a country of beer, cycling, early dark nights and short distances between country and town?

Another cycling legend – one that does have equivalents in British folklore – concerns the old-timer. In song and story he is not awheel but is encountered at the side of a road. He wears unfashionable clothes, carefully washed and stitched where necessary. He is not the sort of person who takes his rest in a haystack. He might be a ghost. The old-timer's bike is ancient. Some of its accessories, in this story usually the mudguards, are held to the frame by twisted pieces of wire. But the transmission – chainset, chain and back sprocket, the heart of a bicycle – is expertly and beautifully maintained. The old-timer has climbed off to eat his sandwiches or to smoke a pipe. Other cyclists riding the same road instinctively brake and stop to say a word in fellowship or homage. He replies only with the words 'It's a grand life'. Just as no one has seen him ride, nobody knows where he comes from. But some versions of this myth give the old-timer a Black Country accent.

Is it merely coincidence that the photographs of Reg Harris, advertising his Raleigh bicycle, used to put the world champion in this old-timer pose, on a grassy verge by an English hedge, with pipe in hand, smiling in kindly fashion?

One final country legend. Almost as memorable as the old-timer is the icon of the peripatetic poet. He is on his bike in the countryside, sometimes glimpsed by other cyclists, shepherds and thoughtful rural folk. On occasion he is lying on the verge of the road, apparently asleep. What does this mean?

The cycling figure is surely formed from two more familiar icons. The first is the scholar-gypsy, who, as we know, flits from river to inn to hilly path. The second is the wandering minstrel. Why do minstrels wander? Any bright young Birmingham Marxist of the 1950s will immediately put his hand up with the answer. It is because they have been expelled, by capitalism, from their true home in the feudal hall, and so must endlessly travel, with no warm place to lay their heads and few people to hear their melancholy song. Sir Walter Scott will tell you the same story. And, as the cycling poet recounts,

His head on his battered musette, a dreamy look in his eye,
The cyclist lay by the roadside, watching the world go by.
And his mind went off on a journey, to the land of
    make-believe,
Where the laws no longer run that bind the sons of Adam
    and Eve.

Etymologically, the French *musette* means, originally, a sheep's bladder; then, a bag; then, a primitive form of bagpipes, made from the bladder; and so we have the more familiar notion of the *bal-musette*, a rustic dance or jolly occasion in some *quartier* where country met city, and in which the ceremonies were led by traditional and informal music.

For the modern cyclist, a musette is a small fabric bag slung over the back for carrying provisions such as maps, Mars bars, 'speed mixture' (which is a cake of prunes and rice that wards off the bonk), amphetamines, inner tubes. British cyclists often call them 'bonk bags'*. Leaguers made them from that striped material used in deck chairs. In long races musettes containing food are handed up to riders by someone at the roadside. The professionals then throw them away, while the rest of us fold musettes and keep them in the pocket of a road jersey. I always carry one, just in case; and in autumn days I use a musette to ride home with shaggy woodland parasol mushrooms, or perhaps a pheasant that has been struck dead by some murdering bourgeois in a big black car. A freshly killed pheasant in a musette gives a little warm nudge to the lower vertebrae, a strange feeling that I suppose is known only to cyclists – and poachers, now I come to think of it.

---

* 'The bonk' is a cycling term for a sudden loss of power and energy. It is accompanied by depression and sometimes tears. The condition is unknown to other sports and therefore to anyone who is not a cyclist. It can hit you very suddenly, when a cyclist will say 'I've blown'. There are many other demotic terms. We speak of 'The knock', 'hunger knock', 'the sags', and fear the time when 'Old Mr Saggy comes knocking at the door'. The rather official French word is *défaillance*. Bonk is caused by a lowering of the blood sugar level. The remedy is in food and drink. Hardriders always carry bonk bars, in former days prepared to gruesome recipes. Try oats slowly baked with syrup, lard, margarine and cocoa powder, together with chopped mixed fruits previously soaked in Guinness. But never eat anything that will make your handlebars sticky. *Always* have a bonk bar after two hours, even if you're not hungry. The first time my son had the bonk (aged 12) I got him home, my arm around his shoulders. Then he had four giant helpings of Coco-Pops and milk before falling asleep, still wearing track mitts. No bonk is worse than the bonk you suffered as a teenager.

79

IX

A typical drawing by Frank Patterson.

The connection between cycling and Georgian rolling-road mythology found a visual poetry in the art of Frank Patterson, which captures the spirit of cycling in the years before the motor car occupied our highways and byways. Patterson drew illustrations for cycling magazines for half a century. His career coincided with the period of the bicycle's most popular appeal. Drawings by Patterson first appeared in *Cycling* in 1893. They filled its pages until his death in 1952 and are still reproduced, for this unique artist had neither a rival nor a successor.

It is said that Patterson produced some 26,000 drawings for publication. I believe this figure. Patterson was fluent, regular and knew exactly what he was about. His style, established early in life, was constant. Very thin pen lines, often elongated, each line close to the next, describe rural scenes, landscapes and quaint country buildings. Patterson never used cross-hatching or a wash. His line, though not distinguished, did everything he needed. The original drawings were three or four times larger than their published reproductions, so readers of *Cycling* and the *CTC Gazette* marvelled at his virtuoso penmanship.

Patterson's drawings always included a cyclist or a bicycle. They depicted the things that old-fashioned cyclists like – a drovers' road over Welsh hills, Lakeland passes and Peak District rough-stuff tracks, the Great North Road at Eaton Socon, so familiar to time triallists; market towns with coaching inns; castles, wishing wells, thatched country pubs, the Roman Wall, remote parish churches and the final miles home by moonlight.

Sometimes Patterson would make it clear that the cyclist who appeared in his drawing, speeding along traffic-free roads, was riding in a time trial. This was the only kind of cycle sport that he drew. He never shows us a massed-start race, a track meeting or a club run. His cyclists are usually alone. Occasionally they are in pairs or greet each other at crossroads. Very rarely, Patterson allowed a woman cyclist to appear, invariably on the back of a tandem.

'Pat', as he was called by his few intimates, had an enormous but imprecise effect on the nature of English cycling. Both he and his near contemporary Robert Blatchford, founder of *The Clarion* (Blatchford 1851–1943, Patterson 1871–1952), were journalists who established the mood of their era. They did not resemble each other. Blatchford knew that cycling meant comradeship, escape from the city, political optimism, tandems, marriage, the future. Patterson by contrast was reclusive. He scorned the idea of fellowship, never visited a city and had no passion for cycling. Frank Patterson was not the member of any club, not even the CTC. After a little early touring he gave up the bike in 1906.

The purpose of his art was to embalm the England he had known as a boy. He grew up to know old country life, the obscurity of distant villages and the eccentricities of such rustic folk as appear in his drawings. Sometimes they wear smocks. They seldom appear to work. This was the England that Patterson wished to preserve. And, in one little corner, he was successful. Patterson built himself a utopia that was under his autocratic rule for half a century. Pear Tree Farm, near Billingshurst in Sussex, is a rambling Tudor building which Patterson first saw, almost in ruins, in the late 1890s. He rented it, repaired the dilapidated parts and eventually was able to buy the property.

Pear Tree Farm was suited to Frank Patterson's tastes and modest social ambitions. This marine engineer's son from Portsmouth aspired neither to riches nor to a wider fame in his profession. He did not think of himself as an artist. His one desire was to own a piece of English land and to live on that acre or two as a countryman. He did not wish to appear as a gentleman, since he cared little for grandeur or good manners. He also realised that a farmer's life was laborious, so he decided to live on a farm and earn his bread in another, secret way. Patterson's neighbours were never told how he and his family were employed.

The first romantic advantage of Pear Tree Farm was its antiquity. The second was its location. It was inaccessible. No road, nor even a path, led from the farm to the outside world. Visitors were strictly discouraged. Wheelfolk might have come to his door, expecting a genial welcome from a fellow cyclist; but the approaches to the house were difficult, wooded, muddied, over fields. And if a cyclist had managed to arrive at Pear Tree Farm he would have been met by a balding, portly, cantankerous man wearing tweeds and carrying a gun, for Patterson was keen on firearms and had a rifle with him at all times.

Now for the artist's habits. Up from his slumber at dawn, in summer and winter, Patterson's first task was to shoot his supper. Through fields and coppices he roamed. Rabbits, hares, partridges, pheasants, pigeons fell to his fire. The game was carried back to the house. As far as was possible, Pear Tree Farm was self-sufficient. Its owner wished to be isolated from the wider market economy. Ground was cleared for vegetables, berries and fruits. Patterson's wife dug his potatoes and tended his hop bines. Her husband drank her beer throughout the day, even when he was in bed.

Lighting was by candle, rush light and oil lamp. The children were disciplined within the house, though they could do as they wished in the fields and woods. Patterson had dogs and a horse. I do not know whether he kept a pig. Conceivably not. To own a pig was the sign of a cottager. Patterson was of no social class, but he was sure that he was not a peasant.

Patterson's wife died in her early forties. Then his two daughters ran away from home. He married the woman who had been his wife's nurse and she bore him two more children. Family traditions were always maintained. Every day, without fail,

Patterson did his artistic work after lunch. The heart of Pear Tree Farm is an antique room with a huge inglenook fireplace. In Patterson's day it was decorated with crossed muskets, pewter tankards and an ancient clock. In the middle of the room was an oval table. Patterson spent the afternoon at this convenient surface, where were placed his pens and ink, to the right, and his visual aids to the left. Nobody was allowed to see him draw.

Every week ten elaborate illustrations were made into a package. Patterson did not care if he never saw them again and never made a collection of his art. His wife took the drawings, on horseback, to Billingshurst, where there was a train service to London. Soon they would arrive at the offices of *Cycling*. And this routine was maintained for forty years.

The public-house inglenook that so often appears in Patterson drawings – where a cyclist sits on a curved oak settle by a log fire, enjoying his pint – in fact depicts Patterson's favourite place in his own home. Pear Tree Farm was not merely his house; it was his local. He did not have to ride to a country pub, because his home was the perfect hostelry – the more so because travellers and strangers did not cross its threshold. Patterson never even met the writers of the touring articles he illustrated, though they were colleagues for years.

His two magazine editors, H. H. England and George Herbert Stancer, did make an annual visit to Pear Tree Farm. Every Christmas they brought Patterson presents and were allowed to sit in the inglenook. It was in their interests to keep their illustrator content. That was surprisingly easy: Patterson never complained about the wretched fees that the Temple Press, the publishers of *Cycling*, paid to the magazine's most popular contributor. 'G.H.S.' (as he was always known) and the reactionary Harry England realised that their visits to Pear Tree Farm should be few and that Patterson's secret had to be guarded. They ensured that the many thousands of people who loved his drawings never knew that Frank Patterson, who seemed to embody the spirit of cycling, was not a cyclist at all.

Even today, few cyclists are aware that Patterson was not really of our number. But he does belong to cycling, and to cycling alone. His art, which is unmistakable and resembles no one else's, has no recognition at all beyond the world of British clubmen. The drawings are not reproduced in surveys of illustration, are not sent to auction and are never found in galleries. Most of Patterson's output was destroyed by a fire in the Temple Press building in the Second World War. There may be some sheets somewhere and if there were opportunities to buy Patterson's original work some people would pay large sums, for all cyclists beyond a certain age have a bit of Patterson in them.

The reason for his place in our hearts is uncanny, and without parallel. Patterson's drawings give the impression that, wherever you ride, he has ridden there before you. We feel that his wheels had explored every lane in every English county. On hundreds or even thousands of occasions, we imagine, he had paused before some view and had climbed off his bike to take a sketchbook from its saddlebag. The truth is that Patterson scarcely went anywhere beyond the purlieus of Pear Tree Farm. His knowledge of places and scenery came from photographs and picture postcards.

Patterson's life coincided not only with the era of popular cycle touring but also with the golden age of the picture postcard. He must have had an immense collection of them, no doubt supplied by Harry England or someone else at the Temple Press. Patterson made good use of his sources, so good that we don't realise what those sources were. One can usually tell when a drawing has been copied from a photograph. Not so in Patterson's art: his style is so distinctive that the photographic origin is erased. Patterson is also immemorial. Although we feel that he has visited the places he portrays, the drawings seem to record the spirit of some past time, not an actual moment.

Consciously or not, Patterson evoked the period after the First World War. The emptiness of his drawings, which make much use of white space, reflects a real emptiness in rural England. Fathers and sons from so many villages had left for foreign fields, never to return. Like so many parents of his generation, Patterson was interested in ghosts. Some drawings include spectres from another world, while many more have a generally ghostly quality. Here is another reason why they appeal to cyclists. We all have quasi-spiritual memories that come to us when we traverse roads we have known before, quietly gliding between hedgerows, changing rhythm with the lie of the land or the strength of the wind, rising a little from the saddle to catch a glimpse of a stream. Pedestrians do not know these experiences. Neither of course do motorists. Only cyclists know what I'm talking about and it's useless to try to explain it to anyone else.

*   *   *

The mood that Patterson represents was also captured by a group of writers famous for their touring articles. Some were staffers on cycling magazines. Others had 'day jobs' and wrote in the evenings. The touring writers were also the lecturers who went round halls and clubrooms and institutes with heavy boxes of lantern slides. Often these lecturer-writers used pseudonyms. Here are some of their assumed names: 'Kuklos', 'Chater', 'Wayfarer', 'Winona', 'Cotter Pin', 'Ragged Staff', 'The Gangrel', 'The Potterer' and 'George a'Green'.

'Kuklos', the most interesting of them, was a man called Fitzwater Wray. His writing was held to be authoritative until about 1950, partly because of his great age. (One of his stories recounted a ride from Bradford to London in 1898, when the Great North Road still had grass in the middle of its rutted surfaces – or so he claimed.) 'Kuklos' was shrewd. He acted as an agent for sending 'city dwellers' on farmhouse holidays, so he has a place in the history of the tourist industry. He wrote a cycling column for the *Daily News* (some of his pieces were collected in *A Vagabond's Notebook*, 1908) and he had enough

French to recognise and translate Henri Barbusse's *Le Feu* (1916), a classic story of the Great War.

These cycling writers were most active in the years when soldiers came home after the two world wars. 'Wayfarer' (Walter McGregor Robinson) was a Merseysider who had fought in the trenches. His peacetime job, in Birmingham, was with an insurance company. He wrote in his dinner hours, published his work in *Cycling* and served for many years on the councils of the CTC. Touring articles by 'Wayfarer' led many Birmingham cyclists to previously unknown tracks among the mountains and lakes of North Wales. After his death in 1956 the Rough Stuff Fellowship (a body devoted to off-road riding) erected a memorial to him on the lonely highway over Pen Bwylch Llanrillo.

Not often, is it, that a simple part-time writer like 'Wayfarer' receives such a tribute. He has his monument because he gave heart to so many unassuming people and led them away from the dullness of their working lives. Touring writers were genuinely appreciated in the old days, even if they were as little talented as 'Ragged Staff' (Rex Coley), another Birmingham man, whose columns are gathered in *Cycling is Such Fun!* (1950) and *Joyous Cycling* (1953). Coley was the founder of the Cape Wrath Fellowship and issued certificates to cyclists who made the journey to the lighthouse at the north-western tip of the Scottish highlands. I remember him as a revered lantern-slide lecturer in the clubrooms of the Birmingham CTC. By mistake, I heard his talk 'A Warwickshire Lad'. It was about Shakespeare. I thought it was dreadful. Who would wish to look at pictures of Anne Hathaway's cottage when the excitements of the British League of Racing Cyclists were all around us?

X

A boy and his bike.

Time for more poetry, this time modern BLRC verse. 'The Veteran's Song' is so good that on this occasion I give the author's name. He was John Leeson. My quotation comes from a poem of much greater length, which begins:

> The time has come, the veteran said, to talk of many
>   things:
> Of thirty-four tooth sprockets and twenty-six tooth
>   rings:
>
> Of bicycles and bikers, of barns and bridleways,
> Of back roads and of bridges we knew in yesterdays:
>
> Of handlebars once popular, in shapes no longer seen:
> Binda and Capo Berta, Ventoux and Azureen:
>
> Of curly stays by Hetchins and curly forks by Bates;
> Of chromed and convoluted lugs and sleek
>   bilaminates;
>
> Of Taylor's touring tandems and Higgins' racing
>   trikes,
> Of sidecars and Rann trailers on vintage family bikes:
>
> Of youthful window-gazing at rows of gorgeous
>   frames –
> Arrays of chrome and colour crafted by famous
>   names;
>
> Of frames by Russ and Rotrax, Claud Butler,
>   Ellis-Briggs,

Frames brazed with fancy lug-work or welded in
    bronze on jigs:

Track frames with angles seventy-five, road frames at
    seventy-two,
Road-track frames for double lives, and short-based
    specials too.

Frames with orange, heavenly blue, or purple flame
    with jade:
Diamond-panelled, barber's poled, chequered and
    blended fade:

Heraldic badges, stylish script, chevroned Olympic
    bands,
And lugs picked out by sable brush by dedicated
    hands;

And canopied by pendant frames, pictures from
    magazines
Of continental heroes in sun-drenched racing scenes;

Of Coppi's blue Bianchi with Campagnolo gears,
Of proud Bartali's triumphs and Rene Vietto's tears;

Of battles on the pavé and tactics by the team,
Of frantic tyre changes and sprinting for the prime . . .

Now you know how to pronounce 'prime'. The French word
means an intermediate sprint within a longer road race, often
simply marked by a chalk line across the road, perhaps in a
village where cafe patrons or a shopkeeper put up some money
for the first rider to zip through their main street.

A wealth of internal evidence suggests that 'The Veteran's
Song' invokes the culture of BLRC cycling in south Yorkshire
in about 1954. It has a possible antecedent in Lewis Carroll's
'You are old, Father William', which parodied Robert Southey's
'The Old Man's Comforts, and How He Gained Them'. But

in the main the poem is doggerel – by far the most common verse form used by cyclists, jogging artlessly along just as the writer fancies. I am glad that doggerel has never been examined by literary historians. There is no reason why the poets who write happily in this mode should be criticised. It is a fact that doggerel cannot be written by an educated person. And here I see a danger. For if the whole population were educated in such a way that doggerel was eliminated, a goal that some politicians see before them, where then would we be?

So let us look at 'The Veteran's Song' in more detail, starting with the title. Everyone knows what a veteran is: someone old. It also denotes someone who has fought in a war, as Leeson perhaps had. In cycle racing, a veteran is a person who has reached the age of forty. We are given some seconds of allowance in time trials and occasionally are treated with respect.

Line 2 is wrong. Nobody ever had twenty-six teeth on a chainring, nor thirty-four on a sprocket. Leeson, just getting into his poem, hastily put down some incorrect numbers. The poet mentions barns in line 3 because he remembers sleeping in haystacks.

Lines 5–6. Some handlebars were named after great riders who introduced or popularised their shapes. Alfredo Binda (1902–86, racing 1922–36) was one such person. Some shapes were named after famous climbs. The *capi* are the coastal hills encountered at the end of the first classic of the year, Milan–San Remo. The Capo Berta is one of these hills. Mont Ventoux is the Provençal mountain of evil reputation. The 'Azureen' handlebar, known in Britain as the 'South of France' bar, was favoured by riders from the Mediterranean hinterland – stylish and often difficult people. The handlebar created a fashion but was no good. You couldn't ride properly on the tops and the brakes had to be fitted at a slant. What slaves to fashion we were.

The family firm mentioned in line 7, Hetchins, was based in Seven Sisters Road in north London and latterly in Southend-on-Sea. It made highly finished frames with curly back stays and elaborate lugwork. Eccentric front forks were a feature of frames built by E. G. 'Basher' Bates in Plaistow.

Line 9. Jack Taylor was a tandem specialist. Bespoke tandems are still (in 2003) built by his family firm. The Higgins firm made tricycles. Fred Higgins's workshop in south London was visited by all lovers of the trike, known to us as 'barrow boys'. Mostly they are mad, but some are elderly and infirm. I suppose I might end my days on a Higgins. When barrow boys die their widows sell their trikes to slightly younger men.

Line 10 refers to the practice of putting infant children into sidecars. When they were slightly older they rode a Rann Trailer, which is attached to the back of an ordinary bike. It has a tiny wheel and a separate transmission. Nowadays they are marketed as 'trailerbikes'.

As line 15 indicates, steeper frame angles are used for track machines, more relaxed angles for road bikes, while (see line 16) a road-track frame has track ends because it uses a single fixed gear. A 'short-based special' is a tandem built with the shortest possible distance between its two wheels, often achieved by curving the rear seat tube.

Lines 17–18. The colour and finish of racing bikes were of great concern. Sometimes we copied continental styles. 'Heavenly blue', for instance, probably refers to the colour of Bianchi bikes, a colour fancifully said to be that of the queen of Italy's eyes. The barber's-pole motif – always on the seat tube – was I believe indigenous. At the period of which Leeson writes, practically all of our knowledge of continental cycle sport came in the form of photographs in French cycling magazines, and this explains the allusions in lines 21–2. Pages from *Miroir-Sprint* and *But et club* were pinned to the walls of all good bike shops.

*   *   *

I know how Leeson felt about Bianchi frames and Campagnolo gears. I desired such things with a longing by which I am still

92

possessed. They were before me – but unobtainable – when at the age of twelve or thirteen, still riding an ASP, I began to spend hours and days in a Birmingham racing bicycle shop, Wilson's Cycles, at the city centre end of the Aston Road.

Wilson's Cycles was neither large nor small, just crammed full. Racks that went all the way up to the ceiling held frames. From the ceiling itself were suspended further rack-like constructions for wheels. Wilson's dealt exclusively in racing bikes. A customer would have to go elsewhere if he wanted an everyday bicycle or a 'sports model'. You couldn't even buy the products of such craftsmen as Claud Butler or W. F. Holdsworth, though they built decent machines within the British tradition. Wilson's was an outlet for imported racing equipment. Most of the stock was French or Italian, and it was of dazzling beauty.

The style of the shop was owed to David Wilson, who had been at Worcester School of Art before inheriting the business from his father. I doubt if he knew foreign languages. In Birmingham nobody spoke another tongue, except perhaps Welsh. No doubt he got his stock from the annual cycle show at Earl's Court. Wherever the equipment came from, this man with a shop on the Aston Road – which was still cobbled in places, and had malevolent tramlines – was an adventurous aesthete.

I already had a 'photographic' memory for paintings and was surprised when the satanic grown-ups who interested themselves in my education could not remember, as I could, the exact position of every work of art in a museum. This gift, however, did not mean that I could discriminate between paintings. Wilson's Cycles made me into an aesthete. I marvelled at the racy elegance of forks and stays, the delicacy and precision of the tooling, the perfect carpentry of wooden wheels, the Byronic brake levers capped with neat rubber pads, the jewellery of gear mechanisms, the saddles like flying greyhounds and, perhaps most of all, the wonderful daring of the colours mentioned by John Leeson, for at Wilson's were frames in plum – not maroon, which Sickert calls 'pink trying to be purple', but *plum* – scarlet, pearlescent grey, duck-egg blue, deep yellow and, most daring of all, pink.

At Wilson's Cycles on Saturday mornings racing men showed off the novelty and panache of their bikes. They gathered in dozens, all dressed in radiant club colours, before speeding into the country. I was too young to join these groups but had a privileged role at Wilson's, for I became the shop's errand boy.

As happens in any workplace, a lad who hangs around is given jobs to do. My tasks were to open boxes, sweep the floors and take things to the post office. I also rearranged the window display, the best job of all, and polished frames whose chrome had been left grubby by the handling of our local connoisseurs. Wilson's gave me no proper wage – fair enough since I did only bits and pieces of work; but I got a few shillings' reduction on the price of equipment, a Campagnolo rear mechanism my ultimate goal.

Two men were in charge at 217 Aston Road. I have forgotten their names. One lived in Coleshill, up the road from Aston at the northern end of Warwickshire (read this sentence aloud, and you will begin to have a Birmingham accent). He was a kind person. The other, quite a nasty man, had a blonde wife somewhere at the back of the shop who sent me out for her patent medicines. The ways of this couple made a mark on my adolescent mind. It was interesting to realise that they disliked each other. In the shop one day the husband showed me some dirty drawings printed on a sheet of pink cardboard. They depicted, in rows, about twenty types of women's breasts: fat or thin, full or sagging, nipples protuberant or sunken; breasts that were voluptuous, or lovely, laughable or painful to see. The jocular comments under each drawing weren't funny at all, but the draughtsmanship was remarkably good, within the limits of cartooning art. Anyway, by looking at these breasts I had been put through some kind of initiation ceremony. 'We're all red-blooded men in the League,' said the Wilson's shopkeeper.

XI

The Red Star Club.

How to become a red-blooded man? In my mid-teens I sometimes thought of the future. Life to come would have to include women, but for a time the bike took precedence over girls. Books were often interesting. You could get them from libraries. But I didn't like the experience of formal education. In any case, the communist intelligentsia wished their children to become members of the working class, so the purposes of education were confused. A career as a postman beckoned me, and for a time I became a telegram boy on a red roadster with a metal basket, delivering news of births and deaths to houses without telephones, mostly in Balsall Heath, Saltley and Nechells.

My hours in Wilson's gave me the idea that I might enter the cycle trade. It was a naive way of looking at the future. My qualifications as a shopman were as follows. For a teenager I was fast and strong. I could not sprint but in those days I could climb. My time trialling was uneven but promising and I could hold my own in the massed-start races around disused aerodromes – a feature of cycling life in the 1950s. Because of my family connections with the *Parti communiste français* I spoke understandable French and was able to read and translate French sporting magazines.

Like all racing cyclists, I was a connoisseur of the photographs in *But et club* and *Miroir-Sprint*. We became aficionados of the Tour de France through a love of magazine illustration. Not only the Tour, but other continental races too; for while French cycling was obviously classic in every way, and the Tour the pinnacle and epitome of its classicism, we learned also of the lesser French races – the Paris–Nice, the Critérium National, the Dauphiné Libéré, the Grand Prix des Nations – and were able to glimpse the far more distant world, beyond the Alps and the Pyrenees, of the Giro d'Italia and the Vuelta a España. There was a woeful omission in this self-education. About the great riches of Belgian cycling we knew next to nothing, though you can almost throw a stone from Kent into Flanders.

When I was with these cycling friends we talked about bikes and cycle sport and nothing else. The more we talked and exchanged information, the more certain we were that cycling was a separate world which nobody else could understand. I suppose all sports have their secrets and interior histories, but British cycling has been particularly self-enclosed. Apparently there are non-cyclists who think that we are eccentric. Even the old-fashioned and surely obvious principles of the club run appeared bizarre to some outsiders. One of them was the poet Edmund Blunden. He gives me my last example of pastoralism in British cycling, which I think was often a reaction to the experience of war.

Blunden's book *Cricket Country*, published in 1943, is about Englishness. Blunden believed that all people who did not share his interest in cricket were foreigners, or peculiar in some other way. At one point in *Cricket Country* we find its author in Belgium, receiving particularly good service in a restaurant. He got chatting with the waiter, and when he asked what the waiter did on his day off, discovered that he was talking to a cyclist. Here now is the Walloon waiter's reply to Blunden's question, and the English writer's comments:

> He answered glowingly, '*Je roule dans la campagne*' ... We, too, have our townsfolk who '*roulent dans la campagne*' with complete devotion to their deity, the wheel. They forge away and make their circuits as though no other sport or byplay existed; I should not like to ask them whether they thought the West Indies

would win the Oval Test, or anything so remote from them as that. They pursue some vision which clearly never disappoints them, which excites no greedy ardours, no envies . . . on they ply, he and she, a dozen perhaps in a drove, exactly dexterous, in a world of their own . . .

Ha! Does not Blunden's use of the word 'drove' indicate that he thinks cyclists are like sheep? Had it never occurred to him that cricketers far more resemble sheep than do cyclists? Their arena is like a fold and their umpires and scorers employ tally sticks. He is however correct to imagine that cyclists are usually indifferent to other sports.

Let us not forget the Belgian waiter. Let us indeed reflect for a moment on his position in life and his liking for the bicycle. There is much sympathy between racing cyclists and people who work in cafes and restaurants. In Belgium the regulars of a local cafe will have a kitty to support a young cyclist, probably a lad from the neighbourhood but maybe a visitor, even a British visitor. These supporters' clubs are often organised by waiters and the informal system usually works out well for all concerned. The cafe has its protégé and the lonely aspirant cyclist appreciates the warmth and welcome of the bar on the corner.

Waiters resemble professional cyclists in wider ways. They are good at noting the state of play in the peloton or the dining room. For months on end they may be far from their homes or their homeland. Their quarters are in small rooms, their possessions in suitcases. There is a lingua franca of the kitchen, which is French, just as the first shared tongue of the peloton is French. Waiters and racing cyclists quickly learn foreign languages, though seldom to the point of eloquence. Champions apart, most racing cyclists accept their humble role in life. They are, like waiters, *domestiques*.

Anyway, *Cricket Country* goes on to discuss the Tour de France:

I dare say you have heard of the Tour [yes, Mr Blunden], which in ordinary times catches the imagination of France in a manner beyond that of even a Cup Final or Grand National here. It has the advantage that, lasting four weeks or so, it goes the round of the country, it is everybody's at one point or another, and it exists as the grand highways do in their national unity, and business of life; these cyclists, while they strive for their prize, trace out the glorious map of their land, so various and so single . . .

This isn't so bad. A number of things should be said in Blunden's favour. His writing was formed by experiences in the First World War. Just twenty-one when he was sent to the Western Front, he was in the trenches for three whole years – and survived. In the 1930s he, the English poet, was able to travel to northern continental Europe as a free and living man. Alive, sentient, filled with memories, he walked and drove across the fields where so many of his generation had fallen.

Blunden saw their graves and then was served lunch by the cycling waiter. Living is better than mourning, and the pieties of his expedition would not have been complete without the pleasures of a restaurant. Good fortune to him; and perhaps there was a happy old age for Edmund Blunden, and more visits to Belgium, for he died as lately as 1974. That was one of the years when the Bruxellois Eddy Merckx won the Tour de France. I doubt, though, whether our cricket lover ever understood that Belgian cycling is grippingly concerned with life and death, if only as memory and metaphor.

*   *   *

I'm also wondering how many people of the British cycling classes returned to Europe on holiday – or to revisit north Africa, in the case of the Buckshee Wheelers – after their experiences in 1939–45. They cannot have been numerous. There was no money or time to spare. Holidays were limited to a summer fortnight. Cyclists took short family tours at Easter and in June they went to Isle of Man week. That was all. It seemed to be enough. The cyclists I knew who had returned from the desert or the Normandy beaches, or some other theatre of war, were simply glad to be home. The lanes had been waiting for them, and so had their loved ones.

Cyclists are said to have carried two photographs with them during their active service: one of a wife or girlfriend, the other of their club (a ragged line-up, unlike the official formations of cricket or soccer teams). Then Jack from the Wobbly Wheelers comes back to England to be reunited with his Jill and to get his bike out of the shed. He finds that he's in the same job, in the same factory where he worked before the war. Perhaps things are a little better than they were, despite the rationing. Jack and his wife might have a new council house on an estate. But they won't have much besides their home, and Jack certainly has no wish to return to France.

Many people of that sort were provincial and conservative – or so I then thought, being a bumptious young person. Today, I mourn for them. In the later 1950s, not with much fellow feeling, I observed one of their rituals. In May every year they rode to the cyclists' memorial service at Meriden in Warwickshire. In its church they remembered old comrades. Meriden, nowadays almost a suburb of Coventry, is reputedly the geographical centre of England. It has been a special place for cyclists since the end of the Kaiser's war, when the tradition of the service began. In 1921 there were 21,000 cyclists at Meriden. That is an astonishing figure. Nowadays there are about 500 of them. I rode down to Meriden only if a race had been organised. It was strange to see so many bikes, often of an antique sort, within the churchyard. After 'Onward, Christian Soldiers' the churchgoers left Meriden for a run to some quintessentially English shrine, Shakespeare's birthplace or Warwick Castle. I went elsewhere.

100

Not until years afterwards did I appreciate the way that cycling veterans rebuilt their broken world. Sometimes club cyclists did actual and literal rebuilding. After a day's work in a city, an hour or two awheel on Friday evenings might take them to a youth hostel that required their skills. In the war years its roof had been left in a damaged state. Pipes leaked, cables carried no power, the calor cookers had no gas. So the artisanal cyclists worked on their communal weekend home. They were good men. Just as I wouldn't go inside the Meriden church I avoided giving any help in these tasks. Of course I was a member of the Youth Hostels Association – we all were – but my use of the YHA was pretty selfish. I just wanted a place to stay and, with any luck, the opportunities to become a 'red-blooded man' as well as being a boy who sang 'The Red Flag'.

XII

Vietto's tears.

One more comment on *Cricket Country*. Its remarks about the Tour de France were made in a vacuum. By 1940 the great race had ceased to exist, its international aspect having already been lost in 1939. In that year (when the winner was the Belgian Sylvère Maes) there were no teams from Germany, Spain or Italy. In 1940 Henri Desgrange died. He had not followed a Tour since 1935. There was a natural successor as *directeur de la course* in Jacques Goddet, but this ultra-capable man refused to organise any cycling event during the Occupation, and it is in any case inconceivable that the Nazis would have allowed a Tour to take place.

There was still some bike racing during the war, more in Italy than in France, with quite a lot of track meetings in neutral Switzerland. A year after the Liberation Desgrange's old paper, *L'Auto*, reappeared in a new form as *L'Equipe*, a daily paper devoted entirely to sport. *L'Equipe* then made an alliance with another newspaper, *Le Parisien*. Between them they planned a rebirth of the Tour de France, to take place in 1947. There was an interesting rehearsal in 1946, a race known as the 'Petit Tour'. It was rather like Paris–Nice in reverse, for it began in Monaco and ended in Paris five days later. There were difficult passages through the Alps, where some roads had been mined, and indeed all roads had been neglected; and then there was a long last stage from Dijon to Paris.

The 'Petit Tour' was won by a new star belonging to the glamorous, controversial group of riders from the Côte d'Azur known as the *azuréens*. Apo Lazarides was the child of a Greek immigrant family. The French called him *l'enfant grec* and also, because they liked a touch of folk religion with their cycling, made him a nickname from his middle name, which was Apôtre.

Other people were wary of riders like this godlike youth from the Mediterranean, swarthy or olive-complexioned, reputed to be adventurous fishermen who had also known mountain combat. The *azuréens* were never to be comfortable members of the French national team, but they were often admired for a mixture of toughness and glamour that recalled the nature of their home territory. During the war the land behind the beaches, never very productive, had become desert. With peace, wealth returned in different forms. France saw the wonders of the new Côte d'Azur: the socialites, the casinos, the daring jewel thieves, the Cannes film festival (which began in 1946), the great villas, Picasso's riviera-style communism and the buzz of different languages. Many of the *azuréen* cyclists spoke the local dialect, not easily understood by anyone else, of Nice and its mountain hinterland, a patois whose territory extended to the lower Alpes Maritimes and Ventimiglia, just over the Italian border. A number of these riders, though French, had Italian surnames.

Apo Lazarides, *l'enfant grec*, had been coached and advised by the most able of all the *azuréen*, René Vietto. To tell his story, and to explain the reference to 'Vietto's tears' in John Leeson's poem, my narrative must dive back to the years before Hitler's war.

Vietto was born in Cannes and in all ways was a son of the riviera. Like so many others in his home town he had been brought up to work in the luxury hotel industry. He was a lift boy and a waiter. Rich people called out *Garçon!* and René hastened to do their bidding. He took orders, balanced cocktails on his tray, emptied ashtrays, accepted tips. His hours of duty over, René Vietto took off his long apron and black-and-white uniform. In seconds he was in the clothing of a racing cyclist. Then he got his bike from the back of the hotel and went off to train in the hills. Freedom! The promenades, wedding-cake hotels, terraces, cypresses and tennis courts were left behind, and forgotten, as Vietto rode up to the rough territory of the Massif de l'Esterelle or the Gorges du Loup.

This was in 1933–4, when Vietto was twenty. He didn't have a coach, which is why, a decade later, he so cared for *l'enfant grec*. But his earliest results were so dazzling that he seemed not to need advice. People had heard of Vietto even in distant Paris. He was invited to join the French national team that would contest the Tour de France. Thus the *garçon* from the hotel became a *domestique* for the team's leader, the commanding Antonin Magne, who had won the Tour three years earlier and was likely to do so again. In 1934 Vietto's role was to be at Magne's service. His work for his captain allowed Magne to win his second Tour and made the young Vietto the hero of the race. His heroism was in self-sacrifice, and therein lies his legend.

The 1934 Tour covered 4,363 kilometres in twenty-three days – a programme that could break the heart and health of a young man, however talented and fit. That year the average *moyenne de vainqueur* was 29 kph. During the first flat stages, which went from Paris to Lille and then southwards through Charleville and Evian to Aix-les-Bains, the speed was much higher. Vietto was disconcerted but held his place in the peloton. By Aix the French team had lost two of its most experienced riders, Maurice Archambaud and Charles Pélissier, both eliminated after crashes. Vietto therefore came much closer to Magne, who was riding with aplomb and had taken the yellow jersey at the end of the second stage.

This was still the position when the Tour approached the mountains. Magne was in yellow, his neophyte lieutenant well down on General Classification, bewildered but surviving. Then, as soon as the race began to climb the high Alps, everything changed. Suddenly, as the peloton tackled the first of the big mountain passes – they can be 20 kilometres long – Vietto was on his own. He had been riding at the front of the bunch, which then thinned behind him. Soon there was nobody who could follow his pace. Like all the supreme climbers, Vietto went uphill as though oblivious of the general state of the stage, and as though he could not ride more slowly. For a time a couple of Spaniards – climbers from a nation of climbers – organised a pursuit. Vietto was unaware of them, for they were a couple of kilometres further down the mountain. He finished this stage at Grenoble 3 minutes and 23 seconds before the Spaniards. Other leading contenders were even further adrift. This exploit took René Vietto from forty-third place on General Classification to third.

Now we must join our friends in the cafes and bars of Grenoble and listen to their conversation. 'Supposing,' said the *amateurs* of cycle sport, 'that the stage had been longer than its 229 kilometres and had included another mountain? Vietto might then have won by an even greater margin and might even have taken the *maillot jaune*!' Yes, but I think we hear the voices of the younger men in the cafe, about twenty years old, like Vietto, expressing their dreams.

More cautious people in the Grenoble bar argued as follows. 'My dear young friends, *soyons sérieux*. Here is a newcomer who is riding his first Tour de France, and it is unthinkable that he should displace the most senior and acknowledged leader of his team, the renowned Antonin Magne, who has all the qualities of a man from the Auvergne!' A further group of conservative thinkers agreed, though with the reservation that food in the Auvergne is the worst in France. 'This *azuréen* will cause difficulties in the national camp. And if he takes the yellow jersey there is no guarantee that this unknown twenty-year-old will have the necessary strength, let alone the tactical wisdom, to hold his position for another fortnight. Furthermore, his exertions in the mountains today will have drained him of strength, and now he is less likely to be able to perform his duties as a *domestique* to Magne, *ça va sans dire . . .*'

Conversations like this took place throughout the land, wherever Frenchmen gathered. On one point there would be agreement: the racing cycling team, especially in a long stage race, is a structure with its own rules and hierarchies. It has a leader. Some members of the team have particular abilities (the heavily built man is a sprinter; this short and light person is a climber) which enable them to win stages. But their main role is to protect the leader of the team, so that he can enter Paris in triumph. Vietto's astonishing talent threatened to break this understanding.

In the years when I began to learn about cycling it was often said that the model for a cycling team was feudal: all members of the team give their loyalty to a leader, king, captain or baron. In the view of a certain teenage Marxist there might be a better analogy in primitive capitalism, in which hierarchies are broken asunder. For in their young careers the best new riders must supplant their elders. They beat and sometimes humiliate not only cyclists from other teams but also their own comrades and even captains. Had this time come for 'Tonin' Magne and his servant Rene Vietto?

Vietto's riding was that of a new champion, but his devotion to his captain could not be questioned. The next day's stage, from Grenoble to Gap, was still in the mountains. Vietto rode strongly, yet within himself, and not once did he leave Magne's company. Shoulder to shoulder, the two Frenchmen looked closely at the Italians, and especially at Gianni Martano, for he was a potential winner of the Tour. Martano took the stage. But Magne and Vietto, riding together, were only seven seconds behind. The yellow jersey had been defended. *Le roi René*, as the newspapers now called Vietto, had been content with service.

The Tour had another day in the mountains after Martano's stage victory. Vietto now performed another aerial feat. On the Col de Vars he rode everyone off his wheel and was the victor at Digne. He had conquered the highest Alps and the road ahead led to his home on the Mediterranean, for the next stage ended at Nice. When the time came to tackle the awkward Col de la Turbie, Vietto was first at the summit, way in front of other people. At the top of the climb he sat up. The peloton, which included Magne, overtook him. Vietto settled into the bunch and acted as a member of the French team until the finish.

Vietto's magnificent Tour was crowned with a stage win in his home town of Cannes. How sweet that victory must have been! For a night, he was the most honoured guest in one of the hotels that, only a year before, had employed him. When the race entered the Pyrenees Vietto took his fourth stage victory at Pau. Magne was still race leader but was constantly harassed by the Italians. All of France looked on this Tour with growing excitement and anxiety. The outcome of the race was in a fine balance and its leading riders were desperately tired. One of three of them would take the ultimate prize: Magne, if the French team stuck together; Martano, if the French faltered; and Vietto, if he decided to strike against his captain.

He did the opposite. On the second day in the Pyrenees Magne fell on a mountain descent and damaged his wheel. Martano saw his opportunity and sprinted away. Vietto saw the situation, skidded to a halt and gave his own wheel to Magne. A service vehicle should have quickly arrived to give Vietto a replacement. It did not. Minutes passed. The wonderful waiter from Cannes chafed at the delay, then began to weep. Exhaustion and frustration had unmanned him.

These were Vietto's famous tears. The obvious interpretation of his *douleur* is that he had just lost the Tour by gifting the race to Magne. Other emotions must have also prompted Vietto's sobs, including rage at the driver of the support car. In any case, there is an unforgettable photograph – a French national icon – of Vietto's wait by the roadside, captioned in newspapers the next morning '*La vivante image du désespoir*'. Vietto is slumped on a stone wall, his bike is without a front wheel and he is crying like a child.

The next day Magne punctured, Martano attacked and Vietto

once more gave his wheel to his captain. A week later the Auvergnat rode into Paris as winner of the 1934 Tour de France. The cheers were louder for Vietto, who was fifth. It seemed certain that the new French hero, *l'ex groom d'hôtel*, would one day win the Tour. He did not. He briefly wore the yellow jersey in 1935 and for nine days in 1947, the year that the Tour was refounded. In the later 1930s Vietto had begun to suffer from knee injuries and operations. Somehow he lost all his money. It is said that he died (as a small farmer in the hills behind Cannes) an embittered man. Yet he must have known that he had a place in the hearts of his countrymen. In the year 2003 they still sigh and shake their heads with the memory of his brilliance and desolation.

XIII

Biagio Cavanna and Fausto Coppi:
a partnership in shades.

Vietto had become legendary: his story had more resonance than the plain facts of his life. Many cyclists generate a sort of mythology, especially if they have often been a part of the Tour de France. They stand for something in the minds of their admirers – bravery, ill fortune, magnanimity or, often, the nature and virtues of their native places – and their victories and defeats are recounted time and again, until the stories of their adventures on the road become exciting folklore.

The most 'legendary' of racing cyclists is Fausto Coppi. Everyone responds to Coppi's name, though it is forty years and more since his death. Stories about him and other cycling heroes were mostly gathered and dispersed in the press, and it is to the credit of the old journalists that they sensed the nature of the sport's popularity. For these pressmen of the people, Coppi was an inexhaustible subject. Their comments were not simply about his exploits on a bicycle, but concerned Coppi's unfathomable nature, his acquaintance with good and evil, the baffling contradictions of his character. It was said that he could never be understood, not by anybody.

Writers often began their stories with poetic speculations about Coppi's unusual and perhaps disconcerting Christian name. He was in fact christened Angelo-Fausto. This conjunction, said the newspapers, was an augury of Coppi's fate. He was to soar so high, yet fall so low, that he gave sorrow to the Pope himself. The cyclist was both an angel and a man from the realms of sorcery. His parents knew this, though unconsciously, and that is why they named him Fausto.

Thus ran the newspaper story. It is not likely, however, that

111

Coppi's father and mother, who were peasant smallholders in Castellania, near Novi-Ligure, thought of Goethe's necromancer when their son was born. Look at the etymology. The latin *faustus* means 'auspicious', 'favourable'. Look at the wider family. Coppi's paternal uncle was also a Fausto – and was the bearer of good fortune because he gave the future godlike champion his first racing bicycle.

*　　*　　*

Castellania would always be home to Fausto and his younger brother Serse, home whatever riches came his way. Home with its tiny village, stony fields, poor crops, thin wine; home with the vines and olive trees in the beautiful grey mountains above the blue Mediterranean.

But Angelo-Fausto does not wish to be a peasant like his neighbours. He tells his father (the old journalists often fell into the present tense at this point in their narratives) that he does not wish to till the bare fields of Castellania. For him, there must be other things in life. He dreams of his uncle Fausto, who left Castellania and became a seaman, who sailed in huge ships from Genoa and came home with gifts and amazing stories. Luckily for the world, the younger Fausto feels no call from the sea. He will not be a peasant, no, but neither will he be trapped in a boat. He will become a delivery boy for the butcher in a nearby town.

By bicycle, Fausto goes to work and makes his deliveries. The long journeys from his home to the butcher's shop are more satisfying than his employment. He begins to long for a better bicycle, perhaps even a racing machine, for the thought has come to his mind that cycle racing is within his power.

Enter now Uncle Fausto, returning to visit his old family home. The uncle feels an especial affection for the boy who bears his Christian name, so young Fausto benefits from a rush of love and the generosity peculiar to seamen. Before going back to his ship, Uncle Fausto says to the family, 'You have land, your house, the vines, the olives, the goat, your stove in winter and the priest. You may rise and sleep when you will, for although poor you are free in a way that a seaman is never free. I have money. Here is some, and I will give you more. Here is especial money for Fausto, to buy a racing bicycle.'

The money is given, and Fausto has his racing machine, a Legnano, the marque represented by his idol, the champion from Florence, Gino Bartali. We are in 1935, and Fausto Coppi is fifteen.

Fausto began to race and sometimes he won. Back to the little house at Castellania he brought the trophies of his victories and gave them to his wondering mother. One day it was a salami sausage, then a few lira, his first prize money from cycle sport. On another occasion he brought his mother an alarm clock. It was curiously made, the face supported by the crouching figure of what the Coppis took for a hunchback. My theory is that the seated, bowed figure, with the weight of time and the world on its shoulders, was the god Chronos, whose iconography is also that of Saturn.

For a while, life under the little ticking figure of Chronos had no surprises. Toil, sunshine, night, rest, sunshine, toil. Fausto's successes in bike races were particularly welcome to his family since the boy's physique had given anxiety. Like many children among the poor of Piedmont and Liguria, he may have suffered from rickets or a related disease. All his life, people remarked on Coppi's skinniness and a disproportion in his body. His arms and legs were very long, he had no torso, nor were his shoulders broad. His back had a hunched look, as though he had some curvature of the spine.

Because of his body shape and his long, pointed nose, Italians sometimes called Coppi 'the Heron'. Only when he was on a bike did Coppi find ease and physical assurance. Off the bike, there was an awkwardness to his frame that may have been congenital or perhaps came from generations of malnutrition. But there is no doubt about the infirmity that marred Coppi's racing days. It was osteoporosis. His bones were so brittle that whenever Coppi crashed, something within him was broken.

*   *   *

A day in 1938 was to change Coppi's life. The circumstances are still mysterious, and it was whispered in the village that Fausto had made a compact with a man who had come from the devil.

It is a bright morning in midsummer. Castellania is quiet. The men are in the fields and their womenfolk are indoors. Fausto Coppi has been out training. He is still in his cycling clothes, a road jersey and shorts. His mother is preparing a meal. Then a car is heard. A stranger appears and takes a place at the kitchen table. He has the brutal, knowledgeable face of a boxer and wears dark glasses, for he is blind. It is Cavanna.

By touch he learns Fausto's face. His hands test every muscle in the young man's legs, his arms, his sunken ribcage. Coppi is silent as the strong fingers explore his body. Then the blind man calls for his servant and is led back to the car in the farmyard. Fausto's mother is frightened.

*   *   *

To this day, there is something unnerving in the hundreds of photographs of Coppi in the company of the man with dark glasses and a white stick. The blind Cavanna was Fausto's discoverer, and became his *soigneur* and manager. We know of Cavanna's rages, of his dominion over Fausto, his uncanny knowledge of a sport he had never himself practised. But nobody knows how the former boxer was struck blind; and least of all how he directed a champion he had never seen ride – indeed had never seen at all. What was the nature of their relationship? Did Coppi pay Cavanna? No, it was whispered, no money was exchanged. Coppi had struck his bargain in a different coin. This man from a place lower than the earth and its seas had been given Fausto's soul.

With such a beginning to his career, Coppi was of course the topic of superstitious talk, not only in Castellania – which had just ninety inhabitants – but also in a wider peasant community, and finally in Italy as a whole. Peasants said that Cavanna came from another part of creation, a region to which, probably in the night, Fausto had been conducted. More rational lovers of cycle sport wish to penetrate the fog of secrecy that protects top riders and their coaches. Contemporary photographs give us some clues. Cavanna is so often present, even when Fausto is in a hotel bedroom with his young wife Bruna, a lovely girl from Genoa whom he had met on the roadside during a training ride. The snap is like this: Bruna demurely looks aside while the blind man massages her husband's legs. She is pretty, and seems sad, perhaps because she can never enter the complicity between her Fausto and his enigmatic manager.

The history of modern sport – ancient sport too, no doubt – often tells us of men who form a passionate, half-paternal relationship with a younger athlete, a passion both protective and urgent. The athlete must be driven on, or he will not excel; and protected – for the older man is most inspired when his protégé is in a sport with an emphasis on solo endeavour, such as boxing, Cavanna's own background, or cycling, which is sometimes a team sport but also produces riders like Coppi who excel when they ride alone.

There is another aspect of the Fausto Coppi legend; the matter of the dark glasses. Coppi has an individual and leading place in the unwritten history of this fashion accessory. Photographs show Coppi and his *soigneur* both wearing dark glasses, Cavanna because of his affliction, Coppi for other reasons. He took to wearing tinted lenses in his mid-twenties. He even wore dark glasses when racing, first adopting them in (I think) 1948 or 1949. There may have been a quite ordinary reason for their use: to replace the goggles worn by many riders in those days to protect themselves from glare and dust. However, only a very few other riders took up Coppi's innovation.* The dark glasses were his alone, part of a style of contemporary stardom which he shared with film actors and, in distant New York, modern jazz musicians. The peasant in shades both acknowledged his fame and asserted a kind of privacy by not allowing strangers to see his eyes.

Accompanied always by Cavanna, the teenage Fausto made an electric début in his professional career. In June 1939 he entered the Tour of Piedmont and lined up with the greats of Italian cycling. Among them was Gino Bartali, whom Coppi had always admired. The imperious Gino, winner of the Tour de France in the previous year, was evidently the leader of the field. His bearing both on and off the bike was that of a man who gave orders, who knew the value of discipline. He was a *duce* of cycling, blessed by the Pope, well liked by Mussolini's Minister of Sport (and president of the Italian Cycling Federation), General Antonelli. Fausto, still only nineteen, was not at all cowed. Two-thirds of the way through an arduous race he was in a leading group which included Bartali and the Italian road champion Olimpio Bizzi. These two men were watching each other. Nobody knew who Fausto was.

With the lightning-like strike for solo victory that would always be his trademark, Fausto Coppi escaped from this leading group. On a climb he went to the front and attacked. Not for some time did he dare look behind him to see what damage he had done. He was alone. Coppi might have continued his unaccompanied ride all the way to the finish in the Turin velodrome had his gearing not been so primitive. The mechanism failed, the chain unshipped and Fausto was forced to halt. Flus-

* Except in the United Kingdom. British cyclists, imitating Coppi, wore dark glasses as a badge of their allegiance to the BLRC. The large number of riders wearing *lunettes de soleil* in the mid-1970s is attributed to the use of cortisone, a drug which causes (among other side-effects) irritation of the eyes.

tered, he put the chain back on in too high a gear. Just as he did so Bartali flew past him. Fausto was congratulated by Gino when he finished in third position. This was probably the only time that the older man gave a compliment to his future rival.

*　　*　　*

Coppi's first hostilities with Bartali occurred among the confusions of war. There was no Tour de France in 1940, but the Giro d'Italia was run. It was more than ever an insular race, for the only non-Italian riders were the Swiss. Widely regarded as national property since its foundation in 1909 (by the *Gazzetta dello Sport*) the Giro had never been won by a foreigner – nor would it be until Hugo Koblet was victorious in 1950. The Giro's stars were often men who had no great success or renown beyond Italy's frontiers. One of them was Giovanni Valetti, the winner in 1938 and 1939. Gino Bartali had taken the Giro in 1936 and 1937. Now Italy expected a final battle between these two giants of the sport.

But the winner of the 1940 Giro d'Italia was an unknown newcomer from Castellania. Coppi had been signed by the Legnano team on the understanding that he would ride in Bartali's service. He was fortunate to be riding at all: instead of the olive-grey of the Legnano *maglia*, he might easily have been in the olive-green of an army uniform. Coppi had been conscripted, but the Italian army had allowed him leave to ride the Giro – and would continue to allow him to train and compete for some time to come.

The 1940 Giro unfolded in the following way. Its start was in Milan, and the first stage went off without incident. Then, on the second stage, between Turin and Genoa, Bartali came to disaster. He crashed on the descent of the Scoffera pass, remounted in pain and limped to the finish. How serious were his injuries? In the two days after the crash it seemed that he might recover if he was nursed by his team. Then he could regain time in the mountain stages, for climbing was his speciality.

Now there was a confusing situation for the Legnano team, its manager Ettore Pavesi and its newest recruit. For Coppi, officially a water-carrier for the senior members of the squad, was riding with all the panache and assurance of a champion. Was ever a rider less of a *domestique* than Fausto Coppi? He was a servant for only four days, in this first multi-stage race of his career, before he decided that he would not ride within himself, as a *domestique* should, and that he would abandon his duties towards Bartali, his team leader.

As so often in cycle races, the deed was done with a few shouted words between a man on his bike and his manager in a car. Some managers are better at betrayal than even the most ambitious water-carriers. Bartali was sheltering in an elongated peloton. Some riders were going off the front. Obviously there was going to be a split or maybe many splits. Coppi felt his strength and knew that he could catch and outclass anyone in a breakaway group. He asked Pavesi for permission to go to the head of the race. Pavesi could have, maybe should have, told Coppi to pace the stricken Bartali. Instead he told him to chase. Coppi took off, nearly won the stage and found himself in second place in the General Classification.

A few days later Coppi took the *maglia rosa* on the road to Modena, finishing alone in the lead after a day of climbing in cold and sleety weather. He defended the jersey for twelve days until the finish, back in Milan. On the flat stages and in the Dolomites he controlled the peloton with sheer speed. Bartali lost more and more time and spoke of abandoning. Pavesi told him that it would look more generous and sportsmanlike if he remained to support a teammate who was clearly going to be triumphant. This Bartali did, with the modicum of good grace that he could summon. Fausto became the youngest ever winner of the Giro d'Italia, having humiliated his captain in the process. Then he went back to the army and his uniform.

XIV

Coppi during his hour record at the Vel Vigorelli.

The Italian army was kind to Coppi. Mussolini's fascist state had always wished to be associated with the nation's sporting prowess. However, cycling is not a sport that lends itself to political ideology. In the years of Mussolini's power cycle sport continued and was seldom troubled by the dictator and his Roman henchmen. There was a little cycle racing in France and Belgium, but nothing of much consequence. In France, I think, the bicycle had another important function, especially in rural areas. The humble and ubiquitous *vélo*, silent, easily hidden and the means of free movement, was almost a symbol of resistance, or at least of non-compliance. The revival of cycling after the Liberation was in part the legacy of simple thankfulness to the bike.

Between 1939 and 1945 Switzerland was the only European country in which cycle sport was maintained, and almost flourished. Many Swiss professionals had been active in France and went home after the German invasion. Switzerland was suited to professional cycling. The country is compact, centrally located, mountainous, linguistically sophisticated, and rich. In the war years the country's Classic, the *Championnat de Zurich* (otherwise known as *Die Zuri-Metzgete* or *Kampionenschap van Zurich*) was held every year. There was professional track racing at the Oerliken velodrome. This situation encouraged the two most prominent Swiss riders, Ferdi Kubler and Hugo Koblet. Kubler was to win the Tour de France in 1950 and Koblet in 1951.

Apart from the Swiss, Italian racing cyclists probably had the easiest passage through the war years – if they were champions.

Coppi was encouraged to train and compete until 1943, when he was sent to the north African desert. He raced all through 1941 and 1942. In 1941 he was the Italian road champion and won the Tour of Tuscany, the Tour of Emilia and the Tour of Veneto. In 1942 he again won the national road championship and accomplished one of his most remarkable victories, the capture of the world Hour record.

Unlike Bartali, Coppi had a relish for track racing. Gino had the wrong physical build and pedalled as though he were competing on a treadmill. Coppi was lighter and had a more vital and supple style. In the first years of the war Gino and Fausto often travelled to Switzerland to race. The conservative and prosperous atmosphere of Zurich suited Bartali and both Italians liked Swiss money. On the Oerliken track Coppi beat Kubler (who was his exact contemporary) with ease. At tracks in Turin and Milan he had already defeated Bartali as well as Olimpio Bizzi and Fiorenzo Magni. These track victories gave Fausto Coppi even more self-confidence. This boy of 21 suddenly began to think of one of the ultimate tests of cycling, the Hour.

*   *   *

The Hour record is a complex and agonising trial that requires months and even years of preparation. A cyclist is going to ride to the extremity of his powers. He needs to be mentally mature, at the highest point of physical development, and must have a team of advisers and doctors. So we nowadays believe. But the young Fausto made his attempt at the Vel Vigorelli in Milan on 7 November 1942 while not fully recovered from a broken collarbone. The Vigorelli track – used by the Italian army – had been bombed. An especially light track frame had been made for Coppi's attempt. He had Cavanna to encourage him. That was the extent of his support team.

In 1942 the *recordman de l'heure* was the Parisian Maurice Archambaud. In 1937 he had recorded 45.840 kilometres on the same Vigorelli track. That translates as 27.5 miles in an hour. Coppi knew what he had to do, broadly speaking, and this was his plan. He would get up to Archambaud's pace in the first half lap of the track by a violent effort out of the saddle. Then he would exceed that speed. Then he would hold his own higher pace for the next 59 minutes, finishing if possible with a sprint. There were other possibilities, but this was the sensible way to ride the attempt.

A gun was fired. The Hour began. Coppi started fast, too fast. By the 30th lap his initial speed had failed. On the half hour he was slower than Archambaud's time. Fausto fought back. He was chasing an abstraction, Archambaud's ticking phantom. He caught that phantom, was in front by two seconds, then by one second. Fausto was like a man hanging by his fingernails over a precipice. His style disappeared in a final desperation. He could not sprint, just lunged over the bars to ride out his time with just 31 metres of advantage over his French predecessor.

*   *   *

Four months later, the army ended Coppi's easy ride within its ranks. His regiment was sent to Africa and then to the desert, where they were defeated by the forces under General Montgomery. Coppi was a British prisoner of war until May of 1945, a period which damaged his health. He was then able to return to Castellania to recover from a malarial fever. Coppi married his Bruna. He resumed his cycling career, signed a contract with the Bianchi firm and began an even more intense rivalry with Gino Bartali.

*   *   *

It happens that we have an outsider's testimony to the nature of Bartali, Coppi, their rivalries and the meaning of Italian cycle racing after the war. Our document comes from the daily reports of the 1949 Giro d'Italia written by Dino Buzzati. The columns were published in the *Corriere della sera* of that summer. The descriptions of each day's racing later became a book, though not within their author's lifetime; for he died in 1972, by which time his career was mostly forgotten.

Buzzati was a literary man. He was also one of the few high-brow writers who came to realise that cycle racing had a place in cultural life. Like the Tour de France, the post-war Giro d'Italia presented the nation's war-torn condition, from the Swiss border to Siracusa, and hoped to proclaim that the country had a shared soul. Buzzati had always wished to be a poet of his native land. But he had been appalled that Italy could produce fascism and, personally, was gripped by psychological unease. To make his daily living Buzzati was a journeyman writer on the feature pages of the *Corriere della sera*, whose editor decided to send him to cover the Giro and the long-awaited battle between Gino Bartali and Fausto Coppi.

In his first report Buzzati confessed ignorance: 'He who today writes this article as a reporter assigned to follow the Giro has never seen a bicycle road race.' Why then was he given his job? Probably because his editor had been taken with the French sporting press, whose reports of the Tour de France had a literary flavour and dragged in all sorts of classical allusions. The yellow jersey, for instance, often became *la toison d'or*, the Golden Fleece. Buzzati could surely file prose of that sort. He was a poet, wrote short stories and, in 1933, had published a well-received regional novel, *Barnabo della montagne*.

The queer nature of Buzzati's reporting was however at odds with the Giro d'Italia. That is because he was a follower of Franz Kafka, whose peculiar vision informs Buzzati's short stories and, in the *Corriere della sera* of 1949, all his brief sketches of the day's events on the road. We can safely say that Kafka has a negative influence on sports journalism. For everything in the Czech writer's world is preordained by mysterious and implacable forces. It is a world without history or geography. Its actors are helpless. They can resolve nothing, and nothing is brought to a conclusion in Kafka's universe. So his actors do not act. They scarcely know each other and they are not free. In all these respects Kafka's imagination cannot hope to understand cycle sport, which depends very precisely on geography, is drenched in history and encourages heroism, leadership and camaraderie.

This said, we must praise Buzzati. He quite modestly left his library for the discomforts of the press car. On the way through Italy he came to realise that a long stage race nourishes the minds of the poor as fully as literature diverts the minds of the cultivated. After the Giro he preferred reality to fancy metaphors. He had begun with the idea that Gino Bartali was Hector. His rival Fausto Coppi, who wishes to supplant him, was Achilles. Then Buzzati had toyed with military and artistic parallels. The leading cyclists on the road were the avant garde. Behind the breakaway was the bunch, a battalion that had somehow become separated from the greater army of the people. Behind the riders, silently and often cruelly directing operations, were the despots of the general staff. They were the team managers, the police and the autocrats who had devised the Giro's route.

When he had finished his play with metaphors Buzzati saw wonderful things and developed a genuine interest in racing cyclists. That was natural, since he witnessed their travails over a period of nearly three weeks. Like everyone else, he awaited the grand finale of the race, which surely would be in France. This year the Giro was routed through the French Alps on roads between Cuneo and Pinerolo. This stage was 254 kilometres long. It is an immense distance, but within the compass of voluntary effort. Cyclists often rode as far. But consider also the mountain terrain. The stage included the Cols de Vars, de l'Izoard, de la Madeleine and du Montgenèvre. Then, before returning to Italy, the race went up the Col de Sestrières (Sestrieri) before a 55-kilometre run into the finish at Pinerolo. The weather was cold and misty at the start and became worse in the mountains.

Fausto Coppi's ride through the Alps that June 10 of 1949 may count as the most hellish and glorious triumph of his life. We think so because we use imagination. There are so few records. Not many people witnessed Coppi's superlative break-away. Many thousands, perhaps even a million people, had cheered the Giro as the race passed through sunlit country. In the remote mountains there were few spectators. On the Col de la Madeleine, a *Miroir-Sprint* journalist tells us, there were just 'a few dozen Italians from France who had climbed up the valley, several mountain shepherds and a handful of privileged journalists . . .' These were the pressmen who saw Coppi make his audacious departure. For many days he and Bartali had been watching each other. Now, at the bottom of the Madeleine, Coppi accelerated and left the front of a struggling bunch. Bartali could not hold his wheel. Fausto leapt further away as the gradients steepened. There were still 190 kilometres to the finish. Coppi obviously meant to ride them alone, in the rain, over five more mountains.

The bunch could not organise a chase. Bartali set off alone, stamping on the pedals. He rode like an enraged and cornered animal. Cars following Coppi could look down the hairpins and sometimes see Bartali's pursuit, way down the mountain. Gino was in sight of his rival but could never catch up. Coppi was in 'a state of grace', as cyclists used to say. He climbed at immense speed. He ascended 15,000 feet that day and therefore descended around another 15,000. Fausto flew to the tops of passes then flew down as though careless of any hazard. Never before had he seen the Izoard; but Coppi scaled its fearsome slopes and then rattled and skidded down the descents – dropping at 60 or 70 kph for twenty kilometres – though he could have fallen to his death on many of the precipitous corners. He never relaxed when he reached a valley, as lesser riders do. At the end of the day Coppi had twelve minutes' advantage over Bartali. Thus he won the Giro for a third time.

*   *   *

Dino Buzzati was in the press car behind Fausto's breakaway. Of course he realised that he was the witness of an epic. Maybe there would be a new Italy and Coppi would be its hero. But our Kafkaesque writer could not see a new society. Anything might happen: revolution, earthquakes or another war. And there was something eternal in the Alps, a way of life he hoped would never change. Buzzati was himself a son of the Alps. He came from Belluno, in the high northern part of Venetia, and so he had his epiphany, and found the most heartfelt image of his writing on the Giro d'Italia.

During Coppi's breakaway Buzzati had seen something that was neither grand, nor political, nor menacing. It was just the sight of a little shepherd boy who appeared in the mists of the high mountains, an illiterate boy probably, a kid who in his nine years of life had never seen anything like a bike race going through the narrow roads of his home – and a boy who could not imagine why the great cyclist had drunk from his aluminium bottle and then thrown it on the road.

The peasant boy, Buzzati reckoned, would always keep the feeding bottle – *bidons*, we call them, even the British and Italians using the French military term – strapped to his waist. The bottle might have come from the sun or the moon, not those magnificent men chased by motor cars. But how did Buzzati know this? He could not have done. All the writer could remember were some shouts as Coppi rode higher and higher towards the summit. The boy was gone. He would have been born in the war. Perhaps his life would improve and he would learn to read and write. Nobody could know. The bicycle race went on without him. As the poet writes:

How little we learn from the goatherd's hand,
Yan, tan, tethera, pethera, pimp,
Whose tongue has no letters, whose charges no
    names,
Sethera, bethera, hovera, covera, dik.
What do you say for Nanny and Billy?
Yan-a-dik, tan-a-dik, tethera-dik, pethera-dik, bumfit.
Count with your fingers, not the right thumb,
That is the dead goat who does not come home.
Yan-a-Bumfit, tethera-bumfit, pethera-bumfit, figgit!
Words on the mountain, cries in the valley,
No stories, no escape, all tethered among stones.

*   *   *

I come down from the mountain tops to southern European life, near vineyards and gleeful streams. Coppi and his fellow cyclists remind me not so much of poetry as of shabby little southern towns *en fête*, towns with their hotels that are places of rest and intrigue and in whose markets and bars we once heard an especial kind of music. Classic cycling was a link between the old ways and the new, as was the accordion. Who can appreciate cycle sport who does not also love this instrument? I know that it was once disliked by purists who could remember when kermesses and feast days featured ancient fife and bagpipe music. But the accordion served cycling well. It took the place of the traditional small country bands and its tunes and intricate variations (often performed by a young woman in local dress) preserved the music of traditional small country bands. Sounds of the accordion linger still, and to this day I sometimes hear the strains of its music in the *Dauphiné-Libéré* loudspeaker vans that follow the quasi-competitive rides in the lower Alps that are known as *étapes du Tour*. Perhaps the nostalgic music is chosen because so many of us who enter those events are veterans. But it is perfect music when we cross the finishing line, shake hands and head for the fountain. I never go to track meetings where modern disco music is played, *never*. This brands me as a fogey. I don't care. Bright young people are entrancing but their fun is not mine.

A pleasure of later life is to discuss Coppi's races with other elderly cycling experts in the cafes of rural France. I say France because in Italy the *Bartalisti* become too vehement. A problem with the more stately French seminars is that we cannot remember dates or details, quite apart from (in my case) language difficulties. Which were Fausto's greatest achievements? I have just nominated the Cuneo–Pinerolo stage of the 1949 Giro d'Italia. But Coppi won so many races of all sorts that one can scarcely prefer one to the other.

There was the Paris–Roubaix of 1950, for instance. Coppi was not to be seen in the tented 'village' set up at the start of such a Classic, a place for autographs, interviews and predictions. He was on a warming-up ride of no fewer than 60 kilometres so began the race with a steaming head of adrenalin. Fausto passed in first place over the hill at Doullens, ignored the feeding station at Arras, for he had crammed his clothes with bonk bars, left everyone else as they were dealing with their musettes, attacked in 52 × 15, time-trialled all the way to Roubaix and was out of the showers before the next man (Maurice Diot) entered the velodrome.

Or we could mention Coppi's 95 pursuits between 1939 and 1955, of which he won 84. We could add other wins in the Classics, particularly in the Tour of Lombardy and Milan–San Remo. And let us briefly add Coppi's victories in the Tour de France in 1949 – just after he won the Giro – and another Giro d'Italia and Tour de France victory in 1952 before, in the next year, he once again won the Giro d'Italia and took the World Road Race Championship. Only Eddy Merckx has a comparable record, if we take all branches of the sport into account. But Merckx was a child of peacetime. Coppi would have been stronger and would have won even more races if he had not been a prisoner of war.

XV

Reg Harris.

Coppi's *palmarès*, or list of honours – like Bartali's – would be even more outstanding if the war had not interrupted his career. So also with Reg Harris, the only British cyclist whose name was familiar to the general public. Harris and Coppi were contemporaries, born within the same twelve months, Coppi in 1919 and Harris in 1920. Fausto and Reg, Reg and Fausto . . . the names do not sing in unison. Neither did the two men, though they met often enough and were not rivals, since they had no event or cycling discipline in common.

How eloquent their Christian names are! Just as Fausto signals a dark magic in Coppi's character, so the name Reg seems to be a token of Harris's nature, his northern and bloody-minded Britishness. He was never called Reggie, as happens to some Reginalds. The abbreviated form of Reg suited his class. It also has a geographical note, often belonging to a person from the East Midlands, the Potteries, the Wirral and Manchester, which were indeed the power bases from which this superb sprinter made his forays to the European continent. Reginald means 'Wielder of power' and was originally a warrior's name.

> Reginald, bold in the tourney, the first and last in the
>   field;
> Reginald, mighty of arm and the cleaver of helmet
>   and shield;
> Reginald, last of the line of the crest blazoned never
>   to yield!

sings Clinton Scollard in his 'The Banquet of Sir Reginald'.
But Reg Harris was never going to be dubbed Sir Reginald.

No one in the establishment would have put him up for a knighthood. In many ways he had the qualifications. Reg was successful, bold in every tourney, and was a former Olympian. He made a genuine contribution to British industry, for his connection with Raleigh helped the Nottingham firm to sell bicycles all over the world. Both in 1949 and in 1950 he had been 'Sportsman of the Year', easily beating Stirling Moss and Gordon Richards, both of whom received knighthoods in their later years. Reg was a world champion who vanquished foreigners; but there was a dangerous autonomy in his character, so no honours came his way.

A number of Reg's tricks were on the borders of legitimate business and some of his activities (smuggling watches, for instance) were illegal. Harris was disliked by the cycling hierarchy. He especially provoked officials who were southerners. The blazer brigade knew that he meant trouble and took issue with such minor matters as his place of birth. In fact he came from Bury. Reg was himself unsure about his natural background, though he knew where he lived. In truth his name was Reginald Hargreaves. The surname Harris came from his stepfather. Reg liked to think of himself as Reginald Hargreaves Harris and always used the initials RHH, which were displayed on the seat tube of his bikes.

I can just remember how he rode. To see Reg on the track was to marvel at his speed, guile and crushing strength. Often he wore the world champion's white jersey with a rainbow band, the *maillot arc-en-ciel*. That was because he won five world sprint titles, the amateur championship in 1947 and the professional crown in 1949–51 and again in 1954. In many respects Reg was an icon of our national pride. The Brylcreemed hairstyle, plain features and wide, slightly cheeky smile were familiar from many photographs, from Raleigh and Dunlop advertisements and from the sports coverage of the Pathé News. For ordinary wheelfolk, however, there was something alien about him, and that was because one could not believe that Reg was a club cyclist.

Or not a clubman in the usual way. No weekend tours or gatherings at the tea place for Reg Harris. He was solitary because he was a ruthless winner. Reg was a trackman, and the most aggressive of all trackmen are the sprinters. Reginald Hargreaves Harris realised early in life that he was a sprinter and nothing else. He could of course do some other wonderful things on the track. He had awesome ability in the kilometre time trial, for instance, usually covering the distance in between 1 minute 9 seconds and 1 minute 10 seconds. In 1955 he set a long-standing world record of 1 minute 8.9 seconds. But the kilometre is a solitary effort. Reg mainly excelled in combat against one or two other riders; and he learnt how to crush other people in the Lancashire of cotton-mill times.

*   *   *

Harris began his career in the late 1930s at the Fallowfield track in Manchester and the Herne Hill track in south London. It is more significant that the young man was racing and winning at dozens of venues in the north of England. In these places, I believe, he learnt how to make money: lots, but in small amounts, so Reg had to be continually busy.

At the same time, far away in north Italy, Fausto Coppi was astonishing bike fans when he won road events. Both Reg and Fausto quickly showed their superior talents. No other riders could stop either of them. So, in different ways, they had to leave their local cultures in the quest for victories and wealth. Coppi wanted fame to release him from the meagre vineyards of Castellania. Lancastrian Reg smelled the money of his own part of the world. He was greedy for the prizes to be won in his neighbourhood. When he had taken them all he would go on to other achievements.

I am curious about these British prizes. Often they were timepieces and their accessories. One of the first things

Reg won was a heavy gold watch-chain. The young Fausto's saturnine alarm clock comes to mind; and then one thinks of other cultural differences. Fausto's clock was innocently admired by a peasant Coppi family whose members probably did not wear wristwatches and who were called home from the fields by the thin chimes of the Castellania church tower. In northern industrial England, a land of fog, aldermen and factory hooters, Reg Harris had a salesman's desire for the prizes that were awarded after Lancashire track meetings. He began to collect these goods as soon as he started to race, and especially after he left his job in a cotton mill to become a full-time cyclist.

They were trophies, cups and urns in debased Graeco-Roman designs, medals and vases and the heavier forms of domestic ware, like canteens of cutlery and salvers coated with electro-plated nickel silver. Watches he won, granddaughter clocks, cut-glass bowls, all manner of things that could be placed on a sideboard. On tracks in the north and then in the Midlands, at colliery or works sports days, and at every cycle club meeting, after racing on grass, or concrete, or cinders, or shale, Reg triumphed again and again. Then he would go straight to dealers or pawnbrokers who would exchange his goods for cash.

These specialised establishments, the earliest dating from the 1880s, are called trophy shops. They are found in the centre of cities, but not in high streets. Look for trophy shops in older populous areas such as Camden Town or Lewisham, Ancoats, Cowley, Walsall and the part of Bristol known as St Paul's. Trophy shop owners sometimes also run angling shops, and they are always interested in darts. As a general rule their shops are in the same areas of urban Britain in which coarse fishing and darts still flourish, or were slow to perish. All trophy shops specialise in cheap metalworking and engraving. A cup or urn will be inscribed with the name of the victor of a competition. But the craftsman-engraver also knows how this inscription can be removed. A victor can take his cup to the trophy shop and have the name erased so that the cup can be resold.

Such were the rewards of effort and fame in the lower reaches of professional sport. The world of the cinder track and the trophy shop was the milieu that shaped Harris's racing and, subsequently, his dodgy life as a businessman. He was never truly an amateur, only belonging in that category because he signed no contracts before he joined Raleigh in late 1948. He was officially an amateur when he had his first experience of cycle sport on the continent, having been selected for the 1939 world championships. The track events were to be held at the Vel Vigorelli in Milan. Reg went to Italy and was amazed. The track was constructed from hundreds of thousands of polished larchwood planks and had banking of 45 per cent: steeper by far than anything he had known in England. There were splendid facilities for riders and spectators alike. For hour after hour Reg circled the Vigorelli, sometimes in company but mainly alone. Then a message came from the British consul. War was to be declared at any moment, and the British cycling team must leave for Switzerland. And so Reg changed his track jersey and shorts for uniform.

*   *   *

Catterick first, a unit in Hindhead next, three months on a ship before a tank sortie in the north African desert. Germans bombarded the tank. Harris's comrades got out and were shot but Reg stayed in the tank and when the Germans set it alight he crawled through the flames. He suffered burns, concussion, shock. A field hospital, back to dear old Blighty, Catterick again and then he was invalided out of the army. Thus ended Reg Harris's war. It was a conclusion as sudden and brutal as a defeat in a sprint. I often wonder whether Harris's character on the track was in part derived from his experience in the littered and blazing sands.

*   *   *

What is a sprint? Any extreme effort, generally towards a goal. You sprint when for a short period you ride as fast as you are able. Acceleration is required, then maximum physical power. A track sprint emphasises these things in the form of a contest. Sprints have a gladiatorial intensity, especially when the track has a high banking and the spectators are seated well above the riders, but close to them. The sprints that were Harris's forte belong specifically to this sort of track, which is an arena like no other. Only a special kind of cyclist can excel in a track sprint, and a rider like Harris is always bound to his pitiless speciality.

Other people sprint in different ways. There are the great sprinters who win road races with a final burst of speed after 200 kilometres of racing. These people never win track sprints – nor even bother to try. Nor do track sprinters ever do well on the road. The disciplines are quite separate. Road sprinters, aided by teammates, may start their final approach when 30 or even 40 kilometres from the finishing line. Track sprinting, on the other hand, calls for the strength that provides violent, immediate acceleration. 'Exploding' was Harris's term, meaning that he could go from walking pace to 50 kilometres an hour within ten seconds. When Harris exploded in such a manner hardly anyone could catch him, especially if his acceleration had come by surprise or had begun at the top of the steepest banking.

Non-cyclists who see a track sprint for the first time often don't realise what is going on. Two or sometimes three men (women are not by nature sprinters) come to the starting line. They have drawn lots for their positions. There is quiet around the track. If you have observed the riders in the previous minutes – perhaps doing breathing exercises on the grass *enceinte* – you will have noticed that they seem to be in meditation. They get on their bikes and are held upright. Toe straps are tightened with especial care. No one speaks, except perhaps a *soigneur* or personal manager saying a final word to his rider, who will nod in reply but not speak. A man in a blazer, carrying a gun, walks round the contestants. He returns to his position on the grass within the track, looks again at the riders and is satisfied. The stadium is still silent. Now the pistol is raised and fired for the race to begin.

And then – nothing happens. Or so it may seem, for the riders stay immobile, then creep forward a few feet at a time. Their confrontation begins with menacing slowness, never with speed. Track bikes have a single gear and a fixed wheel. With the aid of this fixed wheel you can balance on the bike without moving. In a sprint, two riders may advance 10 yards or so, then stand still on their machines for as long as twenty minutes. They are going to ride three times round the track. Only the final furlong will be timed, for that is when the sprint is rapid. The beginning and middle parts of the race are slow, tactical and psychological. The sprinter's purpose is to unnerve his opponent and place himself in an advantageous position. It's usually best to be just behind your rival but higher on the banking.

The track sprint resembles no other cycling event. Some sprinters are interested in the way that runners prepare for the 100 metres, but the cycling sprint is *sui generis*. Perhaps some distant comparisons can be made with arm wrestling, especially when stationary riders stare at each other; or with boxing, in the sense that good sprinters are belligerent by nature. Some of them are the nastiest people I have ever met in cycling, a sport which is generally full of equable and helpful friends. Sprinting demands a wide range of hostilities. First there is the cold, unrelenting nature of the standstill. Then there's all the jostling for position. You bear down on the other rider, force him up the banking, baulk him, switch your direction to prevent him from taking his own course; for there are no lanes on a cycle track, except for the 'sprinters' line' at the very bottom, and all sprinters will distort the rules of sporting behaviour whenever they can.

In the final 200 metres – I wrote 'furlong' just now out of nostalgia for Harris's early days – tactics become secondary to the power of the sprinter's legs, augmented by the strength of his arms and torso. The whole body is devoted to a crushing reaction to the slightest sign of weakness in an opponent. It's split-second excitement for the spectators, who are brought to their feet by the electric speed of the finale. These fans are connoisseurs. Like the riders themselves, the witnesses of a good track sprint must be alert to mental warfare, feel the tense changes of pace and position, follow the sallies and retreats up and down the banking, then scream with the final burst to the line, so extraordinarily muscular. Harris's bikes were built with reinforced handlebars and chain stays. Otherwise, it is said, the strength of his arms and legs would have bent the machine when his 'explosion' began.

*   *   *

The track sprint is in decline and people who see it on television think that the event is a minor curiosity. Perhaps they are right. There was a brief revival of interest in track cycling after the British successes in the 2000 Olympic Games, but only a handful of today's riders of the path (to use the old term) have the personality and trackcraft that belonged to the stars of the 1950s.

There are the usual mundane reasons for the current low fortunes of the sprint. All track racing has suffered from the attractions of other sports. There are fewer cycle tracks and, often, hardly any spectators. A Darwinian theory occurs to me. The character of the sprint must have led to natural selection and a dwindling number of competitors. Many cyclists are content with their lot, only dream of winning races and are happy to make up the field. Track sprinters cannot be satisfied with lower places on the result sheet. They have to be uncooperative to a high degree, or they wouldn't be any good at sprinting. And, since sprinters hate losing, those who lose often turn their energies elsewhere, almost always to pursuits outside the sport of cycling.

The height of the sprint game was in the years after Hitler's war. For about a decade a small group of very good sprinters raced against each other on tracks in mainland Europe and occasionally at Herne Hill. These top trackmen knew their business in every way. They had an informal professional club which was also a cartel, an association of physical showmen. They were each other's enemies on the track and in the changing rooms, but hostilities ceased when they combined to negotiate with the promoters who ran track meetings. The collusion helped them to make a good living. If they did not win prizes they had the benefit of appearance money, as well as a retainer from the firms – cycle manufacturers on the whole – whose products they advertised. Reg knew about this nameless club, and his business instincts told him to join it as soon as possible.

He was a professional in other ways. Reg developed a rapport with audiences, especially when his languages improved and he was better able to talk to foreign journalists. Newspapers built up his reputation, attracted fans to the stadiums in which he rode, provided their readers with expertise and compensated for the poor quality of programmes. Harris wasn't generous with journalists but gave them what they wanted and kept essential information to himself – his training routines, for instance, or his thorough study of continental tracks.

Some of that research may have been done on hands and feet, as though he were a surveyor or a builder. Reg liked to know the tracks metre by metre. No two tracks are alike. Most are oval, though some are round and one or two are nearly D-shaped. Some are indoor, most outdoor. Their surfaces might be of wood, or concrete, or tarmac. A sprinter wants to know whether the straights are short or long and how close he will be to the spectators. Above all, he will learn about the banking: how steep it feels and how the gradient diminishes as a rider turns from a corner and flies into the straight, the finishing line in front of him. On these corners many instantaneous and vital decisions are made.

Reg had many secrets. He is mysterious because he wasn't a clubman. We know that he started in the Lancashire Road Club and then (by invitation) joined the Manchester Wheelers. That's fine. But who can imagine Reg on a Lanky Roads club run, or making a weekend visit to the Wheelers' communal hut on the North Wales coast? Who can imagine Reg in a teaplace? Or with a musette on his back? Or – and this is the most important mystery – who can imagine the way he trained?

Some preparations for his early racing are well known. That's because Reg liked to say how, for instance, he would sprint on the road between two lampposts, over and over again, to develop his explosive effort. He repeated this story because in the years of his greatness his training was a private matter, while the lamppost training belonged to his youth, which he romanticised. How did he train on the track? He would not have simply gone round and round. Maybe he did Russian Steps or some similar routine. And a sprinter might be interested in gym work, developing muscles with weights. However, weight training wasn't at all common until the mid-1950s, by which time Reg's career was nearly over.

When questions of this sort arise one looks not to training manuals – which didn't exist in Harris's day – but to cycling folklore and unwritten common knowledge. At the Herne Hill track Reg Harris once told a twelve-hour time-trial specialist that their training patterns were similar. I heard this from a clubmate of the time triallist. They were in the Kingston Wheelers, rather an RTTC club in the 1950s, if I am not mistaken, but I believe what I was told.

Another story will confirm the implausible tale. Reg told the cycling journalist Dennis Donovan, who told me, that he did hundreds of fast kilometres on the flat roads of the Lombardy plain and the Po valley. These would have been the same roads, Dennis remarked, that are followed in the Milan–San Remo, the longest of the classics. Imagine, Dennis Donovan continued, that our man has an engagement on the Vigorelli track. He has two bikes with him, or he keeps a bike in Milan, since he's there so often. Reg does his stuff on the track, probably wins. Then he skims over the Milan–San Remo roads, little breezes making the weather more clement for a Lancastrian in a hot Italian summer, easily pushing big gears, or biggish (in the high seventies, low eighties?)* in a fast cadence so that his legs would remain supple.

Okay, but there were still questions to be asked. 'Would he have been riding fixed?' was the first of them. 'Aha,' said Dennis, who should have asked Reg, but hadn't. Next: 'Would he have been on his own?' Dennis said that Reg was often with Italian roadmen. We agreed that Harris would never have trained in the mountains. His many statements that he loved to meander through the Cheshire lanes were ballyhoo, made up by the Raleigh publicity department. On the question of suppleness, we know that Reg had difficulty in finding the right *soigneur*. An over-heavy massage could damage the tone of his muscles, which were delicate as well as powerful.

When the Olympic Games were held in London in 1948 Harris knew more about training and racing than the officials who were in charge of the British cycling team. He was amateur champion of the world, a title he had taken (after numerous

* The calculation of gears is the abiding legacy of the Ordinary, popularly known as the 'penny-farthing'. On an Ordinary, a complete revolution of its larger wheel would cover, say, 55 inches of road, since that was the wheel's diameter. When smaller wheels, freewheels and variable gearing were developed, a gear was calculated with this ancient principle in mind. Take the diameter of the rear wheel, which today will be 27 inches. Multiply this number by the number of teeth on the chainwheel. Divide the result by the number of teeth on the rear sprocket. Then you have your gear in inches. It is an artificial system but very useful, so long as you have a gear table. Continental Europeans state the number of teeth, back and front, and then say '*soit une développement de* (whatever it might be) *mètres*', using decimals to two or three places. I think our system is more helpful. You can feel the road when you use inches. Old French magazines inform us, for instance, that Fausto Coppi rode the highest mountain passes in 45×25. That comes to 48.6 inches, a very supple gear on the steepest inclines. Today's cyclists climb the same mountains in 39×23, which comes to 45.8 inches. And Coppi had to deal with much rougher roads . . . end of maths lesson.

disqualifications and reruns) at the Parc des Princes in 1947. Later that year Harris competed in revenge matches with sprinters he had beaten in Paris. These matches were in Turin, Milan, Zurich and Amsterdam. They gave him the measure of his opponents, convincing him that he could beat them again.

So Harris looked forward to the London Olympics. A gold medal would sit nicely among his other awards. But then he crashed: not on his bike but in a car. Within Harris's character was a love of motor racing. He wanted to possess all the best sports cars of his day. This one was a Wolseley, a 25 horse power coupé, according to Reg's doubtless accurate memory. Over it went when he was doing 'quite a good lick' on the main road outside Leek in Staffordshire. No seatbelts in those days, so Reg and his passenger were thrown onto the tarmac.

Reg the winner, Reg the motorist, Reg the ladies' man. The girl smashed up in the Wolseley was not his wife. Reg was not a person who took a girl out on the back of a tandem; he separated himself from the domestic and informal aspects of cycling life. Unlike all other cyclists, he proclaimed, 'I had always worn a smart shirt with a silk tie, a well-cut jacket and trousers.' But he was no aesthete, and if he had been more tasteful he would not have been Reg. Personally, I could never stand the all-chrome frames that he favoured in his early days. That scarcely matters, because he had to give them up. After the Olympics and for the rest of his career he was obliged to ride a Raleigh, its frame Lincoln green for his road bike, plum-coloured for his track machine.

Reg had been secretly discussing a professional contract with Raleigh Cycles during the time when, nominally an amateur, he had been preparing for the 1948 Olympics. In years to come, the Raleigh *marque* would gain enormous prestige and sales from Harris's name, though the partnership got off to a bad beginning. After Reg's failure to win gold in the Games, the Nottingham firm tried to pull out of their informal agreement. A betrayal and a disaster, for Reg had already bought himself a new Mark IV Jaguar, the one with the famous P100 chrome-plated headlights! After much talk the contract was mended and signed. The Jaguar had to go but Reg replaced it with a Vauxhall long-wheelbase limousine, a car big enough to take two Raleigh bikes, together with suits and silk ties, racing kit and a stock of wheels and tubulars. In this Vauxhall, with its peculiar contents, Reg crossed the English Channel and passed quickly through customs before driving to Brussels to begin a new life as a continental professional.

XVI

Raleigh advertising: bicycles for all purposes.

When Reg Harris went to the continent he left behind him the old, gritty north of England, but not for ever. He often returned to the tracks where he had made his name. Harris's contract with Raleigh demanded that he should promote the cycle industry at home; and his native ground gave him ideas for a future career as a businessman.

I saw some of those old tracks, which have now mainly vanished. Around 1955, at the end of Harris's supremacy, they still had a local and inescapably plebeian atmosphere. Often, their unpleasant and poorly maintained surfaces were difficult to ride. Here are some:

> Abertillery, overlaid with Canpholte.
> Askern (near Doncaster), red ash.
> Bradford, shale.
> Brighton, tarmacadam.
> Bury, red concrete.
> Cannock, non-skid asphalt.
> Cardiff, red cement.
> Carmarthen, cement.

Clay Cross. Here's an interesting one, especially since it is still sometimes used. The Clay Cross and Danesmoor Miners' Welfare Association had a track that was of grass but with banking that at its height was 3 feet 6 inches. While we are in this industrial area, we should note the track at Staveley, Derbyshire, belonging to the Staveley Iron and Chemical Co., Ltd, offices in Chesterfield Road, cinder; the grass track at Church Gresley Miners' Welfare

Sports Club, near Burton-on-Trent; the Dinnington Colliery Institute's track at Sheffield; and no doubt several more.

> Derby, for instance, cement.
> Ibrox Park, Glasgow, ash.
> Kettering, asphalt.
> Leigh (Lancashire), cinder.
> Portadown, bituminous macadam.
> Palmers Park, Reading, brick dust.
> Wolverton, Resmat.
> Yorkshire Main, Edlington near
>   Doncaster, red ash.

*   *   *

Riding south from Birmingham, through Oxford and the Chilterns or down the A41 through Banbury and Aylesbury, my destination was often the Good Friday meeting at Herne Hill. The numerous events included pursuits, a 5-mile race for roadmen and the entertaining 'devil take the hindmost'. Good Friday crowds mostly looked forward to a sight of the continental professional sprinters. These were Reg Harris's rivals: the Swiss Oscar Plattner, the young Antonio Maspes, a master of the standstill who had been born and bred within the shadow of the Vigorelli, and the Dutchmen Jan Derksen and Arie van Vliet. It was a long afternoon at the Hill: the first heats of the amateur sprint began at noon, and we wouldn't leave until after five. Spectators' bikes were stacked a dozen deep, and their disentangling took some further time.

The track at Fallowfield in Manchester was less welcoming. This was Reg Harris's personal fiefdom in his racing days, especially since, even before his retirement, he had bought the place and renamed it the Harris Stadium. Fallowfield came to a poor end, being sold to the expanding University of Manchester. Urban pressures hastened the demise of many other tracks. If they were publicly owned, cyclists could hardly dispute with the civic authorities, who would point out that the tracks were not used in the winter months. And so we lost Birmingham's Salford Park, the tracks at Leicester, Southampton and many others.

Even at the time of their high popularity in the 1950s many tracks had a faded, abandoned look. One such was the rural Manor Abbey stadium at Halesowen, next to a ruined medieval church and set beneath forested hills in that special part of England where the Black Country merges with the red earth farmland of Worcestershire. I went back the other day. There's now a smart running track, but the old cycle track, which may not encircle the running track for ever, was neglected, cracked, covered with thin, slippery moss like verdigris.

And yet the track is still loved. Maybe I'll be able to ride it again before I go. Probably you can climb over the fence with a bike on your shoulders, as I did when a boy. People keep the Manor Abbey track in operation. A few years ago a nearby stream flooded and washed mud and rubbish over its tarmac surface. Local cyclists cleaned it up and someone has built a wall to keep the stream on its proper course. And Halesowen has a track league, i.e. weekly or twice-weekly evening sessions that combine training with racing and provide a nursery for young riders.

When cycle tracks are covered indoor arenas, racing on the path can take place throughout the winter. This is why European six-day races are so popular. Our native cycling has not often competed with promotions of that sort. A particularly English summer recreation was grass track racing, its season beginning at Whitsun and ending in September – that is, running from late spring until harvest time. Racing on grass had a following in agricultural areas and was still popular in Somerset and East Anglia until the early 1970s. In former days the top grassmen toured the country. They would go to meetings at, for instance, Hereford, Taunton, Knighton, Oakengates, Market Bosworth, Diss and Norwich. Your grassman was a specialised racing cyclist. He often failed on a hard track, but was good in the end-of-season hill-climb events. Bikes for grass had large-flange wheels, 6½ inch cranks and rough or knobbly tubulars, chosen according to the state of the ground.

Grass track meetings were often combined with athletics. In country areas you found these sports at midsummer agricultural shows and fetes, while in towns they would be part of a works, police or colliery sports day. In Scotland, certainly, and probably elsewhere, there was a little unauthorised betting on the outcome of grass events. Racing on grass came to an end in the early 1960s, at about the same time that firms gave up their factory sports days. I have been told that Lord Beeching's policy of closing rural branch railway lines discouraged grassmen, who did not own cars. Numerous old grassmen took up the relatively new sport of cyclo-cross.

Today, track racing on grass survives in only a handful of venues. Enthusiasts gather at Mildenhall in Suffolk for the meeting on August bank holiday. The circuit is marked out by bunting and surrounded by tents. Competitors churn round on their lovingly maintained, outmoded bikes and then rejoin their families' picnics. There's a bit of rusticity about most track meetings, for the simple reason that nearly all British tracks are outside. The future of track racing – at Olympic or world-class levels – probably depends on indoor tracks. If it rains on asphalt you can't race. In 1972 the world championships were held at Leicester's Saffron Lane track. Our native weather led to a bizarre banner headline on the front page of *L'Equipe*, France's sports newspaper. PLUIE A LEICESTER!

*   *   *

A little of the experience of riding the track may be tasted by riding a track bike on the road. At the moment I have two track bikes, both antiques and both of them treasures in almost daily use. They are a Bates – built by E. G. 'Basher' Bates in Plaistow, E8 – and a Carlton. I prefer the Bates, partly because of its antiquity. The frame and most of the bike's components can be dated to 1952–3. The twenty-eight-spoke wheels have been rebuilt on the original Stronglight large-flange hubs. My new rims are for pressures, tyres with inner tubes, rather than tubulars, tyres without inner tubes.

There's another essential addition. Track bikes have no brakes, which makes them illegal on the open road, so we drill a hole in the crown of the frame and fit a front brake. Your own legs will slow the bike when you wish. Experienced cyclists scarcely even touch the brake lever unless they want a position on the hoods. If they do, they fit the stump of a lever on to the other side of the handlebars. I think this is best, especially if you live in an area where hills demand that you get out of the saddle. Some purists disagree. They say that the point of riding a track bike on the road is to be always on the drops. It's a more competitive position, and you are closer to the relentless drive of your fixed wheel.

I say 'relentless' because you can't freewheel. If you stop pedalling the bike will jerk and maybe throw you over the handlebars. Track bikes are recommended for road training by cyclists of the old school. Veterans argue that hundreds of miles on a low-geared fixed wheel encourage a rider to pedal quickly and gracefully. Today, younger people seldom use this form of training unless they are constrained to do so by their fathers. Stephen Roche may have been the last great champion to prepare on a road-track bike. He recalled that pedalling lessons from Dublin cyclists of his father's generation always included long sessions on a fixed. The man who won the Giro d'Italia, the Tour de France and the World Road Championship in one year, his *annus mirabilis* of 1987, still kept a fixed-wheel bike in his Paris house. Whether he used it regularly is a different matter. Certainly, though, Roche informed the cycling world about the converted track bike to show that he had respect for traditional values.

To return to my own track bikes. They are utterly conventional, and their use is also orthodox. I ride the Carlton in the winter and take the Bates out of the shed when spring sunshine has dried the roads after the end of March, which is the month of punctures. Half a century old, is my Bates, and this fine, specialised bike is probably as lively as ever it was in the past. I like to think that the machine combines the virtues and wonders of both youth and age. I ride it on either a 66 or 72 inch gear, though it would be exciting to fit an 81 for a time trial.

The Bates fixed wheel brings the bike up to its tempo in 30 yards or so. Then comes a satisfying whirr from its direct and simple transmission – a sound quite unlike the trilling mechanical ripple of a modern derailleur. I'm reminded by the Bates of early aeroplanes, hand built by aviation enthusiasts, the ones whose propellers were started by hand. This is not totally fanciful. There are technological links between those planes and old racing cycles. The brothers Orville and Wilbur Wright began as bicycle manufacturers, and Wilbur's first plane had parts that were taken directly from his bikes. And it seems to me that an earthbound mortal is closest to man-powered flight when he is on a good racing bicycle.

Returning from the skies to the shed in my garden, I take out the Carlton. Good-looking saddle: a Concor, obviously a later addition. What might be the date of this bike's frame? Early 1960s? One indicator is the bridge. On any bicycle the bridge is the element above the back wheel that unites, strengthens and tensions the frame's two seat stays. Normally the bridge is straight, but on this Carlton it rises in a steep little semi-circle. A nice conception by whoever built it, who also did an elegant seat cluster. One day I might try to find out the name of the frame builder. It's often possible to obtain this information, for the expert little firms attract historians.

This Carlton has mudguard eyes, so it was designed both for racing and as a clubman's winter bike. A machine like this changed its character in October, when the owner fitted more substantial wheels, mudguards and perhaps a saddlebag. In effect there were two bikes in one. It was the racing man's instrument in the noon of the year, the clubman's friend in the months on either side of Christmas. Bicycles of this sort were common until the early 1960s. There were two main reasons for their popularity. First, they were so simple and so good. Secondly, they remained rather British. They were a late expression of our industrial folk art, and there are no parallels in the bicycle manufacture of other countries.

In small, often rather private workshops all over the country – but not in agricultural regions such as East Anglia, or northern Scotland, or North Wales – there were craftsmen who produced maybe only a couple of dozen frames a year. These metalworkers were themselves cyclists. Our builders were attentive to every detail of lugwork, angles and fork rake. They delighted in personal flourishes, were meticulous about decoration and colour and were sure to number each individual frame and to sign their work. The classic road-track frame was built by someone you knew, perhaps a member of your own club. Often you can tell where a cyclist comes from by the craftsman's name on his machine. And how much these names mean to cyclists! Here are some of them:

> Les Ephgrave
> Stan Pike
> Tommy Godwin
> Brian Rourke
> Don Farrell
> Bob Jackson
> Pat Hanlon
> Harry Quinn
> George Longstaff
> Ken Bird
> Geoffrey Butler
> Henry Burton
> Joe Waugh

Pat Rohan
Harry Hall
Malcolm Cowle
Roy Thame

The home-made machines built by such men were serviceable, extremely light and sensitive. There was no need for fancy foreign equipment. And so your road-track bike was cheap, and as dependable as your clubmate and neighbour who sold it to you.

But what does 'cheap' mean, to a cyclist? In the years before (relative) working-class affluence – let us say the era of my Bates and Carlton, the two decades after 1945 – a rule of thumb was that a good racing bike, with ten-speed gearing and other desirable accessories, would cost about twice the amount of a skilled man's weekly wage. The purchase wasn't easy and was hard for a person in an apprenticeship. But neither was the difficulty insuperable. Perhaps it depended on your family. British road-track bicycles cost less than continental machines. Furthermore, they were accepted by wives who did not agree that their husbands needed more than one bike. Today, household accounts are easier for many people. It makes less sense to compare the cost of cycling against a wage. A good bike might take as much money from your pocket as a week's package holiday, or perhaps a year's car insurance for a young professional man. I wouldn't know.

Not myself a motorist, I depend on the Carlton winter bike and sometimes appreciate the library books that are jammed into its saddlebag twice a week. Though the wheels are black and sturdy the frame is a marvellous, almost an insolent, pink. This was a Carlton colour and part of the road-track style.* The Carlton and

* Black bikes always look heavier than in fact they are. Their colour must have a depressing effect on the rider. The earliest pink bicycles in Britain, perhaps copied from the French Mercier marque, caused a sensation, but generally speaking the colour was slow to enter modern life, even in art. The first all-pink sculpture was Phillip King's plastic *Rosebud*, made in north London in 1962.

I go by lanes and B-roads, through puddles, ice and sometimes snow and frozen farm slurry, round the twisting corners and through the bare woods at exactly 17½ miles per hour, which is the regulation winter speed for a *gentleman* such as myself.*

It's best not to linger in a library. Clear January days invite the cyclist to go home by a longer route. Even with books behind the saddle you can lope up the hills with a rhythm and physical pleasure that belong to a fixed wheel. But there is no need to be doctrinaire. Some old-timers say that a fixed gives you a 'live' gear while multiple gears on a freewheel are in comparison 'dead'. I have my own views, but these days never enter disputes with people older than myself. I just listen.

*   *   *

The sight of an old pink bicycle prompts an *excursus* into the history of the cycle industry.

The premises of the small Carlton firm were in the mining town of Worksop in Nottinghamshire. The name comes from Carlton-in-Lindrick, a few miles up the road. Four miles on you come to Harworth, whose most famous son, Tom Simpson, began his career on a Carlton bike in 1950–1. But let us go back to earlier times. The Carlton business was a family concern. The metalworker Daniel O'Donovan was helped by his sons Kevin and Gerald. They didn't build many frames, simply serving local cyclists, often miners. In fact cycling colliers were numerous throughout the East Midlands coalfield, where pits and slagheaps were close to woods and open country, Sherwood Forest or the Vale of Belvoir. If D. H. Lawrence of Eastwood had lived longer – he came from a class that produced cyclists

---

* Italicised because the expression is French. I do not know its origin. It means a former racing man of advanced years, but still active. A famous French race is the *Grand Prix des Gentlemen*, a two-up time trial in which an older person is paced by a younger one, preferably his son. The French firm Clément produced 'Gentleman' tyres and tubulars until the late 1970s, designed for winter training.

– one can just about imagine him riding a Carlton. Daniel O'Donovan would have looked after him. As was always said, cyclists went to their frame builder in the way that more privileged people went to their tailor.

Around 1936, however, O'Donovan wished to expand his business. He reckoned that his high-quality racing bikes could be sold beyond north Nottinghamshire, and he was right. But Carlton Cycles never sought a mass market. Their frames remained the choice of dedicated and knowledgeable riders. O'Donovan's development was part of a trend. Several clubman-builders with firms in the Midlands or London began to market their bikes outside their home territory.

Mercian Cycles of Derby, for instance, sold bicycles to customers who lived far away from the workshop. And then there was Claud Butler from south London. Claud has long since left his little snug bar in Clapham for a similar place in heaven, but his name survives, and not only because of its breezy ring of old-fashioned courtesy. Many are the people who remember having a Claud when young. 'Claud Butlers' are still manufactured, but now by some other firm which uses the name. They produce 'sports models'. In my view the old Clauds were of higher quality. Their maker spread happiness and even had a hand in some marriages, for courtships developed between steerers and stokers on his lively short-wheelbase tandems.

*   *   *

Claud's former renown brings us back to Reg Harris, who was on a Claud Butler frame when he won the world amateur sprint championship in 1947. For the next decade Harris was allied to Raleigh and therefore to the capital of the industrial East Midlands, Nottingham. Anciently a hosiery town, Nottingham grew richer with cigarette manufacture and the ventures of Messrs. Boots. In the Harris decade the town's manufacturing base was given muscle by Raleigh's domination of the national bicycle market: a Commonwealth market too, for bikes were sent from Nottingham to Australia, Canada, South Africa and other anglophone African nations.

By the turn of the century Raleigh already had the biggest cycle factory in the world. In 1951, when Harris won his third world professional sprint championship, the Nottingham firm sold one million bikes in a year. All their advertising was based on a simple slogan: 'Reg rides a Raleigh!' The downturn in sales did not occur until 1957, when car ownership began the sudden decline of the quotidian use of the bicycle. That was also the year when, at the age of thirty-seven, Harris decided to retire from the sport.

He stayed on the Raleigh payroll, but without any clear duties until the still enormous firm bought Carlton Cycles in 1960. Harris's brief was to develop specialised racing bicycles. If I'm right that my Carlton dates to 1961, then it might belong to this period. But Reg was not at Carlton for very long. The prestige of his name was of little practical use. His sprinter's nature made him a bad colleague in the board room and soon he was asked to resign.

Raleigh's best acquisition turned out to be Gerald O'Donovan, the son of Carlton's founder. Gerald's love of cycle sport was allied to inventive technical abilities. Furthermore he could see modern opportunities. In 1974, in response to Britain's entry to the Common Market, he devised ways for Raleigh – now TI Raleigh, after a merger with Tube Investments – to sponsor a professional team on the continent. The team's demanding manager was the Dutchman Peter Post, who quickly rid the new TI Raleigh squad of its British riders, often enough by humiliating them. Then he formed a new team, mainly of Dutch riders, that was capable of winning any continental race.

As they did. Post was fortunate to direct the best generation of professionals that the Netherlands has ever known. Jan Raas and Gerri Knetemann were great champions throughout the late 1970s, as was the ageing Joop Zoetemelk, victor in the

1980 Tour de France, who confessed that he could not have won without the help of the strong TI Raleigh team. That triumph seems a long way from British domestic cycling, so it's good to know that Zoetemelk's bikes were designed and built by Gerald O'Donovan of the Carlton family firm, a Worksop man to the end of his life. Is it possible that my pink road/path frame came from his jig?

XVII

Jean Robic.

Joop Zoetemelk's victory in the 1980 Tour de France interrupted a series of wins by Bernard Hinault. In fact the Breton should have taken the race, but tendonitis forced him to retire; and so, on the fourteenth of the twenty-two stages, the lead passed to a rider who had never been Hinault's master.

As a mark of respect, Zoetemelk initially declined to wear the yellow jersey. He kept to his red and black TI Raleigh colours. This gesture of modesty irritated some patriotic French fans, who said that he had disdained the most honoured place in sport and that his team was an alien and invading army. TI Raleigh certainly had a science-fiction appearance. They introduced one-piece skinsuits, for instance, when they rode to a devastating first place in the team time trial. The style of their victory was precise and military, and their uniform made them look as though they were the identical lieutenants of some superior force. They gave the same impression as they defended Zoetemelk's lead in the week before the Tour arrived in Paris.

The 1980 Tour – whose first four stages were in Germany – was a step towards the *mondialisation* of the great French national celebration. Many Frenchmen felt disquiet about the modern nature of the Tour. It was at about this time that journalists increased the number of 'retro' articles in newspapers and magazines, perhaps in response to French worries about national identity. At all events, there was a French mood that harkened back to the rebirth of the Tour de France in 1947 – and further back, to the brave and suffering image of René Vietto.

*   *   *

Vietto's first Tour de France, in 1934, had been a French triumph. Nineteen of its twenty-three stages were won by members of the national team. Vietto's last Tour, that of 1947, was a French celebration of a different sort, with the nation rejoicing that their race had been resumed after eight long years. The notion of the Tour as *la grande boucle* – the great loop, circle or strap that holds France together – had never been more relevant.

It was clear from the 'Petit Tour' of 1946 that stage racing could be revived, though there were many problems for a full-scale Tour de France. Roads were still in a poor condition, especially in the mountains. Petrol was scarce and the Tour could hardly go ahead without its caravan. There were widespread food shortages, compounded by erratic rationing. These difficulties were overcome, but the 1947 Tour contained no fewer than five rest days or *jours de repos* – not for the sake of the riders but to give the Tour's managers time to forage for supplies.

The renaissance of the Tour owed much to the abilities of Jacques Goddet (who had taken over its direction after Henri Desgrange's death in 1940) and also to the co-operation of the *mairies* in many French towns. Local government clasped hands with the Tour's management, as it still does. The *grande boucle* of 1947 included all of regional France in its embrace. A long stage between Brussels and Luxembourg was a symbolic excursion to previously occupied territory. Of necessity, other stage towns were places that could guarantee petrol, telephone wires, hotels that had not closed down and plenty of shops and markets: Strasbourg, Lyon, Nice, Marseille, Bordeaux and Caen. The logistics of the Tour were, in this way, rather like those of a marching army – except that the army was of sportsmen, reclaiming the land for its people.

The 1947 Tour helped to reopen mountain roads. First-category climbs in remote and wild areas of the Alps and the

Pyrenees included the Granier, the Télégraphe, the Galibier, the Izoard, the Col d'Allos and the Col de Vars, in the Alps; and, in the Pyrenees, the cols de Péyresourde, d'Aspin, du Tourmalet and the Aubisque. Second-category climbs included l'Epine, la Turbie and the Portet d'Aspet. New climbs – within the history of the Tour, that is – were the Col de la Croix-de-Fer and the Col de la Porte. The fearsome Croix-de-Fer rises 6,000 feet from the Romanche valley before descending to the Vallée de la Maurienne. This mountain road therefore took the route of the Tour to France's limits, her Swiss and Italian borders.

The selection of teams was also meaningful. Regional squads could not have the importance of the French national team, but they were appreciated merely for being regional and were especially cheered when the Tour passed through their own part of France. The 100 riders in the 1947 Tour were divided as follows. There were five national teams: France, Belgium and Italy, together with a cobbled-together 'Hollande–Etrangers de France' and 'Suisse–Luxembourg'. Then there were five regional French teams: Ile-de-France, Ouest, Nord-Ouest, Centre–Sud-Ouest and Sud-Est. French riders predominated, and a French victory was more than likely, since riders from regional teams would combine to frustrate any challenge from Belgium or Italy.

Neither Coppi nor Bartali was riding the Tour that marked the rebirth of France. Sylvère Maes, the winner of the last Tour in 1939, was now thirty-seven years old and had pulled out of the Belgian team. The Breton Louison Bobet was riding his first Tour. He had promise but was untried. A potential winner in the French national team was Edouard Fachleitner, 'the shepherd of Manosque', as the newspapers called him. Manosque is in the Basses-Alpes, some 200 kilometres from Grenoble. Fachleitner was an Italian immigrant and his family name was Austrian. The Sud-Ouest team had a fancied rider in Apo Lazarides, *l'enfant grec*. The 'Etrangers de France' team included the powerful Klabinsky from Poland – one of the many immigrant racing cyclists from the coalmines of Alsace – while the Centre–Sud-Ouest team was led by Raphael Geminiani, yet another French rider from an Italian immigrant family.

As the 1947 Tour took the road on its first stage from Paris to Lille the general favourite was the Swiss champion Ferdinand Kubler. In the Italian team was his main rival, Pierre Brambilla, whose Christian name and origins remind us once more of mixed nationality among cyclists in the post-war years. Brambilla came from an Italian family and rode for Italy, but he had been born in Switzerland and in 1949 would become a French citizen. Names, families, countries of origin and countries of adoption tell many similar stories. Professional cyclists, especially in the south and the north-east of France, were quite often the children of immigrants. Sometimes there was hostility towards people of foreign origin; but more among fans, I think, than in the peloton.

Immigrants aside, the Tour of 1947 emphasised that cycling was the sport of rural rather than urban France. Paris does not produce many stage-race riders of the highest rank (of course there are exceptions: the Parisians Maurice Archambaud and Laurent Fignon come immediately to mind). A strong cycling tradition has always existed in Brittany, and this province produced the winner of the first post-war Tour. He was Jean Robic, who rode with the Ouest team. Like many other sportsmen, barmen and soldiers from the northern Celtic fringes, Robic was small, craggy and infinitely pugnacious. In 1947 he was twenty-five years old. A cyclo-cross champion, he knew how to handle his bike in difficult conditions. Not that Robic was a poised rider. He often fell from his machine, probably because of his scrambling and fighting attitudes, and wore a trackman's crash helmet to guard against head injuries.

Robic was a gift to cartoonists. He resented their mockery because he was proud of his abilities. His flyweight size made him a natural climber and he also excelled in other disciplines. Time-trialling ability was to win him the Tour. Three stages before the Paris finish there was a 139-kilometre time trial from Vannes to St Brieuc. René Vietto was in yellow. The *azuréen* suffered terribly in this long test – made ill, it is said, by swallowing a litre of chilled cider as he rode the hot Normandy roads – while Robic came a fine second to the Belgian Raymond Impanis.

Italians had ridden strongly since the Pyrenees and were in command at St Brieuc. It looked as though either Aldo Ronconi or Brambilla would take the Tour. But Robic had them in his sights. On the very last stage he escaped from the peloton and was joined by Fachleitner and the sprinter Lucien Tesseire. This French trio hurtled towards Paris and entered the Parc des Princes to an ovation. The breakaway had gained so much time on the bunch that Robic had won the Tour de France without ever wearing the yellow jersey. A last-stage victory of this kind had never been seen before. This was also the first time that the Tour had been won by a rider from a regional team.

Now began the Tour's custom of inviting the previous year's winner to wear the *maillot jaune* on the first day of the next year's race. Robic started the 1948 Tour in yellow but would never pull on the jersey again. Connoisseurs point to his spectacular rides in the Pyrenees, mountains he preferred to the Alps. He was fourth in the Tour in 1949 and fifth in 1952. These were the two years when Coppi came first, so it is fair to say that the diminutive man fought with the giants of the Tour and was never a failure. Robic did not officially retire until 1961, since he needed the money he could earn from cycling. In the late 1950s he had a cafe in Paris which I sometimes visited. There one might savour, if he happened to be present, the surliness and aggression that had made him so unpopular with his fellow riders. Robic none the less attended reunions of old professionals, rode his bike to the end and died (killed by a motor car in 1980) a national hero.

XVIII

Louison Bobet at
the finish of Paris–Côte d'Azur.

Robic and his compatriots brought joy to France in the 1947 Tour, while the Belgian and Italian teams returned to their homes in disappointment. In the post-war years no Belgian would win the Tour de France before the reign of Eddy Merckx in 1969–74; and no other Belgian has ridden into Paris wearing the yellow jersey since Lucien van Impe's triumph in 1976. The Belgians are not natural stage-race riders – partly because they come from a small country, but mainly because the national sport of cycling descends from the ancient kermesse, a festive local market and fair. Cycle competition in Belgium is almost always in one-day events, often on circuits, and the top Belgian riders are measured in the great European cycle races known as the Classics, which they win far more often than champions from other countries.

There is no hard-and-fast definition of a Classic. We generally mean the fifteen or twenty races for professionals that are held on the hardest courses, rejoice in a long history, have the most competitive atmosphere and enjoy the greatest prestige. Classics are held annually and follow the same or similar routes. Some of the older ones have been lost, like the Bordeaux–Paris. Others have been added, like the Clasica San Sebastian. More have been added and then failed, among them the 'Classics' held in Britain at Rochester, Brighton and Leeds in the early 1990s. The professional world road championship, held on a different course every year, is doubtfully a Classic, while the road race at the Olympic Games, open to professionals since 1996, is certainly not one.

There is no doubt about the status of the major Classics.

They are, in Italy, Milan–San Remo and the Tour of Lombardy; in France, Paris–Roubaix and Paris–Tours; and in Belgium, Liège–Bastogne–Liège and the Tour of Flanders.

To these supreme races we add the Amstel Gold (the one Dutch Classic), the Clasica San Sebastian in northern Spain, Bordeaux–Paris (discontinued after 1988), the Fleche Wallonne, the Het Volk, Ghent–Wevelgem, the Zurich Grand Prix, Paris–Brest–Paris (discontinued after 1951 but still ridden as a trial for *cyclotouristes*) and Paris–Brussels, which has had an uncertain life in recent years, since its dates have clashed with other important races such as the world championships or the Vuelta a España.

The best-established Classics have a fixed place in the calendar. We still see, though faintly, that the premier cycle races responded to the rhythms of the seasons, holidays or saints' days. The first Classic of the year is Milan–San Remo, known as 'La Primavera' or 'La Classique de Saint Joseph', since it is so often run on St Joseph's Day, 19 March. It is very long – 294 kilometres – and proceeds from the square beneath Milan cathedral through Voghera and Tortona to Voltri, which is about the halfway point. There the course turns north to follow the coast of the Italian riviera. A succession of hills, none very high but ridden at speed and often on the big chainwheel, brings the riders to a high point on the Poggio before the final descent to the finish on the via Roma. In the thrilling finale the riders plunge through narrow roads between giant greenhouses, for San Remo is a town of flower markets. It has always been favoured as a springtime resort by wealthy Italians and, formerly, Russians, who idled by day in its cafes and casinos and applauded the artists of *bel canto* in the soft Mediterranean evenings.

Only an Italian can fully grasp the elegant nature of the Primavera, and it is the race that every Italian most wants to win. Milan–San Remo was especially Italian during the introspective and violent years of Mussolini's fascism, when the race's progress towards the riviera seemed to lighten the darkness of politics.

At that period the Italians were always the winners. From the 1950s, to the continued disgruntlement of the *tifosi*, Milan–San Remo has fallen to visitors from the north: the French, then many Belgians, two Dutchmen, an Englishman, an Irishman, a German and a Russian with a Belgian passport.

These riders have been Louison Bobet, Laurent Fignon, Laurent Jalabert, Rik van Steenbergen, Rik van Looy, Eddy Merckx, Fred de Bruyne, Jan Raas, Hennie Kuiper, Tom Simpson, Sean Kelly, Erik Zabel and Andrei Tchmil. They excelled, as do all victors of the Primavera, in tactical awareness on the *capi* of the last 50 kilometres, when the huge peloton (in some years more than 300 riders start in Milan) has finally fragmented and the leading group is down to about a dozen men. These leaders will be riding faster than at any previous time in the race, though they will have been in the saddle for seven hours. Immense physical prowess is required, which is why Italians prepare for Milan–San Remo by riding their March stage race, the Tirreno–Adriatico, a week of effort to get them at their best for St Joseph's Day.

The Primavera's dissimilar twin in the national consciousness is Italy's autumn classic, the Tour of Lombardy, the 'Race of the Falling Leaves'. Since it is held in October or even on occasion in November, the riders will expect mixed weather, especially in the hills. The course has changed over the years. The Tour of Lombardy has started or finished at Milan, Como, Bergamo, Varese and Monza. But the race always has the same heart, in the climbs above the Italian lakes. The crisis of the classic usually comes in the mountains above Bellagio, a little town at the confluence of Lake Como and Lake Lecco.

We are about 30 kilometres from Como and some 100 kilometres from Milan. Behind the clustered houses of Bellagio there is a minor road that does not run along the side of the lakes but rises through woods to the village of Magreglio, which is 754 metres above sea level and has a view across the Swiss border to mountains that never lose their snow. Here, in a distant part of Italy, is the little chapel of the Madonna del Ghisallo. It is the cyclists' church and was blessed as such, in 1949, by Pope Pius XII.

The chapel is a symbol of the link between Catholic consciousness and the sport of cycle racing. The visitor will find that it is decorated with road jerseys, the *maillot jaune* of the Tour de France, the *maglia rosa* of the Giro d'Italia, the rainbow jersey of the world championship. Here also are pennants, badges, photographs, other souvenirs and important bicycles: a bike that once belonged to Gino Bartali, another that was once Fausto Coppi's; one of Eddy Merckx's bikes (who can say which one – he always had thirty-six of them ready in perfect preparation); the machine Francesco Moser used to break the hour record in 1984; and the bicycle on which the young Fabio Casartelli died in the 1995 Tour de France when he crashed on the descent of the Portet d'Aspet.

Casartelli was a local boy, a native of nearby Como. He had been an Olympic champion in 1992, took a lowly 107th place in the Giro d'Italia of 1993, abandoned the 1994 Tour de France and had not quite settled into the professional ranks when he died. This neophyte was much liked. All the winnings from the stage after his death – apparently some $100,000 – were donated to his family by his fellow riders, who also organised memorial services.

The peloton has a solidarity at such times. Most racing cyclists fall from their bikes during the course of the season, so they are aware of their closeness to injury and even death. The loss of Fabio Casartelli reawakened religious sentiments behind generally token gestures. Most European riders make the sign of the cross before a lonely time-trial ride, and we may be sure that all Italian cyclists cross themselves as they pass the chapel of the Madonna del Ghisallo. They need protection, for the chapel is at the highest point of the Tour of Lombardy route and is followed by a precipitous and dangerous descent, slippery with mud and the fallen leaves of the race's title.

Just as the great winners of the Tour de France are those who cross the Galibier alone and in the lead, so the legendary victors of the 'Race of the Falling Leaves' are those who make their move on the Ghisallo climb. Among them we must salute Fausto Coppi – who won the race four times, three times between 1946 and 1949, and then again in 1954 – Tom Simpson, who in 1965 set a record pace for the event after riding away from such men as Poulidor, Motta, Anquetil and Gimondi; Francesco Moser, who was the winner in 1975 and 1978; Eddy Merckx, the winner in 1971 and 1972; and Bernard Hinault, who won in 1979 and 1984.

*   *   *

The mention of such names shows that the major classics are won by major riders. It's good to note Tom Simpson in their company, though we should keep the British rider's achievements in perspective.* Simpson's physique and dynamic competitive manner were suited to events that occupy half the waking day, from nine in the morning until late afternoon. In other words he was built for the Classics, which generally occupy this span of time. Simpson was also more comfortable in cold or rainy weather than in the heat of southern Europe. In this he resembled a Belgian cyclist, and he was indeed an honorary Belgian, as are all cyclists who set up house in that welcoming country. Many were the celebrations in his adopted city of Ghent when Simpson won the world championship in 1965 – a triumph that received much less applause in Britain.

---

* Statistics give a quick comparison. I follow Fer Schroeder's analysis of results in the Classics between 1945 and 1980. Within this time span Eddy Merckx won thirty-five classics, Rik Van Looy eighteen, Roger De Vlaminck sixteen, Fausto Coppi eleven, Herman Van Springe eleven, Rik Van Steenbergen ten, Walter Godefroot ten, Francesco Moser ten, Freddy Maertens ten, Briek Schotte nine and Jan Raas nine. In Tom Simpson's continental career between 1959 and 1967 he won five classics.

Tom Simpson had already become a sort of Belgian citizen after he took the Tour of Flanders in 1961. Perhaps we should say that he became an honorary Flemish citizen, since the Flanders race does not recognise Walloon culture. And in general the Classics are most meaningful when they are rooted in some especial plot of land – the coast road of the Italian riviera, in the case of Milan–San Remo, the *coteaux* of the Loire in Paris–Tours, the mountains above Lake Como in the Tour of Lombardy, the farm roads of the Arensberg forest in Paris–Roubaix. All these races belong to familiar and often hallowed ground; but none of them belongs more to local soil than the Tour of Flanders, the Ronde van Vlaanderen, which is the ultimate expression of Flemish national pride.

The Ronde thrills the heartlands of east Flanders – and not so much the capital of the province, Ghent, as the farming country of the Flemish Ardennes, with its open fields, chill breezes, rain, dust, mud and sudden cobbled hills. These abrupt climbs, not more than a kilometre long, should be noted by every traveller. Some of them charge through the centres of villages or small towns such as Geraardsbergen. Others are rural holloways, sunk beneath two fields. The Flemish call them *bergs*. In towns they are sometimes named *muurs*, and indeed they are rather like walls, so steeply do they rise to block a cyclist's progress.

It is obvious that the Flemish national character is opposed to hairpin bends. The roads of east Flanders don't wind to take a circuitous and therefore easier path but go straight up, rising sometimes to 1 in 5 or 1 in 4. These inclines don't ease off when the road decides on a 90 per cent turn. Often the road steepens. The surfaces are awful: cobbles in the middle, primitive gutters on either side. So these are not climbs for the stylish rider. You get over by sprinting at them in 39 × 21 or 39 × 23. Then you rely on brute strength to reach the top.

The Ronde van Vlaanderen takes place in March. Spring in Flanders is a specialised form of winter, often cold and raining.

The riders of the Ronde also have to deal with hostile winds. The race starts from Bruges and goes north to Wenduine before following the coast to Ostende. On this part of the course bitter gusts from the North Sea split the bunch into echelon formation. Then the route swings south through Wingene and Waregem before turning east to Zottegem. Hereabouts the land is flat, mainly, and sometimes looks as if a prairie had been cut into hundreds of irregular lots – as may be an accurate impression, for Belgium is a land of smallholdings and has no great estates.

The British, it seems, do not find east Flanders a picturesque part of the world. But cyclists will have the impression of a region of enthusiasts, Flemings who love their own soil. You wonder where all the people have come from. Even if there are no houses the roads are lined with fans. It's said that half the population of Flanders comes out to see the Ronde. And what happy hours I have spent on the high banks above the ditches of Flemish farm roads, my son at my side – well fed from a *frituur* (chip van) – clubmates and hysterical locals all around us, everyone searching the sky for the TV helicopters, looking to the further fields for the first motorcycle outriders with their hooters and klaxons – and then for a sight of the bunch or maybe a breakaway, for we are now at the beginning of the cobbled climbs, fifteen or sixteen of them, as the course winds and rewinds upon itself to find the hills that every racing cyclist fears and whose names should be known by every schoolboy! Here they are, followed by their distance in kilometres from the Bruges start.

> Molenberg (151)
> Wolvenberg (161)
> Kluisberg (181)
> Knokteberg (188)
> Oude-Kwaremont (195)
> Paterberg (199)

Koppenberg (206)
Steenbeekdries (212)
Taaienberg (214)
Eikenberg (219)
Kapelleberg (222)
Leberg (229)
Berendries (233)
Tenbosse (238)
Muur–Kapelmuur (249)
Bosberg (252)

The course varies slightly each year so I have used the route of the 2002 Ronde as a guide. The finish of the race is at Meerbeke, which is just next door to Ninove. In 2002 the total distance of the race was 264 kilometres.

Now let's pretend that we are standing next to a *frituur* at the bottom of the Molenberg, the first of the decisive hills. Let us imagine that the peloton is intact, apart from riders who are off the back. The race will have left that big square in the centre of Bruges to travel at touring pace through the neutralised section to the racing start at Sint-Pieters at 10 a.m. Thereafter, if the peloton races at 39 kph, it will reach the Molenberg at about 1.50 p.m. If the speed is faster, at 43 kph, the peloton will arrive at the bottom of the hill at 1.30 p.m. The riders will have had three and a half hours in the saddle, and there are more than 100 kilometres to go.

It is now that the peloton starts to disintegrate and the race becomes the property of hard and wily champions.

The *bergs* are not only steep, with treacherous surfaces, but narrow. Riders collide with each other and fall off their bikes, which they are then forced to carry cyclo-cross style up the rest of the hill, at a run. This can mean a loss of two minutes on the riders who have gone over the top in the leading positions. On the approach to the Molenberg there are 10 kilometres of very fast jostling within the peloton, riders looking for the front of the bunch so that they can enter the climb before anyone else.

So it is that the race leaders sprint for the hill as though its entrance were the finishing line. Up they go through the defile, panting; a snap gear change on to the big ring at the top; no relaxation on the descent, just bumping and skidding; then a few kilometres before another sprint to be first at the next *berg* – and so it goes on, from the Molenberg to the Bosberg, for 100 kilometres. Only the most powerful riders can survive, and the Ronde van Vlaanderen is always won by a man at the height of his physical strength.

As is often said, a Belgian – a Flemish Belgian – would prefer to win the Tour of Flanders than the Tour de France. The Ronde is the Flemish Tour de France concentrated into one day. I grieve to say that there have been a number of top Flemish riders who loathed the French so much (and hated their Walloon compatriots too) that they preferred not to ride the French Tour, even though they could have done well in the *hexagone*. Prominent among such negative-minded patriots was Roger de Vlaeminck, winner of the Ronde in 1977. In a long and successful career he entered the Tour de France only three times and never finished. It wasn't that he couldn't cope; he simply longed to be at home.

I know that at the Ronde it's easy to get caught up in unreasoning local patriotism. For instance, there's one spot where you can run over ploughed mud between two *bergs*. You see the riders come to the top of the first climb, then get across the fields to catch them halfway through the next climb. I have been among a couple of thousand people, all waving yellow-and-black flags with the motif of the Lion of Flanders, on this stumbling sprint across the furrows. Why were we doing it? Because it seemed both a normal and and an exciting part of life. So it is with all venerable festivals.

I do appreciate that such revels appear grotesque to outsiders, a symptom of some national mania. Listen for example to the Walloon writer Paul Beving:

> La Ronde fait partie du patrimoine du peuple flamand au même titre que les processions de Veurne et de Bruges, la fête des chats à Ypres ou la bénédiction maritime d'Ostende. Cette course cycliste est la plus fabuleuse de toutes les kermesses flamandes. Aucune autre épreuve ne suscite une telle ambiance, une telle ferveur populaire.

This is written in slightly aloof terms, but Beving has a point. This French speaker refers to the way that, in one annual festivity, cats (stuffed ones, nowadays) are flung from belfry towers in Ypres, to the parades with fantastic tableaux in Bruges and the ceremony of blessing the sea at Ostend. There are similar religious festivals, which after a few hours become Bacchanalian, all over Flanders. Bike racing is part of any local kermesse, and the Tour of Flanders is a kermesse on a grand scale.

We could make a comparison with Brittany, another region with a passion for cycle sport and which has similar half-religious, half-bucolic fair days. It's a pity that Brittany doesn't have its own Classic, but the province is probably too poor. Classics thrive when they traverse old agricultural territory but begin or end in a rich provincial capital. As we shall see, Classics also depend on regional newspapers published in such capitals.

XIX

On the cobbles in Paris–Roubaix.

Belgium's other major spring Classic, the Liège–Bastogne–Liège, appears less difficult than the Tour of Flanders. Most professional cyclists know otherwise. There aren't so many cobbled stretches and you don't have to fight so fiercely for a good position on narrow roads, but you will certainly struggle on the Walloon climbs, especially on the return journey from Bastogne; and if a rider is dropped on any of those ten hills – which are between 1 and 3 kilometres long – then he'll need much strength to rejoin the leaders.

Strength, and optimism too. My belief is that riders of the Liège race can become depressed by its route. The country between the Ardennes capital and Bastogne is mainly rural. The leading riders in these wooded and winding roads are soon out of sight and therefore have a psychological advantage over their pursuers. It's easy to get lost. I find it an unnerving part of the world in other ways. The isolated farmhouses and small, self-contained towns seem filled with secrets and there's a dripping silence in the wet forests. Coming into this area from the more expansive farmlands of east Flanders, one somehow wishes it to be noisier, and for the fans to shout more than they do.

If we were high above the fir trees it would be possible to see the Ardennes as a vast stretch of forested land running from northern France across south-east Belgium and into the Grand Duchy of Luxembourg and the Eiffel mountains of Germany. The principal river is the Meuse, which flows through the region on its course to the Netherlands and the North Sea. Tributaries of the Meuse include the Semois, the Lesse and the Ourthe, which rise in the higher lands of the Ardennes and have formed narrow valleys and deep gorges.

It's not exactly mountainous, but much of the Ardennes, especially in the east, is quite high. Go there once and you may well decide not to return. Belgium's highest point, the Signal de Botrange, is at 2,265 feet or 694 metres (Scaefell, the highest point in England, is 3,210 feet high) and in this part of the world, easily one of the most desolate parts of Europe, there's a gloomy tundra of peat bog, moor and heathland. The few inhabitants cower behind thick hedges of hornbeam and in their short summer flee from the fires that burn mile after mile of heather.

The route of Liège–Bastogne–Liège skirts this highest and most unpleasant ground, which is known by the eloquent name of the 'Hautes Fagnes', but on half a dozen occasions the riders of the Classic climb to more than 500 metres after delving into deep and shaded valleys formed by the Ourthe. At the end of their seven hours of racing the professionals will have climbed around 3,500 metres. Furthermore, this hilly race is often run in cold conditions and sometimes in snow. So is it tougher than the Tour of Flanders? Ask Eddy Merckx, five times the winner in Liège. 'If the Tour of Flanders had been that hard, I would have won that race more often too.' By this enigmatic and almost boastful remark Merckx meant that the Walloon classic brought out the best in the greatest cyclist of all time, himself.

*   *   *

Somebody has said that Liège is the most northerly of Mediterranean cities. You wouldn't think so in the winter rain. I never go in the arcades or saunter the boulevards, preferring to marvel at the old slagheaps, now covered by grass. They look like modern sculptures, not the sort of art you usually find in Belgium. There's quite a large Italian population in Liège, as people went there from the sunny south to work in the mines.

In Liège bars you can often imagine yourself in France and of course the language of the city is French. Liège–Bastogne–Liège is known as 'La Doyenne', an odd name simply indicating that it is the oldest of all the Classics. Its route was devised in 1892, fifteen years before Milan–San Remo, twenty-one years before the first edition of the Ronde van Vlaanderen.

The turn at Bastogne, a market town pretty well unknown to history before the 'Battle of the Bulge' in 1944, was devised because of the benefits of public transport. In 1892 the town was on the new train route between Liège and Luxembourg. The commissaires of the proposed race could see the riders off, entrain to Bastogne to count the riders through, get on the return train and be back in Liège in time to cheer them home.

It's a nice railway trip, especially if you have a good map and a slow train. In our modern days, however, one surveys crucial sections of 'La Doyenne' from elevated vantage points on Belgian motorways. These marvels of civil engineering – often on piles, as though they were very long bridges – skim over the valleys and head for some distant horizon. I look out of the coach window. Below the motorway, perhaps a hundred feet down, people work (forestry is the industry), children go to school, streams run, a cafe is open; and if you leave the three-lane concrete autoroute on a clover-leaf sliproad to such a place as Remouchamps you'll find a caravan park and campsite, probably a pottery and craft shop, together with centres for kayaking, cross-country skiing or pot-holing. In a number of similar villages 'La Doyenne' meets the *tourisme verte* of our own age.

Sailing along the E2 motorway above Remouchamps one also sees a tiny little road that rises from the village. It's known as the Côte de La Redoute. Other hills on the way back from Bastogne are longer and sometimes steeper, but La Redoute is the climb that most often decides Liège–Bastogne–Liège. I've walked the hill (I had to) and was impressed by its pure nastiness. The road lifts itself quite steadily out of Remouchamps, then rears to a 1 in 5 section, which is quite long, then gives you a further kick in the teeth when it steepens again round a left-hand turn. At that point it would help if you could see the top, but you can't.

The first riders over La Redoute are scarcely ever caught and now must race tactically against each other as well as facing two or three more climbs before the finish. The race used to end on the Rocourt velodrome, but since 1992 the finish has been at the summit of another hill, in the wide main street of Ans, a working-class suburb of Liège. As Sean Kelly (who in 1984 and 1989 won on the Rocourt track) says, the new finish favours an uphill sprinter; and few are the men who can sprint on the Ans hill after 260 kilometres in the Ardennes.

*　　*　　*

Let's consider four wins in Liège, by three Belgians and a Frenchman: Frank Vandenbroucke, Eddy Merckx, Roger de Vlaeminck and Bernard Hinault.

It was at Ans that, in 1999, Frank Vandenbroucke stamped out the most intense and commanding of victories in recent years. 'VDB' – just twenty-four years old, and with a fine but not extensive collection of wins and placings in his young career – began his race at a press conference. There had been snow on the Friday before Sunday's event, but this didn't trouble young Frank, or so he told reporters. 'I go better in bad weather.' Would the course suit him? 'There is no course that doesn't suit me.' Was he ready for the great test of 'La Doyenne'? 'I have a will of steel and legs like fire.' Finally, he told reporters where he would win the race. They should expect to see his triumphant move on the hill of St Nicolas.

This hill is at the centre of the Italian immigrant community of Liège. The local crowds would have been cheering the Pisa-born Michele Bartoli, Vandenbroucke's senior by four years, who had won Liège–Bastogne–Liège in the previous two years and was currently in excellent form. So, was Vandenbroucke being provocative? I think not. At the beginning of his fame his press conferences were as challenging, but also as well managed, as his rides. He spoke Italian to Italian journalists, and French or Flemish to Belgian pressmen, whichever they preferred. Vandenbroucke is himself a Walloon, from Mescrou. He learnt Flemish when he began to race, realising that a knowledge of Belgium's other language would help him as a professional.

Not a lovely-looking boy, this Frank from Mescrou and from the Cofidis team (sponsored by a firm that sells credit over the telephone, *Simple-Souple-Discret* or *Eenvoudig-Soupel-Discreet*). His slicked-back blond hair and ill-judged blond moustache and goatee beard gave him the appearance of a youth who didn't know how to become a man. Or so we old men thought, and we were both right and wrong. Only a man can win the Liège race, yet shortly after his victory Vandenbroucke began to behave like an adolescent. Either way, brash young Frank was a gift to newspapers.

In the earlier part of the 1999 race there were the usual 'suicide breaks' on the way south to Bastogne, nothing of much consequence. Some snow still lay on the verges of the higher roads and in the woods. Otherwise the day was clear, though cold. There was some confused fighting after 100 kilometres, and then a crucial selection on La Redoute. Michele Bartoli came to the front of the leading bunch at Remouchamps and attacked hard as soon as they came to the hill. Usually, nobody could stay with Bartoli when he took off in such a way. The bunch disintegrated. But Vandenbroucke rode up to Bartoli. He didn't follow his wheel or attempt to overtake and drop him. He rode side by side with the Italian champion, almost nonchalantly, as though they were on the flat and had hours to go before the finish.

Bartoli must then have known that he was beaten, and he faltered. A few more riders came up to contest the last 30 kilometres. Vandenbroucke, riding steadily – though the pace was very fast – took little notice of them.

At the bottom of the St Nicolas hill, which is 6 kilometres from Ans, he suddenly switched to the other side of the road, jumped out of his saddle, rode away from his rivals, sat down again and pounded his way to the top. Nobody could reply, least of all the stricken Bartoli. Vandenbroucke gained thirty seconds in a kilometre and kept this advantage to the end of the race. My belief is that he could have increased his lead but kept his pursuers dangling at a distance of his own choosing. That year I was in the crowd at Ans, standing about three-quarters of the way up the final hill. 'VDB' climbed at tremendous speed but looked over his shoulder more than once, not in worry but as though he were inspecting the other riders to see which of them might come second. I think he might even have shrugged his shoulders before raising his arms in victory.

I had put money on him. Ever been in a Belgian betting shop? Mental agility is required. At the press conference Vandenbroucke told journalists that, in the minute or so as he climbed the Ans hill, he had been thinking 'of his mother and his father'. Whether he was being arrogant or pseudo-humble, 'VDB' always had the right thing to say to journalists. They knew that his father, Jean-Jacques Vandenbroucke, had been a professional cyclist and that his uncle was Jean-Luc Vandenbroucke, who had once won the Grand Prix des Nations and was a successful team manager. So Frank came from the heart of Belgian cycling. We thought, in 1999, that here was the young cyclist that Belgium had so long awaited, a genuine successor to Eddy Merckx. It was not to be. Frank Vandenbroucke's career floundered.

*   *   *

It is generally unwise to say to all the world that you're going to win an event. Eddy Merckx, who gathered dozens of victories between 1961, when he began racing, and 1978, when he stopped, did not often predict his triumphs. But he did so at Liège in 1969. In fact Merckx had said all the previous winter that 'La Doyenne' would be his. Then, in the early spring, he won Milan–San Remo, Paris–Nice and the Tour of Flanders. Was it possible that he could add Liège–Bastogne–Liège to these exploits?

There were a number of people who wished to stop him, and two in particular. The more dangerous of them was Roger de Vlaeminck, whom we have already met. He hailed from Eeklo, a small, ugly town between Ghent and Bruges, and had an elder brother, Eric de Vlaeminck, whose success in cycling had lured Roger away from football. The de Vlaeminck brothers were pugnacious, tough even by Flemish standards. They came from a family of travellers, which is why Roger was always called 'the Gypsy'. Roger was a phenomenal bike-handler, able to jump his machine in and out of tramlines or ride it up and down flights of stairs. These acrobatic or fairground skills were combined with a lean and somehow malevolent physique. He worked hard, with long training rides of fanatical intensity.

Eddy Merckx knew de Vlaeminck's qualities and had invited him to join his Faema team. De Vlaeminck refused. He did not wish to be a *domestique* and already sensed that his role in life would be to prevent Merckx's victories. At Liège in 1969 the other major threat to Merckx came from Felice Gimondi. The Italian was three years older than Merckx and had been his rival since they first met at the 1964 Olympic Games. In 1965 Gimondi had won the Tour de France. Then he won the Giro d'Italia in 1967 and the Vuelta a España in 1968. For all Merckx's brilliance, Gimondi was the senior rider. He wanted revenge in the Liège race – the Luik–Bastenaken–Luik, as de Vlaeminck no doubt called it – since Merckx had beaten him by five minutes in that year's Tour of Flanders. The night before the race his fans from the Liège Italian community gathered outside Gimondi's hotel. He would not come down to greet them. He was making his calculations.

Merckx also had a plan. He took no notice of de Vlaeminck or Gimondi, surrounded himself with teammates and went to the front of the bunch. He kept the speed fast, and the peloton intact, until the Bastogne turn (95 km). Then he sent a couple of his teammates, Roger Swerts and Victor van Schil, up the road. They were *éclaireurs*, whose task in a breakaway was to test the resolve of those behind them. The peloton responded, but Merckx was still at its head, carefully and gradually increasing the pace. The Faema leader and an increasingly strung-out bunch had the two breakaways within sight on the Côte de Wanne (153 km). On the Stockeu climb (170 km) Merckx rejoined Swerts and van Schil. All three sprinted, and then they were away together.

So Merckx was in the ideal position: in front with two team-mates. But he might have made his move too early. There were still 94 kilometres to Liège. De Vlaeminck and Gimondi organ-ised the chase and had one of those brief, shouted conversations that so often determine the course of a cycle race. They reckoned that Swerts and van Schil would tire and fall behind as Merckx drove them up the hills. Then the imperious Eddy would be isolated and they could hunt him down.

But the pursuers couldn't get closer than 200 metres. The speed now became intense, and stayed intense. It was too much for Swerts, who dropped back. Merckx and van Schil sped on, Merckx doing most of the work. In 20 kilometres the duo carved out a minute's lead. Then it was two minutes, then three. Gimondi and de Vlaeminck gave up. The defeated chasing group was further slowed by Swerts and two other Faema riders, who sat in and did no work. When they arrived in Liège the Merckx–van Schil tandem was in front by eight minutes. Vic van Schil led into the velodrome, then applauded his leader as Merckx crossed the line in triumph. Britain's Barry Hoban, incidentally, was in the chasing group and won the *sprint des battus* to take third place.

* * *

I should mention here that Liège–Bastogne–Liège has a sibling race, the Flèche Wallonne – a 'little brother' that was created by the French-language paper *Les Sports* in 1935. The idea was to traverse Wallonia on an east–west axis to complement the north–south route of La Doyenne. Initially, the course was between the cities of Liège and Tournai. Then the race was held between Mons and Charleroi, or between Spa and Mons. Nowadays it starts at Charleroi and finishes at Huy, whose steep main street is ridden three times during an exciting final circuit. Whatever the course, the Flèche Wallonne has always confined itself to French-speaking Belgium. It is held in the same week as Liège–Bastogne–Liège and has a similar field. A system of points decides the winner of the 'Weekend Ardennais' for riders who finish both events.

*   *   *

The 1980 Flèche Wallonne was won by Giuseppe Saronni, with Bernard Hinault in third place, under a sky of blue with unbroken sunshine. That was mid-week. Hinault, a Breton who liked Walloon races, had won the Flèche Wallonne in the previous year and in 1977 had taken La Doyenne. He planned to repeat that victory. On Friday and Saturday he did some light training on the Ardennes roads, still in mild weather. Then it began to snow.

As the field left the Place de la République Française there were flakes in the air. A few kilometres beyond the Liège suburbs the peloton rode into a snowstorm. High winds whipped snow into the riders' faces, until they had to hold one hand in front of their eyes. Road surfaces were treacherous, support cars were sliding in the slush and crashes were unavoidable. Real racing was impossible. After an hour of this torture half the field had abandoned.

Conditions were a little better at Bastogne. Hinault decided to stay with the race. Frozen and shuddering, he changed clothes and headed back north into the snow. Tactics were out of the question, and in any case it seemed best to ride as fast as possible, just to keep warm. On the approach to the Stockeu climb (170 km) Hinault saw two men in front of him: the Belgians Rudy Pevenage and Ludo Peeters, who led the race. Who was behind? It was hard to say. The motorcycle outriders and team cars were cut off by the blizzard.

Hinault dropped Pevenage and Peeters on the Stockeu and reckoned that he could not be caught. His struggle was not with other riders but with the weather. Using low gears, he cautiously negotiated the 80 kilometres back to Liège to finish ten minutes ahead of the next man, the redoubtable Hennie Kuiper. One hundred and seventy riders had begun the race; twenty returned to Liège. They were given to the care of doctors. Hinault's hands were frozen to his handlebars and he never afterwards completely recovered feeling in two of his fingers.

*   *   *

A hard man both on and off the bike, Hinault was a champion of cyclists' rights, adamant that those who took part in a demanding and dangerous sport should be respected by that sport's organisers and should not be asked to take unnecessary risks. Two of the northern spring classics, he believed, should be rerouted. The Tour of Flanders was one of these races. Hinault rode it in 1978 (Walter Godefroot's year, with Michel Pollentier second) and had vowed never to return.

He didn't like the buffeting as the riders entered the *bergs*, though he was as good at riding shoulder to shoulder as any Flandrian. Neither did he like the traffic problems in the Ronde. It is true that rogue fans on motorbikes have caused trouble, and so have the following cars. In 1987 the young Dane Jesper Skibby fell on the climb of the Koppenberg. Photos show that he was using toe-clips. A team car just behind him drove over his bike and might easily have crushed Skibby himself, who was still anchored to the pedals. The incident banished the Koppenberg from the race for a few years, until the local council set to work to widen the road. In 2002 the climb, only slightly widened, again became a part of the Tour of Flanders.

Hinault also had strong reservations about Paris–Roubaix, the 'Queen of the Classics'. By winning it in 1981 he became the first Frenchman to be victorious at Roubaix since Louison Bobet in 1956, for this is a French race that usually belongs to Belgians. Hinault was proud that Bobet, then a sick man and late in his life, had travelled to congratulate him as he mounted the podium on the Roubaix track. Nevertheless, unlike Bobet, Hinault was opposed to the event. In Hinault's opinion it was undignified, dirty, unfair to its riders and a relic of a former age.

On all these counts he was right. Yet Hinault was also wrong, for these are among the reasons why Paris–Roubaix continues to be revered. It belongs to an old century and refuses to be contemporary. Today's witness of Paris–Roubaix cannot live in the present, however gripping the race may be. At Arras, Doullens or Le Cateau, he will feel the ancient melancholy of northern France. And then, as his admired cyclists pick their way through mining villages, he will enter the time and the landscape of Zola. He will see the slums of the industrial revolution, battlefields and cemeteries, the wretchedness and despair of those who scratch their living from the soil. No other sporting event has this kind of historical resonance. One cannot imagine Paris–Roubaix in the months of summer. The worse the weather and the state of the course, the more we feel that maleficent skies understand the nature of cycling's most agonising test. Paris–Roubaix is sometimes called 'La Pascale', since it takes place at Easter. Its other soubriquet is more accurate: 'L'Enfer du Nord', 'The Hell of the North'.

The phrase came from the pen of a Parisian journalist – his name, alas, has now disappeared – who, in 1919, had been shocked by the state of the roads leading towards Roubaix and had wept to see the battlefields, trenches across meadows, shell craters, leafless trees, mass graveyards and devastated towns of Picardy and Artois. When this journalist wrote, Paris–Roubaix had not been held since 1914. A sporting event after a war should have marked a new beginning to life. In 1919 that was not possible. A hellish smell of sulphur still hung above the land. The race began with a minute's silence.

*   *   *

Paris–Roubaix had been founded in 1896 by two men, Theodore Vienne and Maurice Perez, *lainiers* who had made fortunes in the Roubaix textile business. In the previous year they had built a velodrome in the Parc de Barbieux, the only leisure amenity in a town of woollen mills. These moneyed men wanted to encourage local pride and initiative, and felt that a sporting event would bring attention to Roubaix. It's surprising that they succeeded. Roubaix adjoins Lille, the capital of French Flanders, a city with an ancient history and many monuments to attract the tourist. Roubaix has nothing of that sort. In the 1890s the town consisted only of factories and *corons*, the local name for its red-brick back-to-back houses. Textile workers in this dismal place did a ten-hour day, six days a week. Their recreations were drinking and betting on cock fights.

More enterprising *roubaisiens* had another hobby. They engaged in petty smuggling. The Belgian frontier is only a couple of kilometres away, and the *douaniers* were easily evaded or bribed. Paris–Roubaix, essentially a race that aims for Belgium, often has an air of illegality. Paris itself has never had much to do with the race, which by nature belongs to the land north of Arras. After 1966 the start of the race was at Chantilly, 50 kilometres from Paris. From 1977 the town of Compiègne has been its host: an unsuitable place, it has always seemed to me, for Compiègne is unmistakably a home for courtiers, while Roubaix is both provincial and plebeian. The wonder is that a Parisian paper, *Le Vélo*, had been prepared to give some money, and a few of its pages, to promote a race from the capital to such an unfashionable location. Messieurs Vienne and Perez must have been persuasive men. As things turned out, *Le Vélo* enjoyed its role and was delighted when 'La Pascale' became a popular yearly celebration.

The aftermath of the First World War gave Paris–Roubaix more significance. In recent years its meaning has been artificially sustained. The 1966 rearrangement of the race, in the year when the start was moved to Chantilly, was made for one compelling reason. Progress in local government led to the resurfacing of country roads with tarmacadam, which was much smoother than cobbles. A sacrilege, said cycling fans. 'L'Enfer du Nord' should hold to its primitive nature. The whole point of the race was that its climax came on farm tracks or roads that went through industrial villages and had scarcely been repaired since they were laid down in the mid-nineteenth century.

So the 1966 Paris–Roubaix looked for obscure sections of *pavé*. They were discovered at Hornaing, Ferrain and Flines-les-Raches, unknown places before 'L'Enfer du Nord' set out to discover the worst roads in France. The organisers of Paris–Roubaix were still not satisfied, and gave Albert Bouvet the responsibility of devising a new Paris–Roubaix. Bouvet, a first-rate pursuit rider in the 1950s, and a roadman, had a friend and former teammate in Jean Stablinski. He asked 'Stab' to reroute the race.

Nobody had better qualifications for this *retardataire* task. Jean Stablinski was a child of the area. He was born there, in Thun-St Amand, the son of Polish immigrants, and now lived at Valenciennes, not wishing to be anywhere else in France. As a young man he had worked in the Arenberg pit. He had been the world road champion (in 1962) and four times the French national champion. He knew his home roads well and used to joke that he knew the Paris–Roubaix route both above and below ground. Stablinski still has memories of a miners' race. 'I can remember the miners cheering me on at the side of the road as we rode through – people who would be underground on the early shift the next day.'

Taking turns, one of them on a bike and the other in the car, Bouvet and Stablinski explored the back roads near Roubaix and drew up a new itinerary. It was and remains horrible, with about 50 kilometres of *pavé* in thirty sections. The cobbles begin at Troisvilles, after 100 kilometres of racing, and with 160 kilometres still to go. The course heads on towards the Belgian border but often twists back upon itself. After the pounding on the cobbles there are welcome stretches of tarmac. Then the pounding starts again and in some places – Quivy to Saint-Python, or Hornaing to Wandignies-Hamage – it goes on for 2 or 3 kilometres. In the Wallers-Arenberg forest and agricultural land the cobbles sometimes do not cover the road, and in the gaps there are big holes filled with water or mud. After the riders leave the forest there are still fifteen or sixteen stretches of *pavé* before the route enters Roubaix – stretches that often seem to madden the men who have already suffered so much.

*   *   *

In search of the Roubaix velodrome, a young man from Birmingham might expect to find a smaller version of Villa Park. Instead, the cycle track – which is open apart from a small grandstand – belongs to a wide and grassy space that is maintained by the council. There is no entrance charge. You simply walk to the track past tennis courts and lawns where families play with their children and boys kick footballs. The track has been patched up, probably many times, since it was built in 1895. The Parc de Barbieux is neither smart nor seedy. Its surrounding hedges are regularly cut, and there are a few small flowerbeds and a boating lake. South of the park begins the residential section of middle-class Roubaix, while quite near its entrance are former woollen mills and factories recently converted into flats or workshops for such modern enterprises as computer graphics or designer jeans.

The one word that expresses the spirit of this place is 'municipal'. There is an indefinable but unmistakable air of concern for well-being and public health. And here we find another aspect of the myth or symbolism of the Paris–Roubaix race. Its exhausted and mud-spattered riders clean themselves up in showers that have always been famous but are now especially renowned because of their appearance in Jørgen Leth's film of the 1975 race, *A Sunday in Hell*. The showers are marble and brass stalls, and you start their flow by pulling a quite hefty iron chain. From the film, you would guess them to date from the 1920s, but they may be of a much earlier date. For the Lille–Roubaix–Tourcoing area, so grimy and sooty, whose *corons* had no bathrooms or washrooms, pioneered showers for the workers at just the period when the Roubaix velodrome was built.

Social historians tell us that crude showers were used by the French army after 1860 and then were introduced to prisons. I guess that there was quite a lot of municipal showering in the industrial north, and have been impressed by J. Arnould's *Sur l'installation de bains à peu de frais pour les ouvriers*, published in Lille in 1879. At what date do we first find British pithead showers? But to return to my main point – we know that riders of the Paris–Roubaix Classic are regarded, even to this day, not merely as sportsmen but as workmen, miners, the foot soldiers of some regiment, or the *forçats de la route* who only sometimes dare to question the system that has made them ride their bikes for more than seven hours in such adverse conditions.

*   *   *

The neat front rooms of some professional cyclists contain one precious souvenir. Among the photographs, road jerseys and other trophies is a cobblestone, usually mounted in a marble base and with a small brass plate that announces its origin. The cobble is a symbol of Paris–Roubaix, and furthermore is not a normal cobble. It is a *pavé du Nord*, pretty much square at 16 × 16 centimetres and weighing 10–12 kilos. Compare such a brute with the cobble known as *le mosaïque*, which you will find in Parisian streets and which is sometimes dug up by students to throw at the police. A *mosaïque* is 7 × 7 centimetres, weighs just 1 kilo and is therefore a minor affair, a cobble for dilettantes, shall we say (French racing cyclists have only limited sympathy for revolutionary students).

Nowadays there are people who try to reclaim roads by introducing new sections of *pavé du Nord*, which takes about twenty-five giant cobbles per square metre. Such organisations as the Amis de Paris–Roubaix have formed alliances with conservation groups and a horticultural college which helps with the preservation of a *pavé* road in the Arenberg forest. These enthusiasts probably won't be able to preserve all the *pavé* sections for all time, but it looks as if the race as we have known it will continue for at least a few more years.

XX

Gino Bartali and Fausto Coppi, together for once.

The immediate danger to Paris–Roubaix probably comes from the very people who might win it. The new class of professionals and their managers are wary of this race. Team sponsors, whose first interest is in advertising, think that it doesn't look modern enough. Paris–Roubaix can humiliate the more elegant sort of champion and the likelihood of a crash is high. Injuries lead to loss of training time. A cyclist might miss two weeks or more, just when he should be starting preparation for the total fitness required by the Tour de France.

Also, racing cyclists born around 1980 are less interested than the older generation in the mythology of the race. And why should they be? They are young. 'L'Enfer du Nord' evokes regional emotions which are felt mostly by elderly cycling fans, supporters who can remember life in villages where coal was mined. There is now little trace of the sentiments that associated Paris–Roubaix with mourning after the Great War or with the consciousness of death and regeneration. There was a famous saying around the Belgian border, now heard no more. 'I would like to see my son win Paris–Roubaix, and then I would like to die on that same day!'

I return now to the contrast between the two greatest Italian cyclists, Gino Bartali and Fausto Coppi, and the disputes between their followers. By the end of the 1940s Bartali and Coppi had more than temperamental differences. They had become involved in a passionate duel that symbolised continuity and change in Italian society. They were public figures, not merely sportsmen, and all their countrymen were divided – many still are – between those who cheered and wept for the temperamental Fausto and those who applauded and saluted the more dignified Gino. The contrasts between the men went further than that, even into the realms of politics and family life.

This is how it appeared to Italians. Bartali was the traditionalist, Coppi the innovator. Bartali was the champion, Coppi the pretender. The Tuscan was reliable while the man from Piedmont was volatile. Coppi was said to be an atheist of the political left, while it was widely reported that Bartali gave his support to the Christian Democratic Party. Coppi was suspected of taking drugs. Nobody could ever imagine that Gino Bartali used amphetamines. He was above such things. The proud Florentine had the demeanour of an ancient Roman statesman – and furthermore he was often welcomed at the Vatican.

Fausto belonged to opera, Gino to the Holy Father. Though many people suspected that he dramatised his piety, it does seem that Bartali was a genuinely religious man. Perhaps it was because 'il pio Gino' made his devotions public that he was the Vatican's favourite sportsman and was personally blessed by three popes. Leading politicians were also eager to claim him as one of their own, but Gino, I believe, felt that the church was a more reliable home.

Bartali set up portable shrines in every one of his hotel bedrooms. Photographs show him in neatly pressed pyjamas, studying maps of the next day's route of the Giro or the Tour. On the bedside table is his statuette of the Virgin. When the Tour de France made its only visit to Lourdes, in 1948, Bartali won the stage and then kissed relics and the ring of the local bishop. That was the year that he won his second Tour, a full decade after his victory in 1938. Gino must have thought that he had been touched by the Almighty. On some mountains, children from *colonies de vacances* sang sweet holy music as he pedalled past, a priest conducting the infant choir.

* * *

The 1948 Tour was the summit of Bartali's career. Coppi did not ride. He had been injured in the Giro d'Italia and, as always, his fragile bones took time to heal. The statuesque-looking broken nose that gives such character to Bartali's face came from a bike crash early in his career. Otherwise he didn't suffer much from accidents. Somehow he was too burly. Bartali's strength was a wonder to all. But in other respects he was an unexpected winner of the Tour. He was thirty-four years old, had missed six years of competition during the war and was confronted with an extremely difficult race. This was in fact the longest of all post-war Tours: in twenty-one stages its contestants would cover 4,992 kilometres.

The 1948 Tour was anti-clockwise, so the Pyrenees came before the Alps. At the rest day in Cannes, after twelve stages, the young Breton Louison Bobet was wearing yellow. Bartali was adrift by twenty minutes. Then the Italian took command, giving the impudent Bobet (twenty-three years old) a crushing lesson by winning three consecutive stages in the Alps: Cannes–Briançon, Briançon–Aix-les-Bains, Aix-les-Bains–Lausanne. On the day that ended at Aix, Bartali was first to the top of the Galibier, then the Croix de Fer, the Porte, the Poret, the Cucheron and the Granier. All these gigantic mountains were contained in a stage that was 263 kilometres long.

At Aix Bobet surrendered the yellow jersey to Bartali. A few days later Bartali contemptuously beat the French and the Belgians in the territory they knew best (and which he usually disdained), the awkward and cobbled roads between Liège and Roubaix. In Paris, only forty-four riders were left from the 120 who had started the race. Bartali finished twenty-six minutes in front of the second man, the Belgian Brik Schotte, and, as he had done in 1938, also took the prize as the best climber, the 'roi des montagnes'.

Has there ever been a more commanding victory in the Tour de France? I think not, though these matters are difficult to judge. It is certain that those three Alpine stages have an unparalleled magnificence – and remember that Bartali rode over rough roads and used, by today's standards, primitive equipment. But then we have to think of Fausto Coppi. How do we compare Bartali's Tour of 1948 with the Tour of the following year, which Coppi won, with Bartali in second place? And how do we judge the overall performances of these deadly rivals?

For the benefit of statistics-minded readers, I present some figures, starting when the two men first met and ending in 1954, when Bartali finally hung up his wheels. *Between 1940 and 1954, in events they had started in each other's company, Coppi claimed 69 victories, Bartali 27. In races that neither won, Coppi finished ahead of Bartali 171 times and Bartali finished ahead of Coppi 151 times.* Surely, a reasonable person might think, here is evidence of Coppi's superiority. But let us enter an Italian bar and put the statistics on the table. I see the image of my much-loved Café dello Sport at the top end of the main street in Sestri Levante – a long way from the beach, thank God. Here was a place where one could play billiards, look at the pink newspaper and watch the Giro on the television. In this cafe would have been found Bartali enthusiasts, though Sestri Levante is in Coppi's home territory. And I know what they would have said. Something as follows:

'We do not for a moment dispute your figures' (the more polite *Bartalisti* would concede) 'but what was the difficulty, the *quality*, of the races that Coppi won? Many of them, my young English friend, might have been end-of-season criteriums, when champions showed themselves to small crowds in such provincial towns as our own. A man as noble as Gino Bartali might not have deigned to contest the final sprint, might often have allowed an apprentice local rider to take the prize! While Coppi was always so hungry for instantaneous glory that he would have scrambled for any victory at all, no doubt in some arrangement with the race's organisers and perhaps indeed with the town's mayor, whose political views are notorious!'

When the *tifosi* leave the roadside and settle in a bar they are expert in the elaboration of arguments. And in this case they may have a point, once we set aside the political insinuations. Many races are indeed minor affairs, their outcomes often arranged before the cyclists come to the starting line.

But let us leave the round-the-town criteriums and look at the sterner tests in the high mountains. Statistics about Bartali's and Coppi's performances in the Alps, the Pyrenees, the Dolomites, the Ventoux, the Puy de Dôme, the Ballon d'Alsace and other major climbs show that the two rivals were most evenly matched in the grand theatre of distant mountain passes. *During their shared careers they rode together over 158 cols. Coppi was in front at the summit 71 times, Bartali in front 70 times.* Unfortunately, details of the other seventeen passages are lost. However, my figures now become more specific, allowing us to study Bartali's and Coppi's rides while also comparing the heights of the mountains that they scaled.

When the col, i.e. the summit of a mountain pass, was lower than 1,000 metres, Bartali was in front 25 times, Coppi 12 times. Bartali was also the superior in passes of more than 1,000 metres. He reached the top of such climbs in front of Coppi 33 times. Coppi led 30 times. But now comes the final confrontation. In passes over 2,000 metres high Coppi beat Bartali 29 times, while at this very high altitude Bartali beat Coppi 12 times. One could brood over these figures for hours, preferably with the aid of the newspapers and maps from which they were compiled. Even without such aids, there is one plain way to interpret the prowess of the two cyclists. Coppi excelled in the highest mountains; Bartali was more at ease in the foothills or the less high mountains.

Fausto may have breathed more easily than Gino as the air became thinner. He may also have been better able to cope with the change of temperature as the road reared up from a temperate valley to a snow-covered summit. Coppi's main advantage was that he was younger than Bartali, and lighter. His legs, massaged morning and night by Cavanna, were more supple. Young legs help a rider to maintain rhythm as the gradients become more difficult in the last 5 kilometres of a mountain ascent, or on the *lacets*, hairpins, where there is often a sudden change in steepness, particularly on the corners – where, in addition, streams have deposited debris and have opened holes in the road's surface.

* * *

Coppi was at his best in such extreme conditions. His rides to the highest points of the Alps, the Col d'Izoard and the Col du Galibier, were a marvel even to such a man as André Leducq, twice winner of the Tour (in 1930 and 1932) and himself a former master of the Galibier. 'Dédé' Leducq realised that Coppi was a climber whose like had never before been seen:

> He seems to caress rather than grip the handlebars, while his torso appears permanently fixed by screws to the saddle. His long legs extend to the pedals with the joints of a gazelle. At the end of each pedal stroke his ankles flex gracefully, a movement which would be wonderful to analyse in slow motion on a cinema screen – all the moving parts turn in oil. His long face appears like the blade of a knife as he climbs without apparent effort.

Leducq – a team manager after twenty years as a professional before 1939 – had ridden against Bartali in the 1938 Tour de France and knew his worth. He preferred Coppi.

Leducq's comments about Fausto's style on the bike bring us to a problem of cycling history. We do have film of Coppi, from the newsroom. But the quality is poor, with uneven, jerky and accelerated frames. None the less it's possible to compare the styles of Coppi and Bartali – their positions on the bike, pedalling cadence and efforts out of the saddle.

Gino Bartali had none of Coppi's *souplesse*. Film shows the raw power and strength of his legs and his broad, muscular shoulders, but it does not reveal the peculiarity of his cadence. Bartali's contemporaries all puzzled over the champion's style. My best witness is Louison Bobet's younger brother Jean Bobet, himself a more than useful cyclist (1st Paris–Nice, 3rd Milan–San Remo, 14th Tour de France, all in the same year, 1955). Jean's fraternal *Louison Bobet: une vélobiographie* (Paris, 1958) – my copy is inscribed in an adolescent hand 'Tim Hilton, August 1958, Rouen', where I must have paused on some teenage adventure – contains a number of good stories and instructive remarks, among which I find this description of Bartali's manner of pedalling.

'Pas spécialement beau à vélo,' Jean Bobet says, 'Bartali progressait dans une style personelle, qui procédait d'un temps d'arrêt tous les deux cent metres environ.' Every 200 metres or so he stopped pedalling for two or three seconds. Why? Jean Bobet does not explain. He says that the interrupted cadence had an agitation (*nervosité*) that unsettled Bartali's rivals in the mountains, and adds that, on the flat, he might pass other riders while freewheeling.

Without a doubt, Coppi was the more cultivated cyclist of the two, not only in style but in his approach to competition. He was dedicated to his training regimes and invented new ways to keep himself at a level of fitness that could cope with either long stage races or the four-minute effort of a track pursuit. Coppi studied other sports to see if they could give him hints about cycling (they didn't); he was an attentive leader of his team, encouraged protégés, learnt French, represented riders' interests if they had to battle with organisers about, for instance, excessively long stages or unfair eliminations; and was courteous and forthcoming when he met journalists.

An early model of the modern sportsman who is also a public figure, Coppi was a forerunner of the new professionalism in many other ways. Take, for instance, his attitude to diet. Even the most highly trained riders of the 1940s had been careless about the food they ate, partly because no one had told them to be otherwise, partly because they had grown up among shortages, mostly because cycling makes you hungry. After a day in the saddle, a good dinner. What could be better?

Gino Bartali used to eat like a Florentine patriarch, which is what he was. He liked good slices of veal with potatoes, stews with beans, masses of polenta. Gino then ate puddings and cakes before coffee and a cigarette. Fausto Coppi's diet had a reserve, a carefulness, some asceticism. He is responsible for the modern racing man's diet of thinly sliced white meat (almost always chicken, never pork), lightly boiled vegetables and quantities of plain pasta. There were no stews or sauces. Salads were undressed. Fausto's meals ended with fresh fruit, but not grapes, for they might upset his stomach. Soups were regarded as useless to a cyclist, as in truth they are. Sometimes Fausto would take a glass of wine, but only to please his old mother.

This diet was devised by Coppi, not by Cavanna, who as a former boxing trainer would be more likely to favour the red meats and proteins that are said to build muscle. Bartali was of the same mind. Indeed he was so wedded to the eating traditions of his native region that he was sure that Coppi could not have abandoned a solid cuisine without taking something else to help his performance. As the riders went to the dining rooms of hotels before and after a day's racing Bartali peered suspiciously (or told a *domestique* to do so) at the contents of Coppi's plate.

For no one, surely, could survive on such a womanish, peckish diet. Coppi must be taking drugs. So thought Bartali; and there were *Bartalisti* who searched through the wastepaper bins from Coppi's bedroom in search of ampoules of some forbidden substance. Or journalists could easily bribe chambermaids to bring them such toiletries as Fausto Coppi might have left behind. Nothing came of these investigations, but suspicions remained. The novelty of Fausto's diet, his unnatural thinness, tortured features and dark glasses gave the impression of a man who used drugs and had 'la bomba', an amphetamine preparation, in his road jersey. Many photographs show him in this light. I wonder whether they were taken by the same lensmen who delighted in their shots of Bartali, that senator of ancient Rome, whenever he climbed off his bicycle for an *arrêt-pipi*.

XXI

Louison Bobet in the Alps, 1953.

Leaving Bartali and Coppi to their essentially Italian quarrels, I turn to the question of French patriotism and the Tour de France in the 1950s. The Tour's renaissance in 1947 gave a popular win to Jean Robic, as we have seen. 1948 was Bartali's year, and he was followed by Coppi in 1949. The next victors were

1950 Ferdinand Kubler, Switzerland
1951 Hugo Koblet, Switzerland
1952 Fausto Coppi, Italy
1953 Louison Bobet, France
1954 Louison Bobet, France
1955 Louison Bobet, France

In the years 1947–55, then, the Tour was captured by two Swiss, two Italians and two Frenchmen. It was a period of complicated national and regional rivalries. France had a national team, but French interests were also represented by regional teams. In some years the Tour was contested by two Belgian and two Italian teams. The Swiss sometimes made a composite team with Luxembourg. Alternatively, Luxembourg led an international team that might include such Australian pioneers as Russell Mockridge and John Beasley; or, in 1956, the Englishman Brian Robinson, who had been part of the weak British team in 1955.

These arrangements could never be perfect. There were too many people from one nation, or too few. The Belgians were divided between Flemish and Walloon riders. Italians had disputes that were often led by Coppi or Bartali. Other national squads were divided because their members had scarcely met before the beginning of the Tour, or because they spoke different languages. In some teams there was no clear hierarchy and no system for sharing prizes. Many teams included riders with dual loyalties and friendships. They rode for their countries in the major tours but for the rest of the year were in trade formations with teammates of other nationalities.

Trade teams replaced these national or quasi-national squads in 1962 as part of the general commercialisation of the sport. *Extra-sportif* products had been promoted by cycling for some years. Fans of those days were able to ignore advertising and were always more likely to know the name of a cyclist's native village than the name of the toothpaste or aperitif that was blazoned on his road jersey. The reason why Frenchmen are nostalgic about the post-war era of national teams is simply because they are French. For there, in the Tour de France, was Europe as the French liked to perceive the continent, with France at its centre in every way: strong, abundant, ever-varied and, whatever differences existed, always and immortally *La France*. Other countries (except Germany) had their place, it could not be denied, but France was the proud leader of all civilised life.

A thoughtful historian of the Tour de France would say that *la grande boucle* reflected the emotions and political fortunes of the Fourth Republic (1946–58). I point to just one aspect of the Fourth Republic's character – its patriotism, led and exemplified by Charles de Gaulle. It is not surprising that de Gaulle liked the Tour and welcomed its riders when they halted to salute him during their passage through Colombey-les-deux-Eglises in 1960. And now let us consider the racing cyclist who thought himself to be the de Gaulle of sport, Louison Bobet, the first man to win three consecutive Tours, from 1953 to 1955, after a period in which he had known defeat and had struggled to regain national pride.

*   *   *

Bobet was born in the village of St-Méen-le-Grand (Ile et Vilaine) in 1925. So he was a Breton, though mainly proud of being a Frenchman. A teenager during the Occupation, Bobet had a strong dislike of Germans and was glad that, after the Liberation (which came later to Brittany than to Paris), he managed to spend a few weeks in French army uniform. He was to have many victories in his cycling career. The one that gave him most satisfaction, he said, was the world professional road championship in 1954. That year the fight for the rainbow jersey was held on the Solingen circuit in Germany. Great was Bobet's joy when he stood on the podium and heard the band play the 'Marseillaise' in his honour.

Bobet had worn the French national colours almost from the date of his twenty-first birthday. He was the French amateur road champion in 1946 and therefore had the right, for a year, to compete in the *bleu–blanc–rouge* road jersey. So he was a proud young man. But Bobet couldn't live on pride. He wanted pride's worldly token, which is status. In this respect he was an aggrandised version of his father, a man who was almost obsessed with his position in the world – though that position was by no means grand.

Bobet senior was quite content with his occupation. He was a baker. Nobody else supplied bread to the 2,000 souls of St-Méen-le-Grand. From his warm shop he surveyed the lives of his customers and let them know that he did not think as country shopowners do. 'My brother has an important position in Paris,' he would often tell the ladies of the village. He himself, Bobet senior allowed everyone to know, held high office in the Brittany table tennis associations. Occasionally he worked wonders. With a couple of middle-class businessmen he formed a syndicate to buy a little aeroplane. And he had two highly talented sons, who also bought themselves aeroplanes when they had conquered the world.

Louis Bobet had christened his son as another Louis, then called him Louison so that the Bobet family would know who they were talking about. There was something childish in the name 'Louison', a sort of fondling term for an infant or *cadet* brother. This quality was seized on by other people, especially in the peloton. Racing cyclists at the top of the professional game are good at finding weaknesses in each other's characters or morale. 'Louison' was a gift to them – a way of teasing or riling Bobet and undermining his self-belief.

Here was an ambitious young man who liked his champion's jersey, who was determined not to be a small shopkeeper and wished to be successful in every way. But there was another side to Bobet, a tearful and petulant part of his nature that often made him give up struggles on the road if a race did not unfold in his favour. The *azuréens* mockingly called him 'Bobette', as though he were a girl. Another nickname, which equally enraged him, was 'Zon-zon'. His French teammates were not sympathetic when he abandoned his first Tour on the ninth stage. They thought he was self-centred and far too demanding of praise.

'In a crowd of 40,000 people,' recalled his teammate Pierre Barbotin, '39,998 applauded him, two hissed – and he heard only the ones that hissed, and then did not sleep that night.' Champions need not be so sensitive. Many people thought that, to be a true cyclist, Bobet should have served a proper apprenticeship. Then he would have learnt how to suffer and would not have so ignominiously retired from the Tour, *n'est-ce pas?*

It is true that a year in a regional squad would have been good for Bobet. But his victory in the 1946 amateur championship enabled him to turn professional and put him straight into the French national team for the 1947 Tour de France, an opportunity he could not decline. The early promotion led to many troubles. Bobet did not realise how hard it was to race at full pressure day after day. He did not have *l'âme vassale*, and so was a poor servant to his team's leader, René Vietto. Bobet may have thought of abandoning the Tour even before a crash in the Gorges des Guillestre gave him a reason to climb into the sag wagon.

He was not popular at the time, except in his native Brittany. But here was a further problem. Bobet had a somewhat aristocratic manner, and this put him at odds with his fellow Breton Jean Robic. In 1947 Robic rode for the Ouest team and won the Tour. Bobet rode for the national team and failed even to assist his teammates. Robic was seen as possessing the virtues of a stony province: grey Brittany surrounded by icy seas, buffeted by Atlantic winds. He was short, ugly, eccentric but indomitable, a lover of *calva*, gritty and immovable as a menhir, a man who would fight to the end. The handsome, susceptible Bobet, so it was said, would always give in and would never be a man of the Tour – whatever his native talents.

*   *   *

What is it, to be *un homme du Tour*? We are talking about personal character as revealed in the most demanding of all sporting events. When Louison Bobet was riding the Tour – between 1947 and 1959 – *la grande boucle* lasted for more than three weeks and always covered nearly 5,000 kilometres. The riders faced every kind of terrain and every type of weather, from blinding Mediterranean heat to freezing cold in the Alpine snows. So a 'man of the Tour' must be strong, with the vigour of youth and the mightiness of age, able to race all day and the next day . . . and the next; and he must be resilient, prepared to ride through fatigue and adversity, looking forward to the challenges of yet more hours on the saddle of his fragile bicycle.

Mental strength is needed to help a cyclist through his physical travails, for the Tour exhausts both the body and the mind. A winner of the Tour has a muscular intellect and probably a deep knowledge of the history of his race. He has to be seen as a leader and must make other riders recognise his authority. He should also be an all-rounder, able to sprint, time-trial and climb, and should be an effortless *rouleur* – a captain who can ride at the head of the race for 200 kilometres or more. Our champion will never flinch. He will suffer but never complain. He will be dignified in defeat, magnanimous in victory, distributing prize money among his reverent teammates. These are the characteristics of the winner of the Tour de France, and a 'man of the Tour' shares them, even though he may not wear the yellow jersey for the Tour's magnificent finale at the Parc des Princes.

Here was the French ideal of a superior man. An unlettered person – perhaps an agricultural worker in the Limousin, a brickmaker in the Pas de Calais, a postman in Arles or a waiter in Toulouse – had a glimpse of the sublime when he looked at racing cyclists. In recent decades the French had found little to admire in their political leaders or their generals. The cult of the Tour de France was partly a dismissal, by a largely rural population, of government. Let us remember a great political truth: most people from peasant backgrounds simply wanted their rulers to leave them alone. They didn't even want to know their names. But they could admire – even worship – the folk heroes of the Tour.

*   *   *

These attitudes contributed to the opinion that Louison Bobet was not a 'man of the Tour'. Few people were confident that he would ever be the overall winner. They could see that he might sometimes be in the placings but were certain that Bobet would succumb when conditions became arduous. Such critics had a point. Bobet was fourth in the 1948 Tour, thoroughly beaten by Gino Bartali in the Pyrenean stages. A photo from that year shows Bartali climbing the Aubisque. Bobet is on his wheel but is grovelling. Bartali looks at the rider behind him with imperial scorn. During the next kilometre, and still some way from the Aubisque summit, Bartali would rise from his saddle, sit down, punch the pedals; and then do the same thing again, as though he were really punching Bobet, who could not compete with the Italian's strength and finished the stage in misery.

In the next year, 1949, Bobet once again abandoned the Tour when it reached the first mountain stages. This was to be Coppi's Tour, and some people suspected that Bobet gave up because he did not wish to be humiliated by Fausto, who was then in his full magnificence. Whether or not he abandoned the Tour through fear, 1949 was the worst season of Bobet's cycling life. By nature and from ambition he regarded all other cyclists as enemies or as servants. Bobet was friendless. Furthermore he had a fault that came from his love of France. He was *cocardier*. His compatriots used the word to say that he was patriotic to a fault – jingoistic, a lover of national uniform rather than national life. Bobet gloried in the thought that he was a man of France, *la patrie*. Yet now for two years he had trailed behind the Italians who had taken his own national Tour. What was he to do?

He began one of those periods of out-of-season reassessment and new training that can sometimes transform a cyclist. In the winter of 1949–50 Bobet looked at himself to see what was wrong. In effect he was practising sports psychology, a difficult thing to do if you are on your own. First, Bobet examined his own character, and came to the conclusion that he ought to be one of the greatest of all Frenchmen. Then he looked at his training routines and the way that he prepared for major races: and it was obvious that he ought to learn from the men who had beaten him.

Bobet's sense of his own worth would not allow him to admire Gino Bartali. Fausto Coppi, however, was obviously incomparable. He was so good, his talent so elevated, that a younger cyclist might follow him as a sailor follows the stars, or as an *agriculteur* looks to the sun. An interest in Coppi's methods might be pursued without damage to Bobet's self-esteem. It was fortunate that the apprentice from St Méen was able to talk to Coppi, who was forthcoming in a way that Bartali was not. Coppi was genuinely kind to other cyclists, even to the young French riders – Jacques Anquetil and André Darrigade as well as Bobet – who were most likely to depose him.

Bobet now followed Coppi by finding himself a personal trainer, a *soigneur* who would be with him at all crucial times. Raymond le Bert was a fellow Breton who advised the Rennes football team. As with Coppi's blind *soigneur* Cavanna, it is difficult to know le Bert's precise duties, but he made Bobet feel more important, even unique. Since he was paid from Bobet's own pocket, and his services were uniquely Bobet's, the moody Breton found that he was further alienated from other members of the French national team. This may have been part of a plan. Le Bert fancied himself as a psychologist and ran a weird alternative medicine clinic at St Brieuc. Unorthodox, 'clean' modern medicine was one of Bobet's enthusiasms. Indeed he was to spend much of his post-cycling life flying his aeroplane between thalassotherapy farms that he owned, one near Biarritz and a couple more on the north Brittany coast.

We know that le Bert was always on hand to give Bobet his massage, and that he refined and prepared the foods that Coppi favoured. Since all cyclists are obsessed with the question of diet I now give a list of . . . 'foodstuffs' might be the right word. For breakfast, chopped steak that had been marinaded overnight in lemon juice. Later in the day, fine slices of chicken breast or maybe a sole. Then rice, noodles, grated vegetables, fruit. As a special treat, calf liver with roasted grains of wheat. No wine, no coffee, no beer, no sugar, never any cake unless you count the bonk bars that our cyclist had to eat all day long, which were rice cakes baked with fruit. This regime Bobet followed every day, 365 days a year, from the winter of 1949–50 to his retirement in 1962.

One feeding bottle contained water, the other rice soaked in chicken stock and mixed with fruit. Bobet's bonk bars were stuffed into his road jersey pocket or handed up in a musette during his training rides. Cyclists will understand the training routines of the winter of 1949–50, but they may well surprise people who come from different sports and do not realise the work that has to be done to succeed on the bike. Here are two of Bobet's exercises.

He was on the Mediterranean coast that winter, used a motor-cyclist helper and trained with other cyclists only on rare occasions. Up early, nice chopped steak tasting of lemon. Period of digestion. Massage from le Bert, who most often was the driver of the *derny* or motorbike. This machine would be revved up, Bobet would go from his middling to his bigger gears, accelerate, tuck in behind the *derny*. Then motorbike and bike would go up to a high speed that they held for 160 kilometres. I guess that they would finish about four hours after leaving home base. Now for a shower and more massage, followed by a super dinner of grains and a small piece of boiled white fish washed down with water. *J'ai bien mangé, j'ai bien bu, merci beaucoup petit Jésus.* And so to bed.

This was an easy day; Bobet had three of these a week. On two days a week he increased his training distance to 230 kilometres. The work became harder, and not only because he was going further. The motorbike would simulate race conditions: sudden accelerations, then a short *longueur*, then another accel-eration, or the kind of chase that is needed to get back to the bunch after a puncture. On the way home there would be a gradual increase in speed through 20 kilometres before an all-out effort in the final kilometre, when Bobet would compete shoulder-to-shoulder with the motorbike. This was one of his ways of training for a bunch sprint at the end of a race.

Shower, massage, a delectable dinner of grains and more grains, maybe even a slice of calf's liver – grilled, never fried – with bread, always toasted, and three or more leaves of lettuce. An apple or an orange for pudding. Bedtime shortly afterwards.

Was his wife with him? Seldom. He didn't much like her and anyway he had to think about the mountains.

On two days a week he trained as a climber. From his Mediterranean base, whose location I must admit I do not know, he went into the foothills – which provide very demanding slopes, especially behind Nice – and then into the higher reaches of the Alps. Bobet would have selected a number of climbs. He would go up a col aiming for pedal revolutions of eighty per minute over, let us say, 10 kilometres. Then he would ride down, which is a skill that must be learnt, before riding up again, this time trying to reach the top with ninety revolutions a minute. And of course he would have tried his exercise with different gear ratios, the use of which allows a cyclist to bring intelligence to a mountain climb, as well as strength. The metaphysical view is that gears on a bicycle are not there to help you over a difficult part of the road. No: they are used to keep your rate of pedalling constant. But of what use are metaphysics when the Alpine winds blow, when you are harassed by your enemies, when you have already ridden 200 kilometres and you don't know how far it is to the summit?

Knowledge of the roads is the best help. Bobet would surely have contemplated the cols that he would have to ride in the next Tour de France, but he would not have been able, in his winter training, to scale these heights. The Galibier, the Izoard, the Madeleine, the Croix de Fer are all closed by snow from October to June. Bobet would have trained on the lower slopes, 10 or 15 kilometres up, then down, starting I presume from a hotel in Briançon or Bonneville (convenient for the Col des Aravis) or the old two-starred auberge at Bourg St-Maurice, not that he would want its excellent food, or the Hôtel du Petit-St-Bernard, which is at the foot of the Col d'Iséran, at whose summit, in 1958, Bobet would set foot on the ground and abandon the Tour for ever – carefully choosing his place, the highest point of the highest road in all of France.

Bobet's training that winter was not absolutely original,

except perhaps in its severe introspection. He had hints from other people, not only Fausto Coppi but (I believe) Antonin Magne. 'Tonin the wise', a respected *directeur sportif* in the 1940s and 1950s, had won the Tour in 1931 and 1934. In 1931, before the Tour began, he had moved secretly into a hotel in Nay, just below the Pyrenees – a tiny town within striking distance of the mountain passes of the Tour's classic Pau–Luchon stage. As well as studying the climbs, Magne examined the descents and decided that he would attack on the way *down*, not up, the dreaded Tournalet. This he did, when the time came, winning the stage and taking the yellow jersey. A marvellous feat! But it was the result of calculation, and Louison Bobet was also a calculating man.

XXII

Charly Gaul, 'The Angel of the Mountains'.

After his winter of intensive training Louison Bobet went to the start of the 1950 Tour de France in hopeful mood. He was the leader of the French team and had an inspiring lieutenant in Raphael Geminiani. Coppi, injured again, was not riding. The Italians were led by Bartali and Fiorenzo Magni, the latter wearing the yellow jersey as the race entered the Pyrenees. Then fighting began. On the ascent of the Col d'Aspin Bartali and Jean Robic were riding side by side. Bartali appeared to obstruct the Frenchman. Probably they bumped into each other while negotiating the final slopes. Bartali fell from his bike. Around him were hundreds of French fans, and one of them had a knife.

Was this man going to stab Bartali? Or was he merely slicing the sausage that he had brought to the mountain for his picnic lunch, together perhaps with some ewe's milk cheese, washed down with the Jurançon wine that is so good in high, cold places? Some said that he was innocent, others that he was drunk. In any case there were many other Frenchmen who created a scene of ugly disorder. They threw stones and wine bottles, and their targets were the Italians. There were two teams from Italy in the race, the national squad and the juniors or *cadetti*, who were protected by their seniors as they rode to the summit. Around twenty riders, in a group, were jostled, spat at, pelted with rubbish.

The race director Jacques Goddet jumped out of his car and laid about him with a walking stick. All was confusion – and the events of the day are still confused. But the differing accounts of the mêlée are agreed on the essential fact: the riot was anti-Italian. Bartali won the stage, then announced that he was quitting the race and that he would never ride in France again. That evening, and way into the night, there was a conference of the Italian teams – and in such a sweet place, alas, under the magnolia trees in the garden of a hotel in Loures, a little health resort on the banks of the Garonne. It is said that Bartali imposed his will on his countrymen, insisting that they all leave the Tour, even though Magni had the yellow jersey and would have been protected in every single kilometre of the road to Paris. Was this really Bartali's position? Nobody knows. In the Café dello Sport the debate continues, even though half a century has passed.

All the Italians went home and the leader of the race became Ferdi Kubler. He refused to wear yellow the next day, becoming one of that select band who acknowledge that the honoured jersey has come by default. '*L'aigle d'Adsiwill*', as the press liked to call him, was a man who liked propriety. He became a florist in later life and offered expert knowledge of tulips to the burghers of Zurich. That was one side of his character. When he was on the bike Kubler went crazy. He was brilliant one day, useless the next. When making declarations he referred to himself in the third person, in several languages. 'Ferdi great champion!' 'Ferdi tired!' 'Ferdi will attack tomorrow!'

Nobody thought that the unstable Ferdi Kubler could win a long and tactical race. Louison Bobet, who was no doubt relieved by the Italian retirements, looked at the Swiss and reckoned that he could be his master. He was mistaken. Two days after Bartali's and Magni's departure there was a flat stage between Perpignan and Nimes. Kubler took off, accompanied by the Belgian Stan (short for Constant) Ockers. This duo took ten minutes out of the pursuing Bobet and Geminiani. Kubler kept his advantage on the next day's stage to Toulon.

The route of the Tour had originally been scheduled to take the race to San Remo. However, there was a fear of rioting if Italians were to seek revenge for the events on the Col d'Aspin, so the stage was ended at Menton. A short farce now mingled with the political and nationalistic menace of the Tour. In the post-war years riviera stages were often treated as *promenades*, a relaxing interval before the efforts required by the Pyrenees or Alps. In Kubler's year the peloton decided to have a real holiday. The riders – led for once by the *domestiques* – climbed off their bikes and ran across the Ste Maxime sands for a swim.

Their dip in the waters of the Baie de Saint-Tropez has entered the folklore of the Tour and is often mentioned as a happy-go-lucky episode. There could be other interpretations. Think first of the white beach and the blue sea. In 1950 that coastline was not yet ultra-fashionable, but it was a place for holiday-makers. The ritual of paid holidays, introduced by the government of the Front Populaire in 1936, certainly did not include a fortnight's leisure for professional cyclists. Symbolically, the peloton in the 1950 Tour took a break from their work at the Ste Maxime beach.

Secondly, note that 29 July 1950 was a day of extreme heat. In hot weather cyclists suffer as no other sportsmen do, especially if they have to face (as on that day) a stage of 205 kilometres. And thirdly, a Tour de France rider always wants water and never has enough. The 1950 peloton laid down their bikes and ran down to the sea as though in gratitude that so much water existed.

The *directeur* of the Tour de France, Jacques Goddet, was a far-sighted man and sensed that the riders' action at Ste Maxime might be the beginning of a future revolt. The Italians had given him quite enough trouble, and so had the drunken French fans at the summit of the Col d'Aspin. Goddet now delivered one of his many rebukes to the peloton, which he was able to do through the medium of *L'Equipe*, thus ensuring that his disapproval was known throughout the land. 'Surely the cyclists should have been acquiring, or re-acquiring, the rudiments of their strenuous profession, instead of indulging in these carnival antics?'

Goddet wanted the Tour to be serious. So did Bobet. Now he made his move, beating Kubler to the top of the Izoard. However, the Swiss retained his lead on General Classification, defended well in all the Alpine climbs and sealed his Tour with an outstanding victory in the time-trial stage to Lyon. It was one of the best rides against the clock that the Tour has ever known. In 98 kilometres Kubler took nearly six minutes out of second-placed Stan Ockers and also passed a humiliated Bobet. In Paris, Kubler mounted the podium while a band played the Swiss national anthem. Ockers was second at nine minutes, Bobet third at twenty-two minutes. Stan Ockers was pleased to have led a Belgian team victory. And, once again, the French team had simply failed.

*   *   *

Bobet's early disappointments in the Tour de France came at the time of especial strength in Swiss cycling; and after Kubler in 1950 Hugo Koblet from Zurich won the 1951 Tour in a style not seen before or since. Koblet was the same age as Bobet but had no experience of the Tour de France. Bobet knew a lot about his country's annual celebration and furthermore had begun the season with impressive results. He was first in Milan–San Remo, second in Paris–Roubaix, fourth in the Flèche Wallonne and had won the French national championship the week before the start of the Tour de France. He was now twenty-six years old, surely the right age to become a 'man of the Tour', and to win it.

But when Bobet was tested, the maturity was not there. He failed when the race went up its first mountains. Moreover, he surrendered to a rider who had less experience and was nonchalant about success. Hugo Koblet was a phenomenon. He was a playboy, a gambler, a lover of fast cars, a young man of magical attractions who made even the toughest cycling tasks look easy. The French, who so love their nicknames and

215

soubriquets for Tour riders, did not at first know what to call him. Then the popular singer Jacques Grello invented '*le pédal-eur de charme*'. That was it. Koblet was never called anything else, from that day to this – when we look back on him with an admiration that still contains surprise.

Blond, handsome and vain, Koblet astonished other cyclists by riding towards an effortless victory, then sitting up to comb his hair before crossing the finishing line. He always carried a comb. So did many men in the 1950s, but not racing cyclists when they were actually on the bike. The practice seems both seedy and conceited, or so we now think. At the time nobody said that Koblet was anything but superb. Other elements of his personal style came from skiing, the national sport of his homeland. The way he carried goggles, *lunettes de course*, on his left arm, for instance: that was an affectation from the ski slopes. Koblet's off-bike recreations and clothing were also rather *après-ski*. He died in a playboy manner (in 1961), crashing his white Alfa-Romeo into a tree. No other vehicles were involved. The road was dry. It is sometimes said that it was suicide.

Koblet's career at the top of the sport was very brief, from 1950 to 1953, but unforgettable. Nobody had ever looked more elegant on a bicycle, whether riding at ease or approaching the heights of threatening mountain passes. Koblet climbed a 1 in 5 stretch as though it were 1 in 10. As for his speed and elasticity as a *rouleur* – look at the Tour of 1951, in which Koblet accomplished one of the most famous solo breakaways in the history of cycling. It is known as '*l'exploit Brive–Agen*' after the towns at the beginning and end of the Tour's eleventh stage.

Not a long stage, about 177 kilometres, but Koblet rode most of that distance on his own, through country that is restlessly up-and-down – *terrain accidenté*, as the French say – on roads that twist and rise, fall quickly, rise again, march across high level land, swoop down, give you a hill, then a long *faux-plat*.

216

Often, you can't see beyond the next awkward corner. These are not roads for the specialists of cycling, who tend to be classed as climbers, sprinters or time triallists. They are roads for the *rouleur*, a man whose momentum is untroubled by the complexities or length of any route.

The Toulouse road from Brive climbs past famous grottoes (but why famous?: grottoes are always horrible, whether natural or artificial) to the first of the *causses*, by which in general the French mean a limestone plateau; and then the road goes down again to the Dordogne valley, passes through Souillac and rises again, with various little hills. Just past Souillac, on one of these hills, Koblet left the peloton. For a little while there was no reaction, presumably because the bunch thought that he was sparring or feeling frisky. Ten minutes passed before the peloton realised that Koblet meant to keep his lead. They began to chase, at first with determination and then with fury.

Koblet knew, when he sprinted away from the bunch, that Agen was about 135 kilometres to the south. It was a hot day. He wasn't familiar with the *causses* or the river valleys. And what a chasing group was behind him! It was a royal assembly of the strongest and fastest men in the world. Fausto Coppi, Gino Bartali, Louison Bobet, Raphael Geminiani, Stan Ockers and Jean Robic made up this company, all doing bit-and-bit, swapping the lead, relaying each other, screaming round the corners and sprinting up the hills.

They too were *rouleurs*. They also had the benefit of each other's company. Hugo Koblet was unworried. Photographs show him riding on the tops, his face both thoughtful and serene. The chase went on all day, but the solitary breakaway remained calm, debonair and by the aid of miraculous strength increased his lead. At Agen Koblet was 2' 25'' in front. He swept into the finishing straight on the Rue de la République, took his hands from the bars, combed his hair, posed for the photographers, received bouquets from local girls and watched with distant interest as other riders crossed the line. But he was never arrogant, our *pédaleur de charme*. He seemed more pleased with his looks than with his victories.

The Tour went from Agen to Dax, then to Tarbes, and from Tarbes to Luchon. The Luchon stage contained the climbs of the Tourmalet, the Aspin and the Peyresourde. The route announced one of those days when destinies are decided, when heroism is rewarded and frailties are pitilessly exposed. First at the head of the race was Fausto Coppi. So far, he had ridden a quiet Tour. His younger brother Serse had suddenly died five days before it began, and he had had to be persuaded by friends to compete. Now Coppi attacked. He was usually beyond compare, and without companions, in the highest mountains. But in 1951 Hugo Koblet stayed with Coppi over all three of the towering Pyrenean cols. He could not be dropped on the descents to the valleys and matched the Italian on the approach to Luchon. There he won the sprint in front of Coppi. In this manner the *pédaleur de charme* became the new yellow jersey.

'He is in a state of grace,' Fausto Coppi then said of Hugo Koblet. Fausto was no theologian, but he clearly felt that the rider who had been able to accompany him to the summits of three mountains had been blessed. Three days before, on the solo breakaway to Agen, Koblet had nearly been in a 'state of grace'. '*Il touchait la grande forme*', as the French put it. And then, when Coppi summoned Koblet to supreme efforts at the peaks of the Tourmalet and the Aspin, where the clouds were below them and all other riders far behind, the playboy had achieved a transcendent condition.

Religious interpretations of the Tour continued when, on the stage between Carcassonne and Montpellier, Coppi collapsed. It was another extremely hot day, but he was used to hot weather. What happened to him? This is still a mystery. We only know that this was Fausto's worst day on the bike. Nobody can explain the cause of his suffering, and although he was a forthcoming man, he could not speak of his misery. Some say that he had a nervous breakdown, brought on by the tension of the Tour and the loss of his beloved brother. He certainly had a physical breakdown. He grovelled on the roads to Montpellier and at one point nearly collapsed into a ditch. Weeping, vomiting and sometimes unable to control his bike, he would have zigzagged off the road if his loyal teammates had not stayed with him. They sheltered the stricken *campionissimo* and rode on either side of him with their arms around his shoulders.

That was the role of Coppi's *gregarii* – to protect their leader. It is heartening to record that other men helped. One of them was the *azuréen* Joseph Mirando, the youngest French professional, who should have been at the service of Louison Bobet. Mirando drifted to the back of the bunch, waited, and then brought water to Coppi. He had a simple reason, repeated in many an interview: he knew that Coppi was 'a gentleman and a lord'. So a ragged group of admirers brought Coppi to the Montpellier finish, half an hour behind the first group. Gino Bartali – who had himself lost a younger brother in a cycling accident – gave Coppi his sympathy. Then Fausto was carried to his hotel room.

The journalist Roger Bastide was among the many people – too many, probably – who found their way to Coppi's bedside. Bastide then wrote:

> He was the sort of person that you would find on a stained-glass window in a church, just as long and just as thin. The lines of his face, witness to his voluntary suffering, were those of an inspired monk. During his *défaillance* he became pathetic. Inevitably, it seemed like a descent from the cross . . .

Though he was not dying, Coppi had the look of someone close to death. Luckily, the Tour had a rest day at Montpellier, giving Coppi a little time to recover. His wife Bruna, in high alarm, sped from Genoa to be with him. She begged her Fausto to abandon the Tour, to give up cycling, to do anything in the world that would end the torture of these races. He gravely told her that he was wedded to his future as a cyclist. And so, the next morning, Coppi went back to his bike. The peloton sheltered him as the race traversed the Auvergne. Then Coppi astonished all the world when he won the Alpine stage to Briançon. Koblet was eight minutes behind him.

This summer there were followers of the Tour who made comparisons between the gaunt, stricken Fausto, inspired by the mountains, and the image of the crucified Christ. These admirers of Coppi were humble people. Ignorant and superstitious they may have been, but they none the less had a right to their icons; and once again we note that the worship of Fausto Coppi was shared between the Italians and the French, especially if they were poor. In his home country there were rifts beteen Coppi's supporters and the *Bartalisti*. At the same time he tended to unite the imagination of the peasantry in Italy and southern France.

Women always left their houses to see the Tour pass by and so did the village children, priests and schoolteachers. Men discussed the Tour with their sons, educating them in the same way that French fathers always taught their sons about agricultural tasks, or honour, or the ways of the world. The effect of this male talk between the generations can't be measured, but we may be certain that father-to-son discussions had more than a hint of moralism, and that they helped to form the conservative attitude of the French towards their national fête. In 1951 the cyclist who lost most esteem in the post-war conversations was Louison Bobet. He rode into Paris 1 hour 24 minutes down on the winner, Koblet; and no fewer than seven French riders finished in front of this self-proclaimed emblem of national pride.

Koblet had shaped the Tour, Coppi had lost, Bartali was subdued and Bobet was humiliated. Bobet had a late-season recovery. In the Tour of Lombardy he was in the leading group, feigned exhaustion and then deftly outsprinted seven Italians on the Vel Vigorelli. This win in Milan confirmed one popular view of Bobet: that there was no grandeur in him. He would never be a man of the Tour. And in fact Bobet decided not to ride *la grande boucle* in 1952. That was just as well, for 1952 was the year of Coppi's second Tour victory. Bobet would have been riding for, at best, second place.

* * *

Bobet's absence from the 1952 Tour was the result of deliberations in St-Méen-le-Grand. After the 1951 defeat there was a Bobet family conference led not by the father, Louis Bobet, but by his younger son. Jean Bobet was the intellectual of the family. He could have had an academic career and for a time taught French at the University of Aberdeen. But a future as a *coureur* was more attractive to Jean than a teaching post in the granite city. His career on the bike included an early triumph in 1950, when he was *Champion du Monde Universitaire*. He was wise enough to look into the future and reckoned that his best period as a cyclist would come in about a decade's time, at the end of the 1950s – as indeed turned out to be the case.

Now he urged his elder brother to wait, and not to contest either the 1952 Giro d'Italia or the Tour de France. Louison and his father, together with Raymond le Bert, listened as the Frenchman from Scotland argued somewhat as follows. 'Louison, you have contested the Tour when its recent winners – Robic, Bartali, Coppi, Kubler, Koblet – have been unbeatable. All of them are now approaching the end of their cycling lives, apart from Koblet. All of them are older than you, Louison, again apart from Koblet. But he is a man of loose ways and I have heard from an unimpeachable source that he has contracted a venereal disease, in Mexico or some other place, it scarcely matters. Like a character in a modern novel I have read, Koblet cannot escape a fate that he has brought upon himself. His sex will shortly wither, his heartbeat will be irregular, we will see him as a pitiful figure in the expensive *boîtes* of St Moritz. And who will weep for him? So, my brother Louison, it makes sense for you to wait for a year. The Tour de France is made for clean men in their late twenties.'

Thus spoke Jean Bobet. This family conference typified Louison's requirements in the world of cycle racing. He needed guidance and love, and to have people around him who would work on his behalf and be sympathetic to his misfortunes. In other words he wanted to be the team leader who also had a father within the team. And of course he wished to have his intelligent younger brother as a *domestique* and technical adviser. Some of these demands could be satisfied. But, when the race was under way, who would be his father?

Such was Bobet's emotional situation at the beginning of the 1953 Tour de France. There were two favourites in this fiftieth anniversary race. The first was Hugo Koblet. The other was Raphael Geminiani, who had finished second to Koblet in 1951. Geminiani had recently won the championship of France, beating Bobet. Coppi had refused to ride in the same team as Bartali, so there was a weakened Italian presence. The French national team thought that their main rivals might be among their own countrymen; for the Ouest team was led by Jean Robic and had two emerging stars, François Mahé and Jean Malléjac.

Mahé and Malléjac would work for Robic but might be contenders as the Tour developed. The French national team did not have a designated leader: rightly or wrongly, Marcel Bidot, its manager, had said that 'the course will decide'. So there was much confusion of loyalties. The race was to create a number of enmities between countrymen, and with one surprising result. Bobet was at last provided with a father-figure.

It was one of the anti-clockwise Tours, the Pyrenees coming before the Alps. The most active rider in the progress down the Atlantic coast was another French regional rider, Roger Hassenforder. The Alsatian was an uppity kid who looked like an infant troll, an impudent smirk announcing that he had reason to be pleased with himself. Hassenforder liked to say that he was better than Bobet, and he was in truth a brilliant if unstable rider. Hassenforder's antics gave him the nickname '*le clown*'. He didn't care: he was an entertainer, and when he was riding the Tour could not have the solemnity favoured by such aristocrats as Bartali or Bobet. '*Le clown*' is warmly remembered by French fans, usually with a smile and a shake of the head at the same time.

Hassenforder held the *maillot jaune* for four days before he blew up on the Bordeaux–Le Puy stage. Then it was time for the real champions to come forward. As expected, Hugo Koblet went on the attack, treating the Pyrenean passes as though they were trifling obstacles. Overconfidence was his undoing. Now came a rehearsal for the car crash in which he would die. Descending the Col de Soulor at around 70 kph, Koblet misjudged a corner, went over the side of the road and ended his Tour in an ambulance.

In the 1950s there were many similar crashes. Descending is an art, even on smooth tarmac. In the old days riders fell because of uneven surfaces, grit and little streams across the road. When wheels grew hot from constant braking, the shellac on the rim would melt and a tubular would roll off. For this reason many riders preferred wooden wheels in the mountain stages. But those marvels of carpentry couldn't prevent a back-wheel slide on a corner, or a sudden front-wheel puncture that puts the bike out of control.

Some racing cyclists love the mountain descents. Others are frightened. Personally, I hate descending, even though I am careful and slow. It's not like cycling. I'd rather be on the climb from the other side of the col. Most of all I dislike the tunnels on mountain roads. They are poorly maintained and never well lit. You suddenly go into the cold, from blinding sunlight to blinding darkness. You can't see if there's a footpath, you bump against the slimy walls and can't find the right gear. These difficulties are worse when riding downhill at speed. Thus came Roger Hassenforder's crash, in one of the tunnels towards the top of the Aubisque. So '*le clown*' also left the race in an ambulance.

Next, Jean Robic crashed on the Col de Faurendon. He got up, groggy, and remounted. Four of the Ouest team had waited for him. They brought their captain to the finish of the stage, all of them losing thirty minutes. It was a brave effort with a negative result. Robic could not start the next morning and the Ouest riders now had no hope of the team prize or high individual placings.

The Tour left the Pyrenees and went from Albi to Béziers. Here came the crisis for the French national team – and, I believe, the crisis of Louison Bobet's career. The French left Albi on a preplanned attack. Raphael Geminiani and Nello Laurédi (another *azuréen*, this Nello, naturalised French in 1948) were the first to go up the road. In a few kilometres they were joined by Bobet and his faithful Antonin Rolland. Behind, the peloton was slowed by indecision and blocking tactics by other members of the French team. One or two people got across to the leading group, which at one point in this long stage had a twenty-minute advantage. As the break disintegrated on the run-in to Béziers there were three Frenchmen in front: Bobet, Geminiani and Laurédi. The problem was that Laurédi was on the ride of his life.

Here was a political situation, one of those difficulties that are unique to the Tour. Bobet considered himself to be the team leader, so he asked his companions to let him win the stage. If he did so, there would be a *bonification*. The bonus of a minute would assist him in the General Classification before the race got to the Alps. The three men wearing *bleu–blanc–rouge* screamed at each other as they went into the last kilometre. Laurédi, saving his breath, did not reply to shouts from Bobet and Geminiani. He scented victory and was first over the line. Bobet was third.

At the dinner table that night Louison was simultaneously petulant and imperial. He accused Laurédi and Geminiani of betrayal. Nello Laurédi, who well knew Bobet's hatred of the *azuréens*, merely shrugged his shoulders. Geminiani was incensed. Nobody was allowed to speak to *le grand Gem* in such a way. The mighty warrior overthrew the table, grabbed a fork and held it to Bobet's throat. Laurédi thought it best to remain silent.

So this was not a successful meal. Then a kind of crazy love began at breakfast. Everyone sat down to their pasta and chopped chicken breast. Conversation was impossible. Geminiani saw that they were in an absurd situation, roared with laughter at the tense faces of his teammates, shouted, told Bobet to stand up. Then he embraced young Louison and said that he would ride for him. That is how Bobet acquired a father in the peloton and went on to the first of his three consecutive victories in the Tour de France.

XXIII

Raphael Geminiani: warrior supreme.

Why did Raphael Geminiani put himself in Bobet's service? As is so often the case, this cycle-racing drama tells us about life as well as sport. Geminiani had (still has) a grand sense of life. 'Gem' – *le grand fusil*, 'the big gun' – was a buccaneer, a fist fighter, noisy, extrovert and of immense strength. On a good day, the tall and impetuous man was the equal of anyone in the peloton. Yet there were not many out-right victories in his *palmarès*, perhaps because Gem cared little for guile.

He wore yellow just once, in 1958, at the end of his career and in his eleventh Tour. Geminiani did not think himself a failure; and neither did anyone else, for he was one of those warriors who appear even grander in defeat. Gem made a lot of money and enjoyed good times. The celebration dinner after he won the French road championship in 1953 is said to have lasted for three whole days. But he worked hard on the road, often for other people. Within stage races he found himself a role in which he has never been surpassed. Geminiani was the first and the most inspiring of the *super-domestiques*, the *domestiques de luxe*.

His devotion to this peculiar task was part of a magnificent but complex temperament. With Geminiani as *co-équipier*, even the greatest champion could feel more confident. For a short time the Frenchman rode in the Bianchi team, and Fausto Coppi was glad to have him at his side. Geminiani had a theory that only he could have invented. In his view all champions are frightened men. He looked on them with curiosity, seldom respect. Sometimes he laughed at them. One or two, like Kubler, he threatened. Another, Robic, he held face-down in a bidet. Geminiani the bruiser was also genuinely fond of some people. One of them was Louison Bobet. He was curious, even a little awestruck, about the nervy aspects of Bobet's character, the tantrums, sacred training regimes and obsessive dieting. *'Je n'aurais été capable de mener une vie si monacale!'* Bobet and Geminiani were not alike. But the kindliness in 'Gem' sensed Bobet's need to be relieved from fear.

*   *   *

To return now to the 1953 Tour and the situation at Béziers. Geminiani had in effect made Bobet the leader of the French national team. There was a price: Gem exacted a promise that Bobet would distribute his winnings among his teammates. The French plan was to shepherd Louison through the three stages between Béziers and the Alps. This they did, while the stages were surrendered to three Dutchmen, Wim van Est, Wout Wagtmans and Jan Nolten. Then, for the eighteenth stage, the race entered the mountains, from Gap to Briançon. The French team now expected Bobet to show his worth. He did so with one of the best rides of his life.

The stage profile was as follows. The route went over the Col de Vars and the Col d'Izoard, as well as lesser climbs. The Vars was taken from its southern side. The road there (on the boundary between Provence and Dauphiné) rises about 1,000 metres in 30 kilometres. As the terrain changes so also does the climate. A cyclist emerges from pastures scattered with chestnut trees and climbs through masses of shaly rock, the flat boulders blistered by the sun and rough with juniper bushes. The road gets steeper and more uneven in the last 10 kilometres to the summit. Here our rider will be out of the saddle on two kilometre-long stretches of 1 in 7. There's nothing at the summit, just wind, one of those nasty little Alpine chapels and the way down – a precipitous descent below the treeline to the tiny town of Guillestre and pasture once again.

From Guillestre a reasonable highway leads to Briançon, which is the highest town in Europe. The Tour never takes this road. Its caravan turns east to find the way to a minor pathway or track (hacked out in the Napoleonic wars) that reaches Briançon by a different route. Here is the Col d'Izoard, relentlessly rising 1,350 metres in 32 kilometres. In the days when Bobet climbed this mountain the surface of the road was gravel, a mixture of small stones and flints.

As the road goes uphill on the Izoard, vegetation once again disappears. It's like the Col de Vars, but worse and on a larger scale. The pasturage around Guillestre is left behind. Then the road goes through a gorge, a narrow fissure bordered by white limestone cliffs with blocks of mauve-coloured marble in the rushing waters of a river. There are bridges and tunnels. Chestnut is now replaced by pine. Then pine cannot grow, only the occasional wizened larch. Next, we enter territory where nothing grows at all. Winds scream, or there is silence. No bird calls out, for there are no birds. Looking over the edge of the road you might see a buzzard or an eagle. They live further down the alp, where there is prey.

This is the Casse Déserte, a desert indeed, where the road clings to an amphitheatre of red cliffs, white and yellow sands, scree, rock pinnacles. The Izoard is covered by snow for most of the year and the road is impassable from October to June. In July, when the Tour passes through this fearsome place, there are mad contrasts of weather and temperature. The days are tempestuous or more often volcanically hot, the heat intensified by reflection from white shale. Yet there are still tongues of snow between the boulders above the road.

At the top, the *coureurs* will be well above the clouds. They may still be obliged to ride through bitter mist. The air is thin. Within a couple of kilometres the temperatures can vary between freezing and baking. The cycling fans – and God bless them – who have made their way to the summit have brought newspapers. Not to read. They hand the papers to sweating riders who stuff them inside their road jerseys to ward off hypothermia on the way down the mountain. For as a cyclist sweeps towards Briançon his body may begin to shudder with cold, uncontrollably. This first sign of hypothermia is the most unnerving of all the afflictions to which racing cyclists are subject – all the more horrible because your legs are frozen and you're going too fast to keep warm by pedalling.

It was on this mountain that Louison Bobet, on Wednesday 22 July 1953, won the Tour de France. He was a little way behind the first riders on the Col de Vars, got in touch with them in the Gorges de Guillestre, then took the lead as the Izoard began. In front of him were 30 kilometres of climbing. For a while the Dutchman Jan Nolten was able to hold his wheel. Bobet tolerated his follower for five minutes before he found a more powerful rhythm. Nolten drifted backwards while Bobet pounded on, alone. His ascent was really a time trial: every second counted. There was never a moment of relaxation. Whenever it was possible to sprint on a less difficult stretch of road, Bobet sprinted. Then he sat down again, returning to his tremendously fast average speed. He took the hairpins on the far side of the road, where the slope is less acute, and accelerated on these bends. When the summit was in sight Bobet dashed up the final kilometre as though pursuers were just behind him – but they were nowhere, still halfway down the mountain, and struggling.

The climb from Guillestre would have taken Bobet about an hour. Jan Nolten got to the top five minutes later. By this time the Frenchman was far away down the other side. The rest of the field was in disarray, split and scattered. In Briançon Bobet took the yellow jersey with a lead of eight minutes. Two days later he won the time-trial stage. Paris was almost within sight. A triumphant Bobet rode into the Parc des Princes. On General Classification he was fourteen minutes in front of the second-placed rider, Jean Malléjac of the Ouest team. This was the sixth of Bobet's rides in the Tour de France and his first win.

* * *

Historians of the Tour usually prefer the second of Bobet's three consecutive victories. In 1954 he imposed his will in the mountains and again won the Izoard stage to Briançon. As in 1953 he beat everyone else in the time trial, 'the race of truth'. Bobet was masterful in company as well as in solo effort. He was continually harried by Kubler and Koblet through the Tour's earlier stages. In the Pyrenees and on the Ventoux he had to cope with the amazing climbing skills of a Spanish newcomer, Federico Bahamontes, who was to win the King of the Mountains title for the first time. The Tour was saddened by retirements. Both Geminiani and Koblet had to leave the race. But Bobet rode to a convincing and decisive win. His margin over Ferdi Kubler, second, was fifteen minutes. This was the best year of Bobet's career, for in early autumn he became the world professional road champion at Solingen in Germany.

* * *

In 1955 Bobet started the campaign for his third Tour victory in state. As winner in the previous year he wore the yellow jersey as the Tour began (in Amsterdam). At the beginning of the second stage he put on the rainbow jersey of the world champion. Bobet was clearly the leader of the French team and had the company he preferred. Geminiani was at his side and his younger brother Jean was one of his *domestiques*. A trusted senior teammate was Antonin Rolland, who would lead the race for many days, though quite aware that he could not hope for the final prize.

As Jean Bobet had said at the family conference, the giants who had dominated the sport after Hitler's war were near the end of the cycling road. A new generation was about to take over. It is interesting to consult the sporting press on this topic. Journalists in 1955 could see that Jacques Anquetil (born 1934) would have an illustrious future. Some thought that Federico Bahamontes (born 1930) might win the Tour, while others fancied Jean Brankart (born 1930), the only Walloon in the Belgian national team. He might be capable of great things, especially (according to some French pressmen) if he were to move from his native Liège and become a naturalised Frenchman.

Only one or two far-sighted journalists pointed to the Luxemburger Charly Gaul. The character of Luxembourg cycling was difficult to read, as was the country itself. Luxembourg was of quite recent foundation. It had been a monarchy since 1867. There was a flourishing steel industry but most of the land was agricultural, or given over to forestry. A populace of knotty characters lived in the woods beneath fairytale castles. The French believed that they could understand some of the peoples on their eastern borders: the Walloons or the Alsatians they thought transparent. They did not much consider the people of the Grand Duchy, partly because they had other things to do, mainly because they had no clue about their language.

Despite his Gallic name, Charly Gaul was a German-speaking Luxembourger whose first and favoured tongue was a local dialect, Letzeburgesch, which he shared with three other members of the 1955 Luxembourg-International team. They used the language to keep their plans (including financial ones) secret from other teammates, who in this year included the Australians John Beasley and Russell Mockridge. A fifth and all-important person in this linguistic clique was the team's manager, Nicolas Frantz, still as wily and tough as he had been when he won the Tour in 1927 and 1928.

The Luxembourg-International team was therefore a force separated by language. It was also divided by Charly Gaul's cold leadership. The twenty-two-year-old, who excelled in the mountains, especially in bad weather, was destined to be one of those climbers who are beloved by French women. His youth, slight size, handsome features and daring Alpine rides gave him the popular name 'The Angel of the Mountains', *Der Engel der Berge*. Another soubriquet might have been more appropriate: 'The Butcher's Apprentice', since that had been his original occupation. I can imagine Gaul with a knife. He seldom smiled, he kept himself away from other people and his pale blue eyes were without expression. He may already have been suffering from the personality disorders of his later years.

Louison Bobet loathed Charly Gaul but did not consider him a serious rival. He was mostly wary of Brankart, Wim van Est and Ferdi Kubler. Perhaps it would be best to crush them without delay. As the Tour left Le Havre at the beginning of its clockwise progress into Belgium and then southward to the Alps, the French champion rode with brutal speed. His plan was to get rid of all opposition within the first week; and on the third day he showed imperial strength when he won at the Citadel de Namur, which is reached by a kilometre-long cobbled climb.

The next days contained exciting skirmishes. Antonin Rolland took the yellow jersey on the fourth stage to Metz. Roger Hassenforder organised a breakaway to his provincial capital, Colmar. The French sprinter André Darrigade denied Kubler a victory in Zurich. Then Wim van Est took the leadership from Rolland on the stage from Zurich to Thonon-les-Bains. And now the race was in the Alps.

Charly Gaul was in thirty-seventh place on General Classification as the Tour left Thonon-les-Bains for the first mountain stage. Three major climbs lay ahead before the riders could reach Briançon. After the Col d'Aravis the race had to tackle the Col du Télégraphe, followed by the highest and steepest of all the mountain passes, the Col du Galibier. The northern side of the Aravis presents 11 kilometres of gently rising, quite fast road, not too difficult for any racing cyclist. During these kilometres the Dutchman Jan Nolten went ahead, with Gaul on his wheel. The peloton was untroubled. There were many, many kilometres to ride before the end of the day.

You can almost see the summit of the Aravis when the road steepens and there are hairpin bends that lead to a wide and grassy plateau. On this stretch of road Gaul accelerated and dropped Nolten. It was as though he wished to be rid of the Dutchman for ever, to be alone with his thoughts and with only the peaks and clouds as his companions. Further down the mountain Bobet learnt what was happening. He called Geminiani to his side and began a chase. It was too late. Gaul had his advantage. He held his lead on the descent and through the valleys that led to the Col du Télégraphe.

*   *   *

The Aravis is not a hard climb, by the standards of the Tour. The Télégraphe is longer, higher and has more abrupt slopes, calling for a different approach and maybe lower gears. So we must now puzzle over the question of the gearing favoured by Charly Gaul. In the mid-1950s the general practice among riders of the Tour was to use a bottom gear of 46 × 23 or 46 × 24 for the most difficult climbs. The first of these combinations gives you a gear of 54 inches, the second 51.7 inches. Gaul went lower. It is said that his mechanics fitted a twenty-seven-tooth back sprocket, which would have given him a gear of 45.9, very low indeed for a racing cyclist, though not of course for a tourist.

Gaul's gearing and his climbing style present further problems. By good fortune we have a witness who was at his side: Gaul's Australian teammate Russell Mockridge. A very decent man who could not like Gaul but rode in his service, Mockridge recalled that Gaul's favourite *développement* was 50 inches. Such a gear does not exist, so the information will send us all back to our tables. Looking at mine, I find that you can get 49.7

inches with a 46 × 25. So maybe that's what Gaul was using, and it could be that he saved the 45.9 for the worst bits.

Anyway, a peculiarity of Gaul's climbing was that he used especially low gears even before the hardest parts of any ascent. Mockridge wrote that Gaul spinned his exceptional gears at 120 revolutions to the minute. The fastest professionals go up a mountain at about eighty revs per minute, the slow ones at – maybe – sixty. 'Let any other rider try such rapid pedalling,' Mockridge added, 'and it would kill him in one short ascent.' We see his point. Gaul would have been bumping up and down in the saddle, and who can do that over a kilometre or two, let alone the 20 kilometres of a severe climb?

*   *   *

To my knowledge, Gaul's style has never been imitated. But wait a moment! His technique (which he must have practised) would have worked best on poorly maintained roads. Could it be that he was an unwitting pioneer of mountain biking? I leave the question to clubroom discussion and hasten to the summit of the Télégraphe, back in July 1955.

Spinning away, Gaul arrived at the top with five and a half minutes' lead over Jan Nolten. A chasing group led by Bobet crossed the col thirteen minutes later. The last men of the race were a whole hour in arrears, and there was still more mountaineering to come. On the final climb of the day, the Galibier – 2,645 metres, or 8,677 feet, above sea level – Gaul increased his lead. Eventually, after a stage of 253 kilometres, he rode into Briançon fifteen minutes ahead of the next group of riders, which included Bobet.

Gaul had now risen from thirty-seventh place on General Classification to third. Bobet was alarmed, and with good reason: the silent, impassive Gaul, his eyes full of menace as he caught Bobet's glance, might repeat his performance. And he nearly did. Next day Gaul opened hostilities on the first climb, the Col du Vars. Bobet could not stay with him. By the summit of the Col de la Cayolle Gaul had three and a half minutes. On the Col du Vasson, after they had been racing for 154 kilo-metres, Bobet was more than four minutes behind.

Surely the yellow jersey and overall victory were now within Gaul's grasp? But he crashed on the descent of the Col du Vasson as the race hurtled down to the finish at Monaco. It had been raining, and the road was slippery. More than forty riders fell. Accompanying motorbikes also crashed. Geminiani recklessly sprinted down the slippery pass and won the stage. Bobet came in two minutes later, Gaul after another minute. Rolland remained the leader on General Classification, with Bobet now third and Gaul fourth.

The next morning the Tour and its caravan awoke to blue skies and high temperatures. It was a rest day, giving each team an opportunity to consider its options. The *azuréens* plotted attacks through their home territory. Bobet wished to kill Gaul but did not know how to strike. Perhaps the heatwave would help him: it looked as though Gaul went better in cold and wet conditions. The French champion decided to attack the Luxemburger on the Mont Ventoux in two days' time. It would certainly be hot on the slopes of 'The Giant of Provence'. Gaul, for his part, reckoned that his time would come in the Pyrenees. First he had to rest. He lay on his bed in a shaded room while Nicolas Frantz and a *soigneur* assigned to the Luxembourg-International team looked after his cuts and bruises.

*   *   *

During the Monaco rest day the *coureurs* of the Tour de France would have left their hotels for gentle but quite long rides, to keep their legs supple and to 'sweat the poison out of the system', as many riders put it – in other words the medicines and drugs which they used while racing.

The relentless difficulty of the racing cyclists' calling is easy to describe, hard to imagine. One needs to appreciate the sheer length of the race. The 1955 Tour covered 4,855 kilometres, or 3,017 miles, in twenty-three days. The cyclists had to spend seven or eight hours a day in the saddle, racing at high speeds. They bounced over cobblestones, climbed mountains, pounded along endless roads in *La France profonde* and in Belgium and Switzerland too. They were drenched with cold rain in Picardy, frozen in the Alps, baked in the fierce heat of Provence. They seldom ate enough and were always thirsty. Never could they avoid the nervous tensions of jostling in the peloton, the break-aways for the strong or the struggles to finish for the weak. Nearly everybody crashed at some point. Wounds did not heal. Nobody had enough sleep, even when exhausted. It was a life of extreme physical effort and constant fatigue.

Little wonder that drugs were taken – foolishly, and often in ignorance of their effects. This Tour contained a terrible warning about illicit medicines, and in that sense was a rehearsal for the day in 1967 when Tom Simpson rode himself to death. In 1955 the peloton had to ride the Ventoux mountain in extreme heat, '*sous un ciel de feu*', as the French papers said. One rider – maybe more than one – nearly died. Louison Bobet rode first over the Ventoux, well ahead of a defeated Gaul, took the stage and was poised for his third overall victory. On his day of glory the crowds saw a superb performance by a master of the Tour. But that was not the point. The point was that the Tour could kill.

This is how the lesson was given, and ignored.

After the Monaco rest day there was a stage to Marseilles, with temperatures in the nineties. This year there was no *prom-enade* along the Mediterranean coast. The stage was ridden with a series of vicious breakaways, led by the *azuréen* Lucien Lazarides (elder brother of Apo, and born in Athens), who revelled in the heat and finished six minutes ahead of the peloton. The next stage covered the 200 kilometres between Marseilles and Avignon. Its route included the climb of Mont

Ventoux. The summit of the Ventoux is 1,909 metres above sea level and is reached by 26 kilometres of climbing on a road that, in its final 10 kilometres, offers no shelter of any kind. The heat was even worse than it had been on the previous day.

Russell Mockridge is our best witness to the events on the way to Avignon. He recalled that at ten in the morning, when the race started, the temperature was already over the 100 mark and that 'tar bubbles were popping on the road like jam in a preserving pan'. Several team managers went to the director of the Tour and asked him to delay the start so that the Ventoux would not be ridden in extreme midday heat. Goddet refused. 'The riders are paid for their job. They must get on with it. If it is too tough they will have to withdraw.'

Cyclists cannot prepare for such conditions. In the 1950s they still put cabbage leaves under their racing caps, like peasants. Most of all they needed water. They relied on farmers who turned their hoses on the peloton, or spectators with buckets. If there was a village fountain everyone would dismount and scramble for its cool refreshment. *Domestiques* would raid cafes for anything that could be drunk, leaving the proprietors both outraged and proud. But refilling a feeding bottle could never be enough in such heat – and as the riders went further up the Ventoux there were no fountains, no cafes, no springs or streams, just the white sheets of ancient volcanic lava and the pitiless sun.

Mockridge, faint with exhaustion, had to get off his bike on the lower slopes. In a farmhouse he found shade and water. He ate handful after handful of sugar, then remounted. Further up the mountain he rode past frightful scenes. Brave men were walking and weeping. Mockridge saw Jean Malléjac – who had been second in the 1953 Tour and fifth in 1954 – lying at the side of the road, foaming at the mouth. The Tour's doctor, Pierre Dumas, saved his life with an injection and an oxygen mask.

Many others, whether they were *domestiques* or champions,

were forced to retire. One of them was Ferdi Kubler, who limped into Avignon in maddened pain. The last 2 kilometres took the Swiss hero twenty minutes. In every cafe he drank glass after glass of iced beer, shouting 'Ferdi is finished! He is too sick, too old! Ferdi will never start again. He killed himself on the Ventoux!' This was indeed the end for Kubler. He abandoned, and never again rode one of the national tours, just a few one-day races for two more seasons.

The temperature at noon had been 122 degrees. At Avignon Bobet was unable to savour his victory. He fell against the crowd barriers saying 'a day like that takes years off our lives'. There was truth in his dramatic complaint. It is a fact that many of the men who rode the Tour de France in the post-war years, and beyond that time, died when they were still young. We see the signs of premature age in their faces. Photograph after photograph shows us racing cyclists who were in their twenties but have the appearance of men in their mid- to late thirties. These cyclists were never carefree. They looked like parents. And here is one reason why Frenchmen at the end of the twentieth century did not wish to come to terms with the use of drugs. Those who were boys in the 1940s and 1950s – like me, though I was an English boy – could not bear to think of such transgressions in the men who were not only our heroes but also, in some ways, our fathers.

XXIV

Brian Robinson in Milan–San Remo.

The organisers of the 1955 Tour de France had begun the race at Le Havre, seeing the town's post-war reconstruction as a symbol of new French life. Many speeches were made, speeches in honour of Normandy and also speeches in honour of the British. For it was at Le Havre that we joined continental cycling. '*La plus grande innovation*', it was constantly said, was the '*présence d'une formation britannique complète*'.

That is, our men were not to be part of a composite team such as Luxembourg–International. We were to stand together under the Union Jack. The first Great Britain team in the Tour de France looked impressive on paper, and to this day appears an excellent bunch. Ten riders formed the squad. They were Dave Bedwell, Tony Hoar, Stan Jones, Fred Krebs, Bob Maitland, Ken Mitchell, Bernard Pusey, Brian Robinson, Ian Steel and Bevis Wood. Of these ten, six had contracts with Hercules Cycles. They had a certain amount of experience, though not of long stage races or the high mountains, so Hercules had devised an early-season training programme. Bedwell, Maitland and Robinson showed well in Paris–Nice, the Grand Prix de Cannes, the Tour of Calvados, the Tour of the South-East Provinces and the Tour of Holland.

Good preparation, but none of the British cyclists had experienced one of the northern spring classics, so they had no idea that the Tour could be so much harder and faster than the races they had known. The early stages were a shock. And then, between Roubaix and Namur, the British had the jolting first experience of the cobbled French and Belgian roads. One by one they left the race. Bob Maitland lasted until the Alps but

abandoned the Tour when, after a crash and mechanical difficulties, he could not cope with 250 kilometres through the
mountains on his own. Only two of the ten British riders
managed to get to the finish in Paris.

They were Brian Robinson, who finished twenty-ninth, and
Tony Hoar, who was sixty-ninth and last, more than six hours
behind Bobet's winning time. It was no disgrace to be the
lanterne rouge at the Parc des Princes: anyone who completes
the Tour is a hero. Hoar had survived. In his year 130 people had
left Le Havre, so he had succeeded where 61 other professional
cyclists had failed. Besides, Hoar was no hang-dog loser.
Although he suffered terribly in the mountains the tall lad from
Hampshire – basically a roadman-sprinter and good on the track
– was a lively character on the road and was popular both with
the crowds and with other riders. Hoar's cheerfulness helped
Robinson to survive. And he got his rewards. At the Parc des
Princes Hoar signed many contracts to ride in post-Tour
criteriums.

The first of these took place the next day. After the official
banquets there was an immediate return to work for the weary
cyclists. Here is the first example of the programme they faced.
The 1955 Tour finished on a Saturday afternoon. On Sunday
there was a series of races at the Autodrome de Monthléry, a
motor-racing circuit about 25 miles from Paris. Special buses
and trains brought crowds from Paris to Monthléry. They began
running at 8 a.m., for this was a day out for all cycling fans and
their families.

The first race was the Grand Prix des Minimes, i.e. juniors,
off at 11 a.m. Everybody in every junior's family would have
been there – and how many juniors would have tried so hard
to get onto the same course on the same day as the Tour de
France riders! Second race was the Grand Prix des Vétérans,
with many of the juniors' fathers no doubt on the start
line, followed by the Grand Prix Amateurs et Indépendants,
which began at 1.30 p.m. Now a pause for everyone to enjoy

their *pique-nique* on the Monthléry grass verges. Then, at 3 p.m., the start of the Grand Prix des Champions. You cannot imagine a more wonderful start sheet. The cyclists in this event incuded the Bobet brothers, Coppi, Gaul, Geminiani, Darrigade, Anquetil, Lucien Lazarides, Robic, Willy Kemp (I should have mentioned him, the experienced Luxemburger who had won the Tour's stage to Metz); and among such illustrious men were Tony Hoar from Portsmouth and Brian Robinson from Huddersfield.

Needless to say, this was an exhibition race, though 300,000 francs would be collected by the winner. Everyone at Monthléry wanted to see the riders of the Tour. The riders themselves made sure that they were seen, taking turns to mount three-man breakaways that never lasted for more than a couple of laps. The winner of the race, and the distribution of his winnings, was probably prearranged. Afterwards the caravan of Tour riders would go to other criteriums, throughout France; and if someone was in his home region he would expect to be first over the line to cheers led by his family and old schoolmates.

This local winner might well have made a deal with his rivals. The finances of professional cycling have always been anarchic and secretive. Money was controlled by the top riders and their managers. It was concealed from tax authorities, it was sometimes shared, sometimes stolen, and there was a strong preference for payment in cash. Contracts for the lucrative criteriums were usually organised by agents: cunning, persuasive men who understood the sport and had friends who promoted races.

Racing cyclists were not necessarily within the power of such agents. Young men from country backgrounds had their own forms of guile. They inherited the suspicious self-interest of the peasantry – both in business dealings and in the temporary alliances of life in the peloton. It was mainly the top cyclists who required agents to work on their behalf. Louison Bobet, for instance, had a complex set of bargains with agents and with his team. The French squad rode for him during the Tour; he in turn guaranteed his teammates that he would not sign for an appearance in a criterium unless the agent also provided each of them with a ride and a fee. There were many variations on this kind of arrangement, some of them ruthless.

For instance, Brian Robinson recalls that he was going well in a criterium when Bobet nudged his way through the bunch and rode next to him. 'If you don't let me win you'll never get another contract.' Robinson knew that this was a genuine threat. Bobet was making the rules and taking the money. 'He had so much control,' said Robinson. 'He was Mr Cycling. I was getting £40 a criterium and he was getting £1,000. He was there at every race.' In such ways Bobet earned the money to buy his private aeroplane and finance his thalassotherapy centres. On a more modest level, Robinson's earnings began to add up. But he had to work hard and do a lot of driving with his bike on the back seat of the car. One year he rode thirty-five criteriums in the six weeks after the end of the Tour, and they were all in different parts of France.

*   *   *

Brian Robinson was a terrific pioneer of British cycling on the continent. If the sport had been organised in different ways he would certainly have had more major victories. None the less he had a decent professional career, with some real successes on the road. Robinson came from Mirfield, west Yorkshire, where he still lives. He belonged to a cycling family. His father was a club cyclist and some people say that his brother Desmond was just as gifted on the bike. The Robinsons were builders and carpenters, trades to which Brian returned when he left continental racing.

A standard background for a British cyclist, except that Brian Robinson progressed from local time trialling with the Huddersfield Road Club to the Helsinki Olympic Games in 1952 (he was twenty-seventh in the road race, Jacques Anquetil twelfth).

Then he rode the BLRC-inspired Tour of Britain in 1953 and the Tour of Europe – much less grand than its name – in 1954. Hercules signed him for the 1955 season, when he first went to the Tour de France. But the firm pulled out of professional cycling at the end of that year and Robinson never afterwards had a totally safe place in a trade team.

He rode the Tour de France seven times and finished five times. In 1956 he became part of the Luxembourg– International team and reached Paris in fourteenth place. In that year he was also seventh in the Vuelta a España and ninth in the Tour of Switzerland. In 1957 he crashed in the Tour de France and abandoned. In that year, however, he won the Grand Prix de Nice and was third in Paris–San Remo – the first time that a British rider had taken a podium finish in a Classic. Robinson abandoned the Tour in 1958 but had stage wins in 1959 and 1960. He led a British team when he rode the Tour for the last time in 1961.

Then it was back to Yorkshire and the building trade. His continental career was quite long because he was tenacious. After the disappointments of the 1955 Tour de France a number of British riders – notably Ian Steel – were lost to the sport. The downturn in cycle sales meant that British firms were unwilling to underwrite continental pioneers. There were lean years to come. Brian Robinson alone was able to inspire the few home-grown racing cyclists who dared to match themselves against French roadmen. Those who finished the Tour, during Robinson's time, were Stan Brittain (1958), Vic Sutton (1959), Tom Simpson (1960) and Ken Laidlaw (1961).

XXV

Roger Godeau.

Brian Robinson might have made more money on the continent if he had raced on the track during the winter months. In most years he returned to Yorkshire in October and helped his father's building business before returning to a Mediterranean training camp (an innovation of the mid-1950s) towards the end of January. These were the months when many professionals turned to lucrative six-day racing or other events on the famous tracks at Milan, Ghent, Zurich, Paris and other continental capitals.

In the 1950s the two major Parisian tracks were the Parc des Princes, opened in 1935, and the now demolished Vélodrome d'Hiver, which was much older, in fact a relic of the late nineteenth century. I knew the Parc des Princes but never saw the inside of the Vélodrome d'Hiver. This is a sadness to me, yet another lesson that childhood does not gather enough experience to satisfy memory in wistful age. The 'Vel d'Hiv' must have been a wonderful place. Its architectural history is obscure, but the enclosed cycle track, its roof and seating resembled the functional metal buildings that gave Paris its railway stations and halls for international exhibitions – and of course the Eiffel Tower, which was almost next door to the Vel d'Hiv.

The track itself was of board. All the great men raced on its smooth wooden surface. I didn't witness their battles, being occupied with secondary education in Birmingham and other places. In any case, the velodrome held evil memories for the people who might have taken me to see the racing down on the Quai de Grenelle. In the early days of the Occupation German troops had used the Vel d'Hiv as a holding centre.

For days and weeks 12,000 Jews were imprisoned in the oval at the centre of the track. Some of them were killed. Most were transferred from the velodrome to Drancy, the concentration camp to the north of Paris, before being put on trains to Auschwitz, where they perished. Today you will find the Place des Morts Juifs du Vélodrome d'Hiver just next to the Bir-Hakeim metro station.

*   *   *

I think that the murdered people had another monument and now take the opportunity to clear up a matter that has relevance to Samuel Beckett's play *Waiting for Godot*. For many years it has been rumoured that Beckett took the name for the awful and mysterious person who never appears in the play, but is constantly in the minds of the tramps Vladimir and Estragon, from a racing cyclist. This story appears in many of the lax and unscholarly accounts of Beckett's imagination.

Colin Duckworth, however, who is the editor of a useful edition of the French text of the play, is a little more precise. He was able to talk to Beckett about *Waiting for Godot*, and the writer told him that he had indeed had a racing cyclist in mind. This was not a Godot but a Godeau, whom Professor Duckworth described in 1966 in these vague terms: 'Godeau was (or is) a veteran racing cyclist'. Apparently Duckworth did not know about Roger Godeau, who was born in 1920, became a professional trackman in 1943, retired from the sport in 1961 and died in 2000. Becoming famous at just the time when Beckett's play was written, in the winter of 1948–9, Godeau specialised in one kind of track event, the *demi-fond*. In this event cyclists are paced by a *derny* motorbike, driven by men in goggles and leathers, their faces impassive amid the noise of their engines and the screams of the crowds. It's a nasty kind of racing. Still, people liked it and Roger Godeau was the discipline's best exponent. He was not a roadman, entered only a few sixes and stuck to his speciality. Furthermore, he kept to the track he knew best and where he was best known, the Vélodrome d'Hiver.

That is why he got special applause at the final meeting of the Vel d'Hiv, in 1958, just before the building was closed. His reputation was much more local than it would have been if he had ridden the Tour de France. But his name is widely known through Beckett's immortal play. Godeau's connection with the Vélodrome d'Hiver, site of appalling atrocities, ought to be recorded as a part of the background of *Waiting for Godot*. I write this not only for its own interest but because so many children of the war are also the children of Beckett's play, which we encountered in late adolescence, after its first performance in 1956.

*   *   *

Returning if I may to childhood and early adolescence: I knew about the Vel d'Hiv and Drancy. There were Parisian family friends who had experienced the Occupation. First among them I name and salute Jean Dejeante, a bike fan and a former roadman who had ridden in minor competitions in the late 1930s. Also a communist, he was interned by the Germans but survived. When I knew him, which was between 1949 and 1956, it was clear that he would never get on the bike again. Malnutrition and beatings had given him the look of a man who had shrunk from his proper stature, and his limbs appeared to be joined to his body in the wrong way. He walked with difficulty and I could not see how young or old he might be. My father's age?

Jean's wife, Riri, looked after him. He sat in his chair – the only armchair in the Dejeante establishment – and perused his daily paper, *L'Humanité*. He also studied his collection of old copies of *Miroir-Sprint*. Jean must have known these magazines by heart. No matter: one could look at them time and again, so beautiful and exciting were their photographs. I too spent hours with this archive and learnt the names of all the riders, their achievements and disappointments, *splendeurs et misères*. Jean was a good tutor. He had a white but kindly face and strikingly expressive brown eyes. Nor was he always a melancholy man, in spite of his afflictions. At about two o'clock in the afternoon, when we would be on the third or fourth course of Riri's lunch, Jean would begin to sing – and his songs told of wine and patriotism, love and laughter. Here's a good one (or as much of it as I can remember):

> Pour le repos, le plaisir du militaire,
> Il est là-bas, à deux pas de la forêt
> Une maison aux murs tout couverts de lierre
> 'Aux Tour-lou-rous' c'est le nom du cabaret.

> La servante est jeune et gentille
> Légère comme un papillon
> Comme son vin son oeil pétille
> Nous l'appelons la Madelon.

> Nous en rêvons la nuit
> Nous y pensons le jour
> Ce n'est que Madelon
> Mais pour nous c'est l'amour.

Chorus:

> Quand Madelon vient nous servir à boire
> Sous le tonneau, servir à boire
> Sous la tonnelle on frôle son jupon
> Madelon, Madelon! Madelon, Madelon!

Lierre means ivy, a *tonneau* is one of those huge barrels that hold wine, *tonnelle* means an arbour, *jupon* means petticoat or slip.

'C'est Suzette' is another jolly song. So is 'La Belle Boulangère'. They both go to marching rhythms. But I must press on.

I put these matters on paper because there cannot be many British racing cyclists who knew working-class communist life in Paris in the years after the Liberation. My childhood good fortune took me there, to places to which my mind constantly returns, and to one place in particular.

Imagine that you are by the Seine on its south bank, that is to say the left bank, close to Notre Dame. Now start the walk up the rue Cardinal Lemoine. Everything is different nowadays, but you see where I am. Not far from the river were some very old houses, dating probably from the eighteenth century. They were dilapidated, almost falling down. Their front doors opened directly onto a square – not a formal square, just a wide rectangular area, cobbled, rising quite sharply towards its northern side. There were no cars. Outside the doors of the houses were barrels, baskets for vegetables, bales of straw. I can't remember horses but they must have been a part of the local economy. Anyway there was a feeling of horses in the neighbourhood, which was one of the parts of central Paris that still had the atmosphere of the countryside.

Some of the houses on the square were shops or bars. Jean and Riri's home was a shop of sorts. Above the door DEJEANTE was written in block capitals. There was a counter, though it did not have a till. Behind the counter were shelves, empty apart from jars that contained screws and nails. Near the door were big tins of paraffin for the neighbours. I can't remember any shop window but I do recall that the Dejeantes used shutters, as though by habit.

I suppose that the Dejeante shop could be called an ironmonger's, but mainly it was a home. You went from the front shop area to a passage. This was a kitchen, arranged galley-fashion. The kitchen led to the living room, which was painted a dull green, with a table that could seat eight or ten. Beyond the living room was a place with a hole in the floor, the lavatory. Somewhere at the back were stairs that led to the only bedroom.

At noon every day the shop would be firmly closed and would

not reopen until the next morning. As lunchtime began I was set to my work. I was the *garçon*, the little waiter in a mad restaurant. My first task was to lay the table. Then, when comrades arrived, I served aperitifs. The next job was to uncork six bottles of wine. Riri gave me simple kitchen duties while beginning her magnificent preparations for lunch. I loved Riri, who was a fat, noisy, bossy blonde, kind as a hen. And what a cook! I stood in the passage at her side while she prepared some dish. She seemed first to strut, then to dance – one of those cooks who prepare a meal with the help of her whole body, pouring her humanity into the things we were given to eat.

After aperitifs, the lunch proper began at around one and continued until five or six in the evening. There was always a sense of celebration, as though the end of Hitler's war meant permanent festivity. But there were graver things in the background. Riri had organised her Resistance cell from the modest Dejeante premises. My parents told me many a tale of her wartime bravery – and of her loneliness and anxiety, for in the years of German rule she did not know whether her husband was alive or dead. Now Jean and Riri were making up for their separation. Talk around the table was never serious. It was about food, neighbourhood gossip or the Tour de France. Occasionally there was some reference to the local affairs of the PCF – that is, the *Parti communiste français* – for all the lunch guests would be Party members.

Childless (maybe that's the reason they liked me), Jean and Riri lived for the pleasures of the table, or rather for the especial pleasure of a shared meal. There were never fewer than four courses at a Déjeante lunch. Everything was delicious, though nothing refined. Dishes from Picardy often appeared, for both Jean and Riri came from the north. I remember *flamiche*, bowls of river fish, pigeons cooked with peas, Jerusalem artichoke soup, chicken and ducks.

The ingredients of these meals were not particularly expensive. But they were various and copious in a time of shortages. I wondered occasionally how the Dejeantes earned a living. They caroused through most of the day, and their shop, in the short hours when it was open, had little to sell. Money seemed to have no relevance. Later I discovered the truth. Like many other *anciens résistants*, Jean and Riri were playing the black market. They used their old clandestine networks to buy and sell food and drink. And what more did they want in life than food and drink?

Comradeship, obviously. They were members of the PCF and possessed Party cards but the party line on any issue meant nothing to them. Jean and Riri simply believed in freedom and the brotherhood of man. Their style of communism could only have existed in Paris after the war, and perhaps only in their own home and *arrondissement*. I got to know the layout of some of the streets of the 16ᵉ when I was sent out to buy more bread or wine as lunch approached its crescendo at around 3.30. Back from my errands, panting, I entered the fug of Gauloises and the noise of toasts and communist songs. Sometimes I was put on a chair to sing the great anthem of our movement, 'The International':

> Awake, o starvelings, from your slumbers!
> Uplift, uplift your longing eyes,
> For tumty-tumty tumty-tum-tum
>   And to fight for freedom arise!

Then it would be 'Bravo le petit Tim! Bravo Timoshenko! Bravo!' from all the company, kisses from Riri, handshakes from Jean.

Some meals can inspire you for years. Until 1999 I organised lunches on the Riri pattern and sang 'The International' at table when it seemed appropriate, which was quite often. The extended Dejeante lunches gave me the impression that grown-ups do what they like, all day long. A few years later I realised that the communism of Jean and Riri was unusually natural. In England I felt an outcast, for communists were unpopular people at the time of the Cold War. In Paris, it was as though all the world had the right to be a communist, and somehow I connected that freedom with the bicycle.

* * *

Intellectuals or not, the French communists I knew in my youth had a passion for cycle racing and especially for the Tour de France. Perhaps this is simply because they were French. But the PCF understood the mass appeal of cycling and was always eager to make alliances between cycle sport and the communist movement. A person who spent much time in this endeavour was Jean Bruhat. For a time I was supposed to go to the park with his daughter, Françoise. She had a prissy manner and made notes on her school textbooks. Her piled hair became uncoiled quite nicely, and this seemed out of character.

The whole Bruhat family were correct in ways that were unknown to the Dejeantes. Their neat home, somewhere towards the Porte d'Orléans, was a place of industry and respectability. Its only ornament was Picasso's dove of peace, though there was of course the regulation bust of Lenin that was found in so many intellectual households. Jean Bruhat sat on every committee he could find – one of those communists who wish the whole world to be a system of committees, interlocking and hierarchical. In some ways he was a very clever man, a *normalien* – that is, a graduate of the École Normale Supérieure. I remember my father explaining that this was a sort of French Balliol. Jean was one of the Party hacks who attempted to keep Picasso on the right communist line. He was Picasso's minder when the artist attended the peace congress in Poland in 1954. There is a painting of Picasso's daughter Paloma in a Polish coat he bought for her on that occasion. Françoise had one too, and looked terrible in it. But never mind art history. I must press on! Jean Bruhat was truly impressive only when he applied his mind – the high but supple intellect of the *normalien* – to a minute analysis of the Tour de France. He could tell you every detail of the race in every year, the number of kilometres traversed, the height of every mountain, the name of the home village of every rider.

Jean Bruhat should have written a book about the Tour. It would have been of more value than his other intellectual work. I learnt much about cycling from Jean, even though we had an imperfect understanding of each other's languages. He was the first person to explain to me that many of the *coureurs* of the Tour de France took drugs. What he said was something along the following lines. 'They are the weak ones, the *domestiques* of more feeble ability, and without a doubt they have succumbed to the entanglements of *la droguerie* on one occasion or more because of the demands of the high mountain passes and their obligations to a team leader, which they must fulfil. *C'est dur, le Tour, c'est dur.* Yes, you will see the rider who has taken *un puissant doping* at the beginning of a stage, the movements nervous, agitated, the eyes starting from his face,' (shrug of the shoulders) '*c'est normal*' (shrug of the shoulders) '*c'est dur, le Tour, c'est dur*' (shrug of the shoulders) 'and in the terrible heat of the Midi . . .' etc., etc.

Such remarks were pretty typical of old-fashioned French attitudes to doping, but to me they were terrible, mysterious and enticing, all the more so because I had little idea of their meaning. I should have asked more questions about cycling, but my Parisian elders thought that I was destined to become a communist intellectual. This is why, to fit me into the Stalinist mould, I was encouraged to take serious walks with Françoise, who would ask her young English *camarade* questions like, 'Would you like to come with me one day to work on the youth road in East Germany?'

Françoise no doubt thought that communism was more interesting than cycling. Her father was in a different position. He was convinced that communism was the most important thing in the world – in the whole history of the world – but he could not rid himself, did not want to rid himself, of a fanatical devotion to the Tour de France. How I wish and wish that I could have been recruited to help Jean in his excellent scheme on behalf of French communism. In many ways it was a good plan. Jean thought that he had found a way to combat the increasing commercialisation of the Tour while – how he must have relished the thought – travelling around the whole of France as an accredited part of the race.

*   *   *

The background of Jean's proposal was this. Cycling was a professional sport and had always been used to advertise bicycles and their accessories. Nobody seriously argued that this was wrong. Then, in the mid-1950s, the first *extra-sportif* teams appeared. They were Swiss and Italian. Followers of the sport were astonished by a new team led by Fiorenzo Magni. He and his *co-équipiers* appeared in road jerseys on which was printed the single word NIVEA. Then Gino Bartali started to advertise Brooklyn, which was an American raincoat. A French apéritif, Saint Raphael, cleverly recruited Raphael Geminiani. He led a successful team called St Raphael-Geminiani, which probably helped to gain a new market for the drink.

Along with these developments came the enlargement of the caravan, the procession of vehicles that accompanies the Tour. Let us count the cars by starting at the rear of the race. Behind the very last rider was the *voiture-balai*, the sag wagon, which picked up riders who had abandoned. Then, behind the peloton, were team cars, journalists' cars, motorcycles and various trucks with spare bikes and wheels. In front of the peloton were cars for the *directeur de la course*, Jacques Goddet, his colleagues and an assortment of dignitaries. They did not lead the way: in front of them was a motorcade of converted trucks with loudspeakers and every kind of advertising. Pretty young women in bright suits travelled on the top of these trucks, played accordions, threw free samples to the crowd and generally whipped up the atmosphere. And all this advertising *brouhaha* was in addition to the publicity given to the newspapers associated with the Tour, *L'Equipe* and *Le Parisien libéré*.

The proposal Jean Bruhat put before the French Communist Party in 1955 was simple. The increasing commercialism was a capitalist trick, he said, and would inevitably lead (how right he was, though the process took three decades) to American influence on the Tour, a national festivity that belonged by rights to the French people. So the Parti communiste français, he continued, must claim a place in the caravan. The PCF would have its own lorry, maybe two lorries, decorated with Picasso's dove of peace, the red flag and the hammer and sickle. Perhaps Picasso himself would like to paint one of the lorries. He, Jean, would ask him. A bicycle of peace could be the theme. Instead of distributing sweets, miniature tubes of suntan lotion and other gewgaws, the PCF lorry would give the workers and peasants free copies of *L'Humanité*.

Of course nothing happened to further Jean's plan. Maybe the Party's central committee realised that the Tour had driven him insane. So he was left with a dream. For a couple of years in 1954–5 I too had a dream, the fantasy that I might become a French cyclist. Perhaps my head was not completely in the clouds. With help from Jean Bruhat I could have joined one of the clubs that were front organisations for the PCF. One of them was Le Red Star Club de Champigny, which had great road jerseys (red, with gold bands at the neck and wrists). Its youth section – there is always a youth section in front organisations – combined racing with touring, and perhaps some political activities. I have a box of memorabilia from French cycling in the 1950s in which I have found a photograph of the Champigny club. Its members are at a long communal table in a country restaurant, about to start lunch. Everyone looks happy and fit, as they no doubt were. Underneath the photo are the words

> Lorsque vous avez goûté le charme des promenades à bicyclette dans notre belle campagne française, dans la fraîcheur de l'aurore . . . vous apprécierez l'arrêt sur le bord de la route et vous dégusterez avec appétit la tranche de lard ou le verre du bon vin de France.

All very far from the tradition of the English club run that took its rest in a tea place, preferably of the sort drawn by Frank Patterson. And too far from home for an English teenager. British cycling was to be my life, however francophile I occasionally felt.

XXVI

Fausto Coppi in the World Championship, 1953.

I still have some programmes from the 1950s so I can recon-
struct one or two Parisian track occasions. There is one mem-
ento of a terrific afternoon at the Parc des Princes. To my
embarrassment, I see that I autographed this programme. Obviously, when young, I liked to sign things. What does that mean?
The bold, flashy signature on the Parc des Princes programme
must have been done in the pretence that I was one of the
competitors. I should have been more modest. And yet – what
use is a boyhood that contains no dreams of that sort? Speaking
of autographs, it was quite easy to collect signatures at the Parc
des Princes. There was an area for cars, in which riders turned
up, often in taxis, complete with their bikes. Imagine the won-
derfully Gallic gestures and the handshakes as the driver refused
to accept his fare from a *coureur*. Then a boy could catch the
riders as they walked, frame in one hand and wheels in the
other, towards a door that led to the official quarters.

The little boys who hung around the Vélodrome d'Hiver and
told Samuel Beckett 'on attend Godeau' (I quote the remark
as recorded from Beckett's conversation in Duckworth's edition
of the play) were quite a common sight, not that many people
pay attention to little boys. At the Parc des Princes – as in town
squares all over the country where Tour stages began or ended
– a lad could get quite close to the riders and even *touch their
bikes*. The Parc des Princes was not a big stadium if you compare
it to, for instance, a modern football ground. I believe it held
30,000 people. There were seats for everyone, in green-painted
iron. One side of the track was covered. In general the facilities
were rough and ready, their ordinariness suiting the nature of

cycle racing in the classic days I now recall. The riders were at once godlike men and as normal as a neighbour.

On to the afternoon's racing. First, an omnium for amateurs and independents. An omnium is a competition that includes races of various sorts. Independents were an intermediate class of cyclists who were licensed to compete against both professionals and amateurs. This omnium featured a 5-kilometre time trial, which at the Parc des Princes meant eleven circuits of the track. One name stands out in the programme: 'Elliott' (no Christian name is given), riding for the ACBB club. This was the Dubliner Shay Elliott in his first continental season, learning the ropes with the Athletic Club de Boulogne-Billancourt.

Next came the sprint. There were heats followed by a series of *repêchages*, then a semi-final, then the final. Reg Harris won. His typically pugnacious speed took him past Sacchi, Van Vliet, Maspes and Derksen. The afternoon continued with a succession of pursuits, handicaps and the dangerous races in which riders were paced by *derny* motorbikes, or by the bigger ones, the *grosses motos*. This was the event in which Roger Godeau excelled, but he wasn't there on the day I am describing and I never saw him ride. My purist feelings have never been aroused by motor-paced events. But I remember how the roar of the motors made the crowd cheer and it definitely was exciting to see the riders flashing round the track behind them at suicidal speed.

Now came the event that so many of us had waited to see: another omnium, this time contested by teams of two riders. They had to do four separate races: a two-up kilometre time trial *lancé* (i.e. with a flying start); an individual 5-kilometre time trial; then a two-up pursuit, again over 5 kilometres; and as a finale, 10 kilometres – twenty-two times round the track – behind *derny* motors. A points system determined the overall winners. Superb cyclists were contesting this omnium, including two former winners of the Tour de France, Fausto Coppi (*maillot bleu, ceinture blanche*) and the elegant Hugo Koblet in his Swiss colours (*maillot rouge, croix blanche*), together with a future winner of the Tour, Coppi's brilliant young protégé and rival – now listen to the loudspeaker – 'messieurs, mesdames, nous vous présentons, portant le maillot rouge, ceinture blanche – Jacques Anquetil!' The man behind the public address system was getting just as excited as the spectators.

Then there was a pause before the omnium began. It was the sort of dead interval so common in all track sports. There wasn't any music. We just sat there. After a couple of minutes a man came out of the cabins at the centre of the track. It was Fausto Coppi. I had a seat on the southern side of the stadium, perhaps ten or a dozen rows from the track itself. Someone gave Coppi his blue Bianchi bike. Fausto took the machine by its handlebar and saddle, gave it a little bounce on the concrete, climbed on, pulled tight his right-hand toe-strap, then the left one – gestures he must have made many thousands of times before. With a masterful dig on the pedals he suddenly rose to the height of the banking and began to circle the track next to the spectators, slowly, hands on top of the bars.

Here was a moving sight. Coppi was then thirty-four or thirty-five years of age but appeared to be somehow ageless, or beyond age, his long thin body and melancholy features carved out by years and decades of suffering. The crowd paid him homage. Men and women acknowledged his tribulations and fate. Everyone knew that he was near to his end. There was no cheering. As he went round the track and was recognised there were whispers, 'Coppi, c'est Coppi', and the fans stood up and clapped. Fausto gravely replied with a nod of the head and a smile filled with sadness and dignity. The handclapping followed him round the track, back to the point where he had begun. Then Coppi dashed down the banking, rode at speed for a couple of laps, halted and disappeared.

Those two laps could not have been a real warm-up for the racing. The riders would have been loosening their muscles on

262

rollers. I had witnessed a quite different exercise, a collective ceremony of some kind. Even an adolescent such as myself realised that the occasion had a sacramental air – a ritual in honour of Coppi's age, weariness and fragility. There were those who said that he should have retired when he was still a champion – that he rode only for the appearance money. No doubt there was some truth in this view, but I cannot believe that Fausto was merely a cynical and mercenary man in the last part of his career. My experience at the Parc des Princes told me that Coppi could not simply abandon his followers. Retirement would have been a sort of betrayal. For Fausto symbolised cycle sport itself, the glamour of modernity and the heroism of life.

XXVII

A wet York rally in the 1950s.

It may be thought unusual that an angelic little British subject should have spent so much time, every summer, *chez* Dejeante, learning how to eat and drink and sing rude songs; and odd that I should have known such people in the first place. The simple reason is that the Hiltons and the Dejeantes were friendly because of communism. I don't know when the friendship began. It continued because my parents were bohemian rather than severe communists. They contributed their own songs to the revelries. My father performed his favourite 'The foggy, foggy dew'. He and I did a tableau together as the weaver and his motherless child. Margaret (my mother) had a number of party pieces which amazed the French comrades. In her cups she sang a celebration of Wimbledon High School for Girls, or the following ditty:

> The cuckoo is a pretty bird!
> She singeth as she flies.
> Tra la-la la-la la la
> Tra la-la la-la too
> She sucketh all sweet flowers
> To keep her throttle clear . . .

What on earth came next? The loss of the old songs is a sadness to me. I do not at all lament the fall of the Communist Party of Great Britain and the unutterably awful 'papers' that were read in our house every Thursday evening until, I think, the winter of 1955. By that time I was committed to cycling. But history demands that I should record some aspects of CPGB thought.

The idea that the collective wisdom of the community is better and nearer to the truth than the thought of any of its individual members is a teaching of the Communist Party and lies very near to the heart of the Russian peasant. Does every winner of the Tour de France have his picture on the front of *Paris-Match*? I wish I were on the bike. *That was true of the pre-revolutionary* mir, *and it is true today. After the most hotly contested election for a village Soviet the list of successful candidates is finally presented to the meeting for unanimous approval.* Margaret says that Fanny Hill has been expelled from school. *This must be borne in mind when we come to consider the Soviet electoral system.*

If you are a party member you are expected to conform to a fairly rigid moral code, not to drink to excess, not to be sexually irresponsible. Periodically your private and public life is exposed to the criticism of your party in a public 'party cleansing'. Though he is my best mate I don't want to follow Eric Blakelock into the Solihull CC. I want to be in the Warwickshire Road Club and I know that Albert will help me. *All these voluntary obligations taken upon himself by the party member show that something quite different is understood from the easy-going acceptance of a political label in this country.*

On and on went this comrade, about – as I looked through the window at the pear tree – *the vast educational machine of the Red Army, taking about one third of the young males of the country every year and giving them a superior general and political education for two or three years before throwing them back into circulation again.* Perhaps I could go to the art school in Birmingham, Margaret Street. *In the smallest villages there will be at least half a dozen such men, better educated than their fellows, better disciplined, in touch with the political ideas of the cities.* Next week I could jump on the bike and do the 60 miles to see Fanny and they would let me stay the night at 21 Northmoor Road. *Wages are mostly paid on a piece-rate system, with bonuses and other inducements to good output. Above all, honour and glory are showered on those who squeeze the maximum production from their machines. On the far-distant day when the market ceases to expand the working day can be shortened. Men must be coaxed along the road to communism!*

*   *   *

Fanny Hill was thus christened by her father's decree. He belonged to the severe rather than the bohemian wing of the Communist Party of Great Britain. However, Christopher had been amused by John Cleland's *Memoirs of a Woman of Pleasure* (1748). He knew the book because he was an academic historian. No one else did, not even Fanny's mother, Scarlet Aunty Inez. The little volume was totally obscure before its scandalous republication in 1959.

By that date Fanny was in her late teens and had grown to resemble Cleland's heroine. She was blonde, full-breasted, merrily scornful of any constraint. We had been close friends since early childhood. In fact we were brought up together when our parents shared the Balliol house at 21 Northmoor Road. In some ways we were partners in crime, though Fanny was the more adventurous. I was expelled from only one school, but Fanny was told to leave about a dozen. She regarded each expulsion as a personal triumph. Nowhere could hold her. Finally her father sent her to work on a 'youth road' in Poland. Good old Fanny somehow managed to bring that project to a halt. She escaped with another youth worker, a French boy called Patrice, whom I remember as an excellent chap. There were many diplomatic problems with the Polish police, repatriation and so on. But Patrice and Fanny were brave pioneers and managed to hitch-hike to Paris.

In my teens it was a wonderful pleasure to cycle from Birmingham to Oxford – via Stratford-on-Avon and then over the Cotswolds – to hear what Fanny had to report about life. We also enjoyed criticising our parents. Fanny was often at home since she returned there during the periods between one school and the next. One summer evening I had the miles in my legs and felt like a drink. Fan and I got into a dark corner of the Rose and Crown on North Parade. I had a pint of Morrells and bought my mischievous chum, who had never previously tasted stout, a bottle of Guinness. Fanny drank with two hands. When she raised her head from the glass, her lips had a little wet creamy-brown moustache and her eyes were glazed, deliriously glazed with joy. 'Oh, Timoshenko, how lovely, it tastes just like sperm!'

My memories of Fanny Hill, who is dead now, are not a diversion from my main subject of cycling. I was seventeen when we went to the Rose and Crown so she must have been fifteen. I saw that Fanny was in front of me in some parts of life. But I then realised that she was exactly the sort of girl that a Leaguer deserves. (And what a stir she might have made at a BLRC reunion!) Fanny did not understand cycle sport but had the right attitude to the bike. Here was a good-time girl who – *this is true* – would also sew up my punctured tubulars. I compare the tubular problem with Fanny's understanding of scholarly life. In her home she had set aside a room for study, and would allow friends to sit at a desk there and work with absolutely no disturbances. I for one was in and out of Fanny's house on Leckford Road for a number of years. In the same way she knew about the need to go out training. During the 1970s I did my daily three hours, then Fan would give me a shower and one of her steak sandwiches. I dedicated a book to her and write now in her honour.

Alas, few girls participated in the pastime and sport of cycling after 1956. I shall have more to say about this in a minute. First I wish to recall some of the communist intellectuals who also crashed to the ground in that year. It was interesting to see what intelligence, and also what nonsense, filled the world, and also fun to consider that one could not tell them apart. Listen for instance to George Thomson, one of the comrades who came to 90 Bristol Road every Thursday evening:

Let us consider today's urgent problems with guidance from the ultimate origins of Greek thought in ancient times, long, long before conventional history. Philosophy did not precede poetry, no indeed, though these modes may have emerged in the same era a couple of million years ago. But then philosophy took the lead. Poetry became its younger sibling, so to speak. That is why, in Britain, we have as yet no fully Marxist poet.

The origins of poetry are to be found in the work-chants of primitive men and women. You ask me about the origins of philosophy. Marxism has as yet no full answer to this pressing question. What is certain is this. Philosophy preceded money! Only the most ancient Greek philosophers could understand money. That is because it did not exist. Its non-existence made it more interesting to the Greek philosophical mind. It was evident to philosophers that if money ever took form – and here for the moment I ignore the undeniable beauty of certain Greek coins mentioned by one or two comrades and which of course I have studied in the British Museum, while pointing out to the same comrades that they belong to the 5th century BC, not to the period I now discuss – then, when money lost its abstract philosophical meaning it became merely a tool of commerce and therefore lost its philosophical status! Only the forthcoming revolution will reverse this state of affairs. When we have communism we will have no need of money and philosophy will once more be free.

Some of his colleagues at the University of Birmingham thought that George Thomson was mad. He was short, thin and always dressed like a bank clerk. His eyes had a strange and direct glint, as though he were trying to power a way into your mind through his health-service spectacles. George's wife, a harpsichordist, was rather a wonder, totally in his service. George always stood while delivering his speeches about Marxism and the ancient Greeks, perhaps fancying himself a singer. Behind him, as he spoke, came the trills and then the emphatic chords of his wife's instrument. Apart from the harpsichord the sitting room of the Thomsons' house in Selly Oak was bare of ornament. So it was not a comfortable home. When I visited, terrible thoughts came into my mind. Perhaps this was the way that the world should be, *perhaps everything George said was true . . .*

George Thomson always said that he was a modern Marxist, indeed ultra-modern because he could see that revolution was near. At the same time he claimed that in his youth he had been a member of a neolithic community and that he had an intelligent neolithic mind. Whole aeons of history were contained within his personal experience. 'Look what I possess,' he said, referring to one of those gigantic early tape-recorders. He used to take it to Ryton-on-Dunsmore, near Coventry, where work was beginning on the first motorway, the M1. On the building site he was, so to speak, doing field work, recording the songs of Irish labourers to reinforce his theories about the origins of poetry. The songs would be chants, often no doubt in Irish, their rhythms and simple words both primitive and beautiful.

Was this deluded? One could not be sure. After the collapse of intellectual communism in 1956 George refused to speak to any of his former comrades and transferred his allegiances from Stalinist Russia to the future represented by the China of Mao Tse-Tung. This could be further evidence that he was unbalanced. At this period I became genuinely interested in him, and George then had an influence on my cycling life – an influence that lingers in the mind. My mother gave me his translation of Mauris O Suileabhain's *Fiche Blian ag Fas* (Dublin, 1933). I wish that I possessed or could read his *Breith Bhais ar Eagnaidhe* (Dublin, 1929), which is a translation of Plato into Irish, or his history of early Greek philosophy, *Tosnu na Feallsunachta* (Dublin, 1935). However, Maurice O'Sullivan's *Twenty Years*

A-Growing will do for the moment. It helps one to see life from George Thomson's perspective.

He had an Irish mother, which is why he held that Irish was his native tongue. I do not know about his origins or early life. At one point he was a fellow of King's College in Cambridge, but his crucial time was surely when, in the mid-1920s, he taught ancient Greek in the University of Galway. He did so through the medium of Irish. There were not many students of his subject, so he had ample time to visit the Blasket Islands, which lie 3 miles from the Kerry coast in the extreme south-west of Ireland. About 150 people lived there. The older ones had no English and did not read or write. Some younger men did speak English, though Irish was their first tongue. One of them was Mauris O Suileabhain, Maurice O'Sullivan, who became George's friend and introduced him to the other members of this 'neolithic' society.

In truth it cannot have been neolithic. In the first place, the people of the Great Blasket were Christians. But let that pass. The fruit of George's friendship with the young islander was *Fiche Blian ag Fas*, or *Twenty Years A-Growing*, which is con-sidered a classic of Irish literature. Its first sentence sets the tone. 'There is no doubt but youth is a fine thing though my own is not over yet and wisdom comes with age.' George insisted that the purpose of his translation was to reproduce the manner of the Irish original. I wonder how much of that original he himself wrote. There are a number of mysteries about *Twenty Years A-Growing* and its author or authors. George Thomson himself appears in the book, as a wise, mysterious stranger and as Maurice O'Sullivan's nemesis. The book recounts how, in 1927, George dissuaded Maurice from emigrating to America and arranged for him to join the new Irish police force, the Civil Guard. Why did George do this? What was his motive in forcing a neolithic poet to become a modern policeman?

Maurice O'Sullivan is said to have drowned while swimming, in 1950. Another story has it that he filled the pockets of his uniform with heavy stones, walked out to sea and perished as a suicide. The last native inhabitants of the Blaskets left the islands in 1953. In the mid-1950s, when I was struck by *Twenty Years A-Growing*, and was growing myself, I knew that Maurice O'Sullivan was dead and that life on the islands was dead. It was impossible to ask George to guide my curiosity: he would not have anything to do with either of my parents after they left the Party. So that was a loss. All the same, I decided to get myself and my bike across the sea to Ireland, perhaps via the Isle of Man. Then I could ride to Kerry and see what might be found. On the bike, I might quickly delve into centuries past.

This was at the period when *Twenty Years A-Growing* had its widest or rather its most potent fame. In England there was an enthusiasm for recent but dead Celtic culture. Dylan Thomas, who died in America in 1953 (and whose writing had surely been influenced by *Twenty Years A-Growing*), was admired in ways that would have been impossible had he lived. But that is a matter for literary history and I am concerned only with cycling history. Old cycling magazines show that the south of Ireland was a popular touring destination during the war and for about a decade afterwards. Some people had the romantic notion that they were going to a land in which the bicycle had not yet been ridden. We knew a little about cycle racing in Ulster but nothing at all about the sport in the Republic. Were there places to stay? Or haystacks?

As said before in this memoir, cyclists hankered after primitive or very old ways of life. West Midlands clubmen went first of all to Mid Wales, where with a following wind we could be quite deep into a foreign and Celtic country in a few hours. I said goodbye to England (and sometimes still do) at Bishops Castle, Church Stretton or Clun. You would need to get rations against the bonk because the road would soon rise, the temperature would fall, maybe the moon would also soon rise but without giving light, and nowhere beyond the Welsh-speaking line would anyone find a tea place or a shop with a Mars bar. Perhaps

I could sleep in one of their chapels. Would the country be more hospitable around the Elan valley? How long from the reservoir to a Birmingham tap? Is it all downhill?

I preferred the Marches to the land of Wales. There's more meat in the border country. George Borrow's *Wild Wales* (1862) had a good title though disappointing contents, apart from the descriptions of gypsies. Wales was still an enticing destination for a Birmingham boy. We had cyclists who attended Welsh classes and considered themselves honorary members of a Welsh county. Then they joined, for instance, the Birmingham Montgomery Association. The Welsh came to Birmingham as milkmen, schoolmasters or nurses. So also came their produce. Wednesdays in the Bull Ring Market was known as 'Welsh day'. In a kind of return, Birmingham people retired to Wales, not always happily. I climbed off the bike one morning, went into a pub and met a pools winner from Birmingham who had thought that Wales was the best place for him. He had nothing to do and was drinking himself to death. 'Believe me, there are a lot of people in my situation,' he said.

XXVIII

Land's End and John O'Groats.

Cyclists need the challenge of horizons and I'm grateful that, when young, I thought of Wales, Ireland and the Cornish end of Britain as places within my reach. We live on a compact island. Longer than wide, certainly, but anyone with time to spare can journey between its south-western and north-eastern corners. The expedition has always been attractive to cyclists and the men and women who have held the record for a ride between Land's End and John O'Groats are heroes.

No continental person will have heard of any of these end-to-enders, so I am describing a provincial aspect of cycle sport. I used to wonder who first thought of travelling between Land's End and John O'Groats. For what purpose and in which century? The eighteenth, the nineteenth? Then imagination began its work. Our pioneer might have been a daredevil horseman, the delinquent son of a Truro family, or an ambitious railway engineer. Or was he a cartographer, a student of local dialects, an enthusiast for the Act of Union? Instinct told me that the pioneer would not be a Welshman.

The first end-to-enders were cyclists. H. Blackwell and C. A. Harmon of the Canonbury Bicycle Club travelled from Cornwall to Caithness in July 1880. Their ride, on ordinaries (the correct term for 'penny-farthings'), took thirteen days. No doubt they were encouraged by the opening of the John O'Groats Hotel, which was in business by 1876–7. Other cyclists followed Blackwell and Harmon. Gradually, the long ride became competitive. Then it was treated as a time trial.

*   *   *

I possess a couple of schedules that will take the reader from Land's End to John O'Groats. They belong to record-breaking rides. The first is Dick Poole's in 1965. The second is Paul Carbutt's. He broke Poole's record in 1980. There is one difference in their routes through Scotland: the Forth Road Bridge was built between the two attempts, meaning that Carbutt rode 13 fewer miles. On the other hand he was entangled with traffic on the way to the Bridge and might have lost half an hour among the trucks and cars.

The route is brutal and gives a cyclist few opportunities to relax. Everyone says that they didn't fully comprehend how hilly the course would be. First there's the bumpy ups-and-downs of furthest Cornwall. Then you enter the chaos of the Penzance streets (where the police stopped Carbutt and accused him of speeding: he lost two minutes). Next comes the bleak hostility of Bodmin Moor (57 miles). The West Country hills continue until the route has left Devon and Somerset and skirts the Severn Estuary at Bristol (196 miles). A relatively easy passage follows: there are speedy dual-carriageway roads through Worcester and Kidderminster to Whitchurch (319 miles). By this time, however, it will be night. Our rider will start to have the need, which becomes a craving, for sleep.

When to sleep, and for how long? Let's go back to Cornwall. If the cyclist on a record attempt left the Land's End Hotel at 10 a.m. (which is the preferred hour to start) then he will have paused in the Bristol area to put on a long-sleeve top and strap lights on the bike at about 7.30 p.m. Off he goes again in the dusk. He might aim for a rest at Warrington (353 miles) or Preston (381 miles). Best to have twenty minutes' sleep while it's still dark, some people think. On the other hand it depends on the rider's mood, on the wind and the moon.

A few caffeine pills might help the record breaker through Kendal (424 miles) and the ascent of Shap Fell. Gretna Green

(478 miles) scarcely gives a welcome to Scotland, showing as it does that the nastier part of the ride is still to come. And the cyclist is 400 miles from his goal. Now he senses foreign and forbidding territory (incidentally, no Scotsman has ever attempted the end-to-end), and he can easily go off course. It's when the ride enters Scotland that the tired drivers of the back-up car are most likely to make a mistake or to lose their rider after stopping for petrol.

The weather forecasts received yesterday in Land's End are useless after Beattock and the 2,000-foot climb to the Devil's Beef Tub. The ride down towards Edinburgh is generally windy and cold. Beyond Penicuik there are 20 miles of roundabouts and traffic lights, especially in the Edinburgh rush hour. Carbutt crossed the Forth Bridge (571 miles) at 4.17 p.m. on the day after he had begun his attempt. It was a gingerly crossing. Some riders walk the bridge because they feel giddy. They may also, by this time, have begun to hallucinate with fatigue. Furthermore they fear the lorries. If you wander out of line on this fast and narrow highway above the Firth of Forth a truck will kill you.

By Perth (603 miles) Carbutt was 45 miles in front of Dick Poole's 1965 time and had already experienced the crisis that comes to every end-to-end cyclist. He never went well in the sun. Carbutt's ill fortune was to ride into a Scottish heatwave. The trouble began on his ascent of the Devil's Beef Tub. He attacked at the bottom of the climb and then, a mile or two later, fell off. He wasn't injured but he was unconscious.

What were Carbutt's helpers to do? It was noon. The maps told them that they were somewhere near Glenmuck Height and Culter Cleuch Shank, crazy little Scottish places and anyway there wouldn't be any hospitals in this part of the Southern Uplands. They laid Carbutt on the roadside and put a blanket over him. He was breathing, and quite regularly. So he wasn't dying. The back-up team allowed Carbutt to sleep for another 25 minutes. Then they awakened him, gave him an orange to suck, exchanged his road jersey for a silk track vest and put a wet handkerchief under his racing cap, Foreign Legion style. Carbutt felt quite good as he once again stamped on the pedals.

That had been the crisis. Let the spectator now fly forward to Perth and the road to Blair Atholl (636 miles) and Kingussie (674 miles). At this point Carbutt was three quarters of an hour in front of Poole's time:

> Carbutt at Kingussie, 22 hours 28 minutes
> Poole at Kingussie, 23 hours 13 minutes

– but he now had to ride through a cold and moonless second night. Rain was falling as he passed Bonar Bridge (766 miles), making extra care necessary on the greasy, twisting descents. After Dunbeath (821 miles) it's all coastal road to Wick (841 miles). In this ghostly stretch Carbutt nearly fell behind Poole's figures. But he recovered during the final leg to John O'Groats (858 miles) and was lifted from his bike at 9.20 a.m., a little under two days after his departure from Land's End.

Dick Poole's time had not been much slower. In 1965 he had arrived at the John O'Groats Hotel at 9.46 a.m. Surely this proves that Poole's ride, all of fifteen years before, had set a magnificent record. It doesn't much matter. Anyone who races the end-to-end is a model of athletic courage.

*　　*　　*

Note that Paul Carbutt, unlike Dick Poole, was riding as a professional. The genial Poole (in later years a popular coach in his home area) had carried the road jersey of the Camberley and Farnborough Wheelers from one end of the land to the other. Carbutt was by trade a Birmingham pattern-maker. He had a professional licence because he had signed up with Viking-Campagnolo. This small and short-lived *marque* was a partnership between the classy company from Vicenza and a firm that manufactured good, but not exceptional, sports cycles.

278

Carbutt gave Viking only a little fame. It was a family business, founded in 1907, and had moved from its home in Wolverhampton to take advantage of government subsidies in Londonderry. So the only two pressmen who followed and reported Carbutt's heroic ride were from the local Catholic paper and its Protestant counterpart. For Carbutt there was little money or public prestige to be gained from professional cycling. He went back from John O'Groats to his old friends in the Saracen Road Club in south Birmingham; and that was pretty much the end of his racing career.

Carbutt would have been more celebrated if he had broken the end-to-end record before the collapse of the British cycle industry. He might also have taken more place-to-place records. These were timed individual efforts between one town or landmark and another. They had been popular since the 1930s, not so much because many people were in competition for the records (in fact their numbers were few) as because cycle manufacturers (especially the rival Birmingham firms of BSA and Hercules) used them for intensive advertising.

Land's End–John O'Groats was obviously the most difficult of the place-to-place records. Shorter distances had the advantage of romance, their routes following high roads from London to provincial capitals, striding across the counties and passing through ancient towns. These were the roads that, with the first triumph of motoring, had been designated A1, A2, A3, A4, A5 and so on. Older cyclists still prefer to talk about the 'North Road', the 'Bath Road' or the 'Portsmouth Road', even if they are describing some stretch only 10 miles from Marble Arch.

Until about 1960 it was quite easy to get out of London. When attempting London–York, for instance, a cyclist would quickly find his or her way from the General Post Office in the City (the datum for northern record attempts) to the Great North Road at Highgate, the traditional exit from the capital. Then the record breaker would get up to speed and settle in. Did you know that Barnet church is the highest point on the road between London and York? The climb to Barnet isn't difficult and you can use the big chainwheel if you're feeling powerful – as a record breaker will of course be feeling, in heart and legs. Then, with a following wind, a racing cyclist could travel very rapidly through the flat eastern counties of Bedfordshire and Lincolnshire before entering the South Riding to arrive at the centre of York some eight hours after leaving London.

That's all in the past. Place-to-place record-breaking has lost its poetry and purpose. A few attempts are still made, but traffic conditions have either confused or devalued their success. Sometimes there are ludicrous misadventures. The last rider to attempt the London–Birmingham record got lost. Only 15 miles after starting he found himself riding – at 30 mph – round the South Mimms service station on the M25.

Records have been broken on many roads because of the volume of traffic. Essentially, riders are taking pace from lorries. The romance has gone for ever. Only the Land's End–John O'Groats continues to stir the cycling public. It is a journey so long and arduous that no one begrudges a rider a few miles in the slipstream of trucks and trailers. Land's End to John O'Groats has many mysteries. One of them (in 2003) is its continued attraction for women. Just now I sketched the rides by Dick Poole and Paul Carbutt. Another ride, though slower, is generally held to be immortal. This end-to-end was achieved before the age of traffic and furthermore was the work of a young and somewhat innocent woman, Eileen Sheridan.

XXIX

Eileen Sheridan.

Most racing women entered the sport because they came from a cycling family. Others began to ride competitively because they had a young man who put them on the back of a tandem. Eileen Sheridan, née Shaw, started cycling because she knew such a 'ladyback boy'. That was in her home city of Coventry at the end of the 1930s. A little later she married Ken Sheridan, who was (and is) a London cyclist. Aircraft factories needed his engineering skills, so he had been sent to work in Coventry during the war years.

Theirs was a wartime marriage that grew from the blitz, the fires and the ruins of the Midlands city. When they could, Ken and Eileen rode out of the destruction. Together with other members of the Coventry CC they headed for Kenilworth, Stratford, Warwick, the Malverns. Eileen, with Ken always at her side, was popular on the club runs and a young queen in the cafes, radiating good will. There are legends among wheelfolk about her club life. From that day to this people have always said that she has the happiest smile in cycling. No wonder, they add, that the lads from the Coventry club put her behind the teapot!

Eileen Sheridan's laughter and optimism helped her racing career. Part of the Sheridan magic was her complete lack of guile. Her victories were like generous gifts to the world at large. She never rode a tactical race, even on the track. Neither did she go in for 'scientific' preparation, apart from regular sessions of gymnastics. Her idea of training, Sheridan once said, was to ride as fast as possible at all times, even when she was simply on her way to the shops.

Sheridan preferred longer rides, no matter how long. There seemed to be no end to the distances that she might travel at racing speed. Early in her career, in 1949, she decided to ride a 12 on roads around York and Wetherby. Most people are daunted by the prospect of their first half-day event. To have ridden 100-mile time trials doesn't give you enough experience. A 12 calls for self-knowledge and economy of effort. You also need to overcome the depression that affects riders in the middle of the day, when they have been in the saddle for five hours and there are seven more to come. So say the men of wisdom. But Sheridan had no ear for advice, no taste for precautions. She pushed off after dawn and rode until the sun began to set. Many male riders were astonished as she passed them. When her time ran out Eileen had covered 237 miles and had beaten the women's twelve-hour record by 17 miles.

From the time she began to compete Eileen Sheridan won nearly every race she had entered. She won most decisively when the events were longer rather than shorter. At the start and the finish line there was always the merry smile from the diminutive champion – for she was only 4'11" tall – and long races did not affect her brightness. Despite her later achievements, these may have been Sheridan's best days. A young housewife-cyclist who looked after the house that she and Ken had bought, Eileen also worked as a receptionist in a Coventry motor-car saleroom. She trained whenever possible, raced and won every weekend and always had the pleasure of club life with the Coventry CC.

Then came a summons, all the way from Birmingham. Mr McLachlan from Hercules Cycles wished to see her. This was in 1951. Eileen went to the Hercules office. Would she turn professional? If so, Hercules might be glad to help. The firm wanted only one thing from her: she was to attack all twenty-one of the British place-to-place records. It happened that Eileen herself had been looking at these records – wistfully, for she had not the finances to contest them. Yet it was clear that solo

283

long-distance riding would be the natural theatre for her talents. So the invitation was attractive, and she signed.

* * *

Once her signature was on the Hercules paper Sheridan immediately relinquished her amateur status. Many people were saddened and some were critical. It is true that she lost more than her innocence as a sportswoman. Never again did she take part in a time trial. Nor did she ride any race with other people. Eileen Sheridan's alliance with the Coventry CC did not end, though ties with her club were – well, loosened if not undone. Sheridan was due to ride for the Coventry CC in that year's national track championships. The new professional had disbarred herself from the competition, so her club entered a much weakened team and did not do well.

Instead, Eileen appeared on the Hercules stand at the Earls Court Cycle Show. At that period 'Earls Court' was an important gathering where the trade showed new equipment to both leisure and sporting cyclists. The most interesting stands were occupied by importers of Italian equipment and accessories, which were higher quality than our own. I reckon that the Hercules interest in place-to-place records had a commercial motive: the firm wanted cycling to be as British as it could be. At Earls Court Eileen had a sort of colleague in the sleekly handsome Ken Joy, whom Hercules had persuaded to give up his amateur career with the Kentish Wheelers to ride for place-to-place fame. Joy and Sheridan signed autographs and took part in a promotional film. Then they were sent home to train.

* * *

There now began a three-year period, between 1952 and 1954, that has a special place in cycling history. There was no equivalent of place-to-place riding in other countries, so comparisons can't be made. But Joy and Sheridan weren't alone in their field. There were a few other English professionals who looked towards the records, and some notable amateurs. A number of the amateurs preferred machines that weren't conventional solo cycles. We find records for tricycles, tandems and that unwieldy but exciting invention, the tandem tricycle. Foremost among the amateur specialists were David Duffield (tricycle) and Albert Crimes and John Arnold (tandem trike). All three won end-to-end records and were known to be eccentric. Their favourite machines could scarcely be advertised for a mass market, so they were never likely to be offered professional contracts.

'Amateur' was the word that came to Frank Southall's mind when he first followed Eileen Sheridan. He was a wise man and a record breaker of the pre-war years. Southall had been asked by Hercules to manage their new recruit. 'I had never seen her in action,' he recalled. 'When on her first professional attempt she went off course two or three times with sheer nervousness, insisted on being handed up cold drinks (though there was an icy mist in the early hours) and hammered about all over the road when climbing Hindhead and Portsdown hills on an absurdly high gear, I thought to myself "What have I got here?"'

That occasion had been Sheridan's first record, the 138-mile London to Portsmouth and back. When she finished she was coughing blood. Sir Adolph Abrams, a famous sports doctor of the day, told her to make her record-breaking attempts in warmer weather. His sound advice was ignored, because Hercules wanted Sheridan to take as many records as quickly as possible. She did not wait for summer before successfully riding the London to Oxford and back and, only three days later, the Birmingham–London.

Then followed the straight-out 100 record. Sheridan used a route that started on the A1 and finished on today's A11, the road that goes north-east towards Norwich. Her time was

4.16.1. The ride was filmed by Dunlop, whose tyres she promoted. Next came the Liverpool–London and then, in August, the Liverpool–Edinburgh. This is a dramatic journey for connoisseurs of the bike: from the port on the Irish Sea, England's most foreign city, through industrial Lancashire to the heights of the North Country, then down to Sir Walter Scott's land and across the Yarrow and Tweed. Sheridan would not have been thinking of poetry and romance. The essence of place-to-place riding is concentration. But Sheridan was also learning a part of the end-to-end route. When she next flew along these Lanarkshire roads, on her way to John O'Groats, it would be dark.

The learning went on as Eileen Sheridan triumphed on every type of British main road. Two weeks after the Liverpool–Edinburgh she took the comparatively flat London–Bath and back. In October came the Land's End–London. This is 287 miles of pure difficulty. The West Country hills absorb your strength before you reach the faster roads on the eastern side of Salisbury Plain. It's on these roads that you're liable to fall asleep. Crimes and Arnold, who also tackled this record on the tandem trike, had one advantage. They kept each other awake by singing, by insults, or by blows from the stoker (Arnold) to the steerer.

For Eileen Sheridan, no amount of black coffee could ward off the tremendous drowsiness that comes after twelve hours of physical effort on a bicycle. On her way to London – this was in October of 1952 – she fell asleep on the bike for the first time in her life. Her pedal rate went down, then faded into freewheeling. She veered to one side of the road, then the other. Just before crashing she snapped into wakefulness. In Eileen's following car – trailing her at the regulation 100 yards' distance – old Frank Southall watched and worried. Probably he was a little bit in love.

*   *   *

The hiatus of the war years meant that a number of the place-to-place records were 'soft', ready for the taking. The really hard ones were the property of a former Hercules professional, Marguerite Wilson. We must all be impressed by the few photographs of 'Miss Wilson', as Eileen Sheridan called her. She was blonde, glamorous and just twenty-one years old when, in 1939, she left the West Croydon Wheelers to become the first woman professional cyclist. Her record rides belong to a wonderful few weeks in the summer of that year. Then Marguerite Wilson was lost to the sport, but not to the world, for she became an air hostess – a pioneer in another part of modern life.

Anyway, Eileen Sheridan had to contemplate Marguerite Wilson's Land's End–John O'Groats figures, which were formidable. Wilson's time was 2 days, 22 hours and 52 minutes. The women's record, I should here say, had been established in the previous year, 1938, by Lilian Dredge of the Southern Ladies Road Club. (She was even more beautiful than Wilson or Sheridan: see her photo in the French pub, already mentioned in this book.) Unlike Lilian Dredge, Marguerite Wilson had the benefit of an accompanying caravan. In 1939 she first climbed into its bunk near Bristol, then again near Kidderminster (272 miles). She was back in the caravan at Wigan and slept for three hours at Lanark. Wilson then took no more long breaks until she arrived at John O'Groats, when she rested in the caravan before a tour of the roads of northern Scotland gave her the 1,000-mile record.

Frank Southall considered both Lilian Dredge's and Marguerite Wilson's sleep patterns without drawing any conclusions. Sir Adolph Abrams said that the need for sleep differs with each individual, that there could be no plan and that it was impossible, as Sheridan imagined, to build a 'sleep reservoir' by spending long hours in bed. The fact seems to be that you can't train for sleep deprivation. One or two later end-to-enders (as I write, in 2003, about fifty people have done the ride in competition) prepared by going without sleep for twenty-four hours, twice a week, in the months before their attempt. That doesn't seem sensible. But end-to-enders cannot be careful people. Their project has to come near to cycling suicide and they cannot know whether sleep is a friend or an enemy.

Eileen Sheridan and her manager Frank Southall put the question of sleep to one side, since the problem was insoluble. Other preparations went on for six months. Tubulars had already been matured. Now various pairs of cycling shoes were broken in. Sheridan toughened the skin on her feet and 'saddle area' by twice-daily rubbings with surgical spirit. Above all she put thousands of miles into the bank. I understand that she trained for the climbs by making expeditions to the Malverns and the Welsh borders. For relaxation, Eileen went to the gym.

In the new year of 1953 helpers were organised, a caravan set up, a nurse interviewed and hired. Eileen's bike would have been a familiar old favourite built by a local craftsman. The frame was of course resprayed with Hercules transfers. Today's cyclists will be amazed to learn of its gears, which were the same as the ratios chosen by Marguerite Wilson, fourteen years earlier. In the twenty-first century an end-to-ender would probably use 14 or 16 gears between 56 inches and 120 inches. Sheridan's derailleur, like Wilson's, gave her just three gears.

They were a 66, a 72 and an 84. She would not have been able to pedal on long stretches of downhill road. Perhaps that was a help, since she rested. Her very physical 66-inch climbing gear deserves meditation. Eileen had the natural climber's small size and light weight. It is none the less marvellous that she could turn a 66 on the climbs between England and Scotland, some of them short and vicious, others long and enervating. It could be that her pleasure in gymnastics gave an extra spring to Eileen's body when she tackled out-of-the-saddle hills.

*   *   *

In July 1953 Eileen Sheridan and her support team made their base in a Penzance hotel and waited for a wind that would stand fair for the north.

She started with favourable weather forecasts that turned out to be mistaken. By Launceston (80 miles) there was a malevolent cross wind followed by cold rain at Exeter (120 miles) which persisted until Bristol (195 miles). In this Somerset wetness Sheridan had eaten her first food: chicken breasts and bananas washed down with Ribena. Night fell as she arrived at Gloucester. There was no moon. Sheridan later recalled that she blessed the man who had recently invented cat's eyes. Dawn came at Whitchurch, where once again it began to rain. Drizzle persisted until Preston (382 miles), where she changed into dry clothes.

In her 66 bottom gear Sheridan battled to the top of Shap Fell (432 miles) a little more than a day after leaving Land's End. She didn't get into her caravan until Carlisle (470 miles). There was torrential rain as she made the ascent of Beattock Bank. Late on the second afternoon of her ride she arrived at Lanark (546 miles). At Perth (612 miles) she changed clothes and put on lamps for her second night.

Dunkeld, Pitlochrie, the Pass of Killicrankie . . . It was cold at the top of the Grampians. A far horizon was lit by the midnight sun. On either side were dark mountains capped with unseasonable snow. At Dalwhinnie (673 miles) Eileen climbed off. She had ridden through two nights with only fifteen minutes' sleep. Now she halted for twenty minutes. At Carrbridge (701 miles) Eileen had to stop again. She had twenty-five minutes' sleep before Frank Southall and her nurse, weeping with anxiety, awakened her. It was 7.30 in the morning.

Inverness, Dingwall, Cromarty Firth and the long climb of Aultamain . . . Sheridan had at last changed to a bike that gave her a lower bottom gear of 62 inches, but none the less she had to walk the steeper hills. She was shuddering with cold and fatigue. Southall put his big white boxer's sweater over her other clothes. This is the garment we see in the photographs of her arrival at John O'Groats, 2 days, 11 hours and 7 minutes after leaving Land's End.

An ability to carry on without sleep had been the key to Eileen Sheridan's end-to-end. She had ridden through two nights and right up to the nightfall of the third day with only one and a half hours of complete rest. But the arrival at John O'Groats was not the end of her ride. Another five hours in the saddle would bring the 1,000 miles record. Eileen slept at John O'Groats for 1 hour and 48 minutes before leaving at 11 p.m. for her third consecutive night on the bike. Now she began to hallucinate. Clubfolk were on the road. She stopped to talk to them, but no one was there. She saw animals, especially polar bears. A gigantic wooden platform on wheels followed her, then bore down upon her.

Southall lifted Eileen from the bike and gave her an hour of sleep. She still had 70 miles before the 1,000 was completed. Wobbling as she rode, Eileen was kept awake by supporters who ran beside her. They sang songs, they proposed marriage, they gave her bunches of wild flowers they had snatched from the gorse and rough grass. After 30 miles of this support Eileen fell off. Another hour's sleep. She saw people in the caravan. They were ghosts.

Time for a healthy bacon-and-egg breakfast. Frank Southall and the nurse cut the food into tiny bits, fed Eileen like a baby and carried her down the caravan steps towards her bike and the last 40 miles of her ride. Southall once again was in tears, witnessing the final drama of Eileen's heroism. Slowly, she got back to John O'Groats, sometimes happily, sometimes crying, sometimes zig-zagging into side roads that did not exist. At last she reached the Land's End Hotel for the second time, with 1,000 miles covered in 3 days and 1 hour. The landlord gave her a cherry brandy on the house.

XXX

A women's club run in the 1930s.
Could these be the Rosslyn Ladies?

Eileen Sheridan sounds like a woman in a thousand, or ten thousand. She was and she wasn't. Consider the similarities between Sheridan and her neighbour and contemporary Edith Atkins. Hercules had cleverly, and not untruthfully, presented Eileen as a typical Coventry housewife. She was a young mother who was glad to go shopping on her bicycle. Sometimes, kindly grandparents looked after her children for a day or two while she rode to amazing and unique victories. So said the Hercules publicity. But Eileen Sheridan was not alone.

It happened that Edith Atkins was also a Coventry housewife who had two children, was also a keen gymnast, was also 4'11" and had been introduced to cycle sport by a slightly older husband. Ron Atkins had recruited her to the Coventry Road Club, whose members were the local rivals of Ken and Eileen Sheridan's Coventry CC. 'Edie', as she was always called, began racing in 1946, a year after Eileen. The two women had similarly mundane jobs. Edie was by profession a waitress. She served the mayor and other Coventry dignitaries in their City Hall.

Local and national time trialling was Edie Atkins's weekly sporting activity. She was also, like Eileen Sheridan, attracted to place-to-place records. Unlike Sheridan, Atkins was resolutely amateur. In 1953 she had made an end-to-end ride without any of the back-up that Hercules gave to Sheridan in the following year. Edie's husband Ron was her only helper. She recorded 2 days 18 hours and 4 minutes for the ride between Land's End and John O'Groats. Just now I wrote that Eileen Sheridan rode her end-to-end against Marguerite Wilson's figures. She did. But Wilson's professional record had already been beaten by

Edie Atkins. So her fellow Coventry housewife was Sheridan's real rival.

Edie Atkins (born 1920) raced until she was seventy-six, time trialling in her old age from 10 to 50 miles. She was killed in 1999 when a car ran over her as she was wheeling her bike across the A45, a feeder road for the M1. Ron survives her and is still on the bike. Their son John Atkins is the thirteen-times national cyclo-cross champion. Nowadays he runs a Coventry bike shop.

*　　*　　*

The thought of Edie Atkins's life brings me to the subject of extremely old women racing cyclists. I think the generation of 1950s 'racing girls' was the best. They had predecessors, of that there is no doubt. We find women in competition from 1893, when Tessie Reynolds rode from London to Brighton and back in eight and a half hours with the purpose of demonstrating the merits of 'rational dress'. Since the ride was timed it was to some extent a time trial. Thereafter, many women came into cycling through the Clarion movement and the general expansion of club life in the 1930s.

As always in cycling clubs, leisure and competitive cycling were mixed. One activity easily turns into the other: you just go faster while someone else holds the watch. So it was easy to race, though mainly you were racing against your own personal best. Many women raced independently after deciding that their place was not on the back of a tandem. Others went in and out of the sport because of motherhood. The history of women's racing is confused and incomplete, but I guess that female cycle sport became more determined in the war years, when women undertook tasks that had previously been their husbands'. As in factory or agricultural life, so also in sporting life.

The Road Time Trials Council, as a governing body, began a list of women's records in 1942. Eileen Jordan was the first

woman to be recognised in this way. She had ridden a 25 in
1.6.17, cheered on by her Addiscombe CC clubmates. In 1942
Joy Drage (club not known) had the best figures for a 50 before
Susie Rimmington (Meersbrook CC), later Susie Denham, took
this record in 1944. Then women started riding 100s and 12s.
At the end of the 1940s we sense that they wanted to prove
themselves in the longer time trials. This desire was influential
on the careers of Edie Atkins, Eileen Sheridan and, later, Beryl
Burton.

Susie Rimmington's gears were much the same as those used
by her male contemporaries. She rode an 81 fixed for a 25, 79
for a 50. Furthermore a number of women easily beat their
male counterparts, week after week. Although they were a con-
siderable force, women did not have parity in the sport's governing bodies, scarcely ever rode internationally and were
excluded from the Olympic Games until 1984. Everyone in
cycling knew that they were good, but the men were awkward.
The women had to be celebrated not only for sporting prowess
but also for charm and general femininity. There arose the custom of awarding racing women not with a cup or a medal but
with a tiara. I like the names of women who left club dinners
with a tiara in their handbags or musettes.

Of an earlier generation, emerging from the war years:

> Ethel Thompson
> Betty Perry
> Eileen Newman
> Ethel Brambleby, whom I saw in a 50
> mile time trial when she was in her
> early seventies.

Of a slightly later generation, prominent in the 1950s:

> Susie Rimmington, later Denham
> Daisy Stockwell, later Franks

Stella Courtney, later Farrell (Don had the
bike shop in Edgware.)
Eileen Jordan
Madge Ball
Elsie Horton
Joyce Brooker
Janet Gregory, who married Ken Joy
Joyce Harris
Mary Dawson, Darlington maths teacher
Sue Swetman
Iris Miles, whose husband still uses South
of France handlebars mounted on a
modern Colnago bike
Christine Brown
Jo Bowers, later Shirley Killingbeck
Millie Robinson of the Manx Viking
Wheelers, yet another top cyclist from
the middle of the Irish Sea.

Looking at these names, they read like a party list, or something
to do with a school, or a roll of the fallen. But among ageing
cycle folk these commonplace names may release memories and
trigger talk of Susie Rimmington in the Meersbrook CC, Joyce
Harris in the Apollo, Mary Dawson in the Teesside Road Club.
For cycling clubs are pools of memory when it comes to old
members. Quite muddied pools. Like families, clubs have their
own legends and mythologies, their feuds and their mysteries.

This is nowhere more true than of the most famous women's
club, the Rosslyn Ladies. I have never – knowingly – met a
member of the Rosslyn Ladies CC, do not know when the club
was founded and am not sure when it disappeared. I do know
that the Rosslyn Ladies were renowned: the subject of rumour,
speculation and tall stories. These tales were typical of many
male views of independent female cyclists. In the Rosslyn they
were all lesbians, it was said. Or they were all so voracious that

no man was safe in their company. Warn your son against them. None of them was married. Or, said another story, they kept their club membership secret from their husbands. They kept a list of hated male riders. When someone was on that list the Rosslyn Ladies would gather on a hill to jeer and taunt him. They did a lot of knitting. Or they never knitted but did know how to sew tubulars. And so on. Many of the stories about the Rosslyn Ladies seemed to be contradictory. And nobody knew where the club was based. Some said that the Ladies hailed from Kenton (near Harrow, well known as the setting for 'Mrs Dale's Diary'). Others believed that it was a Hackney club whose operations were mainly in Essex.

They have now disbanded, apparently. By indelicate chance I was given news of their demise by a cyclist I met in the public lavatories at the back of Waltham Abbey. A tap in the lavatories made the building a popular facility for men who had been training on the roads around Epping Forest. My conversation with the other cyclist about the Ladies was in about 1977. 'Did you know that the Rosslyn Ladies finally packed everything in last month?' I said that I thought they had disappeared years before. 'No. They just took themselves out of the handbook.' Because they wanted to disaffiliate? 'I wouldn't put it past them.'

Here was a man with dark views about the Ladies. My guess is that they were a bunch of merry old-timers from the 1930s who went on in their own way until they grew too old to ride, or died. There had originally been a good reason for the existence of the Rosslyn, all-women clubs being founded as counterparts to the numerous all-male clubs (one or two of which, like the Pedal Club, still do not admit women) and because there were clubs whose committees had for years been composed of the same old males. Hence the repeated story that the Rosslyn Ladies were dedicated anarchists who wished to overthrow the settled world of wheelfolk.

XXXI

Jean Forestier in Paris–Roubaix.

The writer J. B. Wadley used to say that however many grand cycling events he had known – and he covered the Tour de France twenty-three times – there was nothing to match the sight of a lone British time triallist on a place-to-place record attempt. This was the sentiment of a clubman of the old school (Jock Wadley was in the Colchester Rovers CC from 1929), and I understand it; but how many more clubmen would have preferred to be at the Herne Hill track on Sunday 14 September 1958 to see Fausto Coppi ride in England, even though he was long past his prime?

That Sunday was the eve of Fausto's thirty-ninth birthday, and the track meeting was in the nature of a tribute. Wadley himself had helped to organise the celebrations. Of course the stadium was packed. It is said that no one in London could find an open Italian cafe: their proprietors and staff had all gone to the Hill.

A friend has lent me his treasured programme of the afternoon's sport. *Always* look at the advertisements in old programmes. I see that the sponsors of the famous occasion were affiliated to London-Italian societies: the Mazzini and Garibaldi Italian Social Club, for instance, with an address in Red Lion Street, WC1, and the members of the Italian Restaurateurs Association, who all give addresses in Soho. Italo Berigliano was the powerful man who assembled the package. He was the London Italian who was the first to import Cinelli and Campagnolo equipment and had a sophisticated bike shop on the Fulham Road.

It was a fine day. Berigliano gave flowers to everyone. The

racing was pleasant, not important. In the pursuits Coppi was supported by Nino Defillipis. Brian Robinson represented England, Shay Elliott Ireland. There was a 5-mile point-to-point race, a 3-mile scratch race and a devil for British amateurs. All ended with a paced 10 kilometres behind Lambretta motors. At the end of the afternoon Coppi was driven away to catch a plane. He had done his work, both as racing man and as ambassador. This was one of the last festivals of the old British cycling culture. A pity that we never got more from the sizeable Italian community (though a couple of ace British professionals, Phil Edwards and Max Sciandri, have Italian family backgrounds). After the Herne Hill meeting Berigliano became disillusioned and turned to the motorbike trade; and Fausto would soon be in his grave.

* * *

Coppi died in 1960. The shock of his passing was felt in France almost as much as in Italy, for Fausto had been the first cyclist to win a truly international following, and Paris in particular had always made him welcome. The journalist Jacques Augendre wrote some memoirs of Coppi's internationalism. In September 1946 he was a young reporter on *L'Equipe* – what a dream of a job – when Fausto first visited the French capital. Representing his paper, Augendre was at the station to meet the champion when he got off the train from Milan. He would always remember Coppi's command of French, his stylish clothes and friendly courtesy towards an apprentice sports writer.

Augendre believed that Fausto Coppi did more than anyone else to improve Franco-Italian relations after the war. Certainly Fausto symbolised the new as well as the old Italy. Some people, especially in Paris, thought that he represented a totally ancient world. For the youthful Augendre, the new Italy meant camparisodas in fashionable trattorias, Alfa-Romeo and Lancia cars, the secular daring of Italian realist cinema. This was not Coppi's way of life. But no matter: if you supported Coppi it showed that you had sophistication.

Coppi made French friends through instinct more than calculation. During this French trip he sought out Maurice Archambaud, whose hour record he had taken on the Vel Vigorelli in 1942. Archambaud had a small bike repair shop in the 15^e. He had nothing else to comfort him and was resentful at the loss of his record. But Archambaud was charmed when Coppi went to his shop. Elsewhere in Paris the cycling fans took to Coppi. They preferred him to Gino Bartali, a devout and apparently fanatical Italian patriot who seldom raced on French roads and never appeared on a French track. In any case, Coppi was – in a profound sense of the word – wonderful. He made you think.

The last year of Coppi's greatness was 1953. By 1955, when I had my sight of Fausto at the Parc des Princes, it was clear even to me that he was tired not by his age but by all the ages of the world. There was an aura of metaphysical exhaustion. Fausto also seemed to be disengaged from those around him. He did not try hard in the omnium. Maybe he was saving strength for a big occasion on the road. Coppi was still a force in the Classics and in his own national tour. In that year of 1955 he was Italian road champion, won numerous other races, was second in Paris–Roubaix and second in the Giro d'Italia.

* * *

The 1955 Paris–Roubaix is still discussed in many a Café des Sports. It had a good winner, Jean Forestier; a man who thought that he ought to have won, Louison Bobet; and a subtle man who did not win, Fausto Coppi.

Nobody knows the motivation of Coppi's ride that Easter Day. Bobet accused him of a cheating betrayal. One view was that Coppi rode towards Roubaix like a master who trifled with his opponents. Or it is said that, in his decline, Coppi competed 'ironically', as though his races were of no significance. Well, nobody can be ironic about 'The Hell of the North'. The merciless route exposes weaker riders and leaves them to grovel, cold and wet, in farm tracks and mud. The six or seven hours of torture contain a high risk of injury, especially for such a brittle-boned person as Coppi.

Furthermore, an Italian starts with the weight of history against him. 'La Pascale' is a French race that is usually won by a Belgian. Taking Paris–Roubaix in 1950, Coppi had been only the second Italian winner – after Jules Rossi in 1937 – since the race's inauguration in 1895. I think it admirable that, in the years of his fading strength, Coppi should have persisted with an event that is so evidently suited to men of the north.

Let us examine the final selection of the 1955 Paris–Roubaix. It is late in the day. The race had passed the worst cobbles. Farmland now merged with the urban landscape of industrial villages. Rain had been falling since morning. There were high winds. Now Jean Forestier came to the front. A twenty-five-year-old in his third season as a professional, Forestier was a swarthy, happy-looking Lyonnais with much popular appeal, especially in his native *département*. The Flandrians, though, had scarcely heard of him. Now Forestier surprised them. On northern roads he had never seen before the Lyonnais suddenly took fifteen seconds' advantage. A small chasing group formed behind him. It consisted of Coppi, Bobet and Gilbert Scodeller, another French regional who had shown (in Paris–Tours the previous year) that he could win a Classic if there was a sprint finish.

Coppi was not a natural sprinter, especially by this late stage in his career. We join the other customers in the Café des Sports. They are trying to read Coppi's thoughts as the four men rode the 30 kilometres to the finish on the Roubaix velodrome. Could the chasing trio catch Forestier? It was certainly possible. Then there would be a four-up sprint. In such a finish Bobet or Scodeller would probably be first across the line. So what should be Fausto's strategy? Maybe he realised that, not in a winning position himself, he could allow the likeable Forestier to be victorious. This was certainly Bobet's interpretation.

After the race, Bobet claimed that Coppi deliberately slowed the pace of the chasing threesome, pedalling easily every time he took his turn on the front. Thus he helped Forestier to a solo ride to glory. It could have been true. Forestier was the first to enter the track. The time gap was still fifteen seconds. Coppi beat Bobet in the sprint for second place. Bobet was incensed. He lost all his former respect for the *campionissimo*, shouting 'This traitor, this coward! If Coppi had been prepared to work then we should certainly have caught Forestier . . . Coppi was playing to lose and wanted to be sure of being second . . . I was riding to win but Coppi was riding with the sole intention of beating me!' Coppi merely replied that he had not yet reached his top form.

It was still early in the season, Coppi said. Probably he said other things too. But these apparently innocent remarks were for the benefit of the press and could also have been designed to needle Bobet, who was easily upset and therefore, his rivals knew, at a disadvantage.

Let us accept that Coppi had gifted the race to Jean Forestier. In doing so he had dealt Bobet a psychological blow. Forestier was nominally Bobet's subordinate in the French national team. Now Forestier had beaten his captain, with Coppi's devilish assistance. After his outburst Bobet had to ride his lap of honour behind both Forestier and Coppi. He did so with ill grace. The Roubaix velodrome's nineteenth-century showers then washed the mud from battle-scarred bodies and the former friends left the stadium without speaking to each other.

The rift was healed a couple of years later. The two men even did some radio programmes together (in French), and in 1959 Bobet was paired with Coppi in the Baracchi Trophy, the two-up time trial that is one of the high points of the Italian season. As in his younger days, Bobet was glad to have Coppi's assistance, even protection, among Italian crowds that had always unnerved him. Friendship was fully restored, but the dispute at the Roubaix track remains in the mind, saying much about the brutal and duplicitous nature of road racing, about cycling intrigue and the riders' use of the press.

And let us not forget Jean Forestier. The brave 30 kilometres of his breakaway brought applause that has not yet subsided. He gained his 15 seconds on the climb through the black streets of Mons-en-Pévèle, an ugly and impoverished mining village. This was just when the day's weather became even more frightful, when the riders competed in '*une course d'Apocalypse*', as the French papers put it. I see from photographs in the next day's *L'Equipe* that Forestier rode up the village's cobbled hill without getting out of the saddle and furthermore that he was on his big chainring. It was the grand physical effort of a conqueror. Forestier was to prove himself yet again as a man who could take the battle to the north. In the next year, 1956, the Lyonnais won the Tour of Flanders. To this day he is one of only three Frenchmen to triumph in the Ronde van Vlaanderen, which has been won more than sixty times by Belgians. His daughter has a bookshop in Lyon, and there the old warrior is occasionally to be seen.

*   *   *

The Tour of Flanders is a national celebration that was invented by a journalist, reminding us yet again of the connections between cycle racing and the press. The newspaperman responsible for the Flemish event was Karel Stayaert, who worked for the weekly magazine *Sportwereld*, later absorbed by *Het Nieuwsblad*. Stayaert dreamed of a northern Belgian Classic that would be the equal of the great French and Walloon one-day races. And so the Ronde van Vlaanderen was born, in 1913.

Most Classics owe their existence to newspapers, even the most recent of them, the Clasica San Sebastian, which belongs to the Basque journal *Il Diario Vasco*. This is a paper with a shrewd response to its native culture. Cycle sport has been an enthusiasm of the Basque people for about a century, for familiar reasons. First, there is the love of a quite small homeland. Secondly, the Basque region was industrialised quite early on, so roads were comparatively good and the bicycle took the place of the donkey. Thirdly, the country people had – and have – the combination of ancient ways and primitive modern technology that we find in all the best cycling lands. Newspapers understand these matters and have been glad to use cycling to increase circulation and advertising revenue, though they haven't been cynical or grasping. Newspapers are on the people's side in ways that television companies are not. It's impossible to think of a classic belonging to television, and no such races exist.

Newspapers responded to national and local sentiment. It is true that they did not always know, in the early days of the classics, how high to pitch their commentaries. There were occasional attempts to make cycling more dignified. Early editions of the Tour of Flanders, for instance, took the race not only through Bruges but also to less well-known Flemish towns in order, as *Sportswereld* claimed, to 'illuminate' their artistic heritage. This quasi-educational charade was soon abandoned. It was obvious that cycling was a populist sport. Proprietors and editors ran cycle races to emphasise the bond between the people of any region and their favourite newssheet. The connection is neatly summarised by the race called after the paper that organises it, *Het Volk*, founded in 1945, amid all the confusions of the rebirth of the Belgian nation.

XXXII

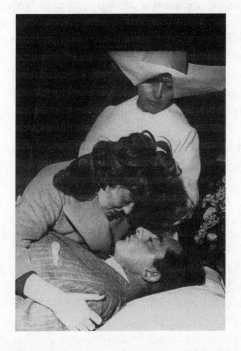

The White Lady kisses the dead Fausto Coppi.

A little more about newspapers, journalists, photography and the role of the press in Fausto Coppi's downfall.

I add the *Gazzetta dello Sport* to the list of newspapers that have given birth to Classics. The *Gazetta*, printed on pink paper (hence the *maglia rosa* of the leader of the Giro d'Italia, which the newspaper also directs), introduced the Tour of Lombardy in 1905 and Milan–San Remo in 1907. The fact that the races are so old makes them even more loveable. Newspapers that support cycling are traditional publications and their reporters always look to history. So we have odd appeals to the past. Seldom, in these newspapers, do we read a preview of a Classic, or even a report of the race, without also reading many invocations of past winners and valiant losers. Today's riders are compared with champions who died some years before the eager new people were born. Some racing cyclists like these comparisons, others do not.

In the nature of things, most sports reporters are older than the sportsmen whose races they report. Young people ride; old people write. In the twenty-first century it looks as though cycling journalists are younger than once they were. Does it matter? Maybe. Early one Sunday morning I was in a misty Flemish square. On its north side was a cathedral, on the east a proud town hall. Top-class professionals were receiving a final massage before a race. The team cars were lined up. Mechanics were loading dozens of brilliant spare wheels; assistants were checking the contents of musettes. The town hall clock showed that there were twenty minutes before the start of the peloton's 280-kilometre journey.

A young reporter was with a group of riders. They were all chatting in a friendly manner. Struck by the reporter's looks, I approached. He looked like me, or me as I had been two or three decades before: ruddy-faced, fair to gingery hair, medium build, a grin and shabby clothes including an overcoat that must have belonged, years before, to some older person. Sticking out from one of his pockets were a paperback and a reporter's notebook. Had I met myself beneath the gothic cathedral? Or could I, on some long-forgotten continental visit, have fathered a child who had grown up to be a cycling correspondent on a Belgian newspaper? I moved closer to this (to me) interesting young man and the cyclists who would shortly dispute a historic classic. To my surprise and disgust, they were discussing new disco music.

*　　*　　*

Veteran journalists gave one real service to young racing cyclists, in more innocent days. They knew the way to towns, and out of towns and through the mountains. Newsmen who had covered many races over the years were guardians of the history and nature of cycling competition. That was good. More specifically, they knew the agonies and opportunities of hundreds of roads. The knowledge was important, especially in long national tours, when stage races took young men far away from their homes.

'So-and-so', a journalist might say to a rider, 'won in 1948 because he attacked on such-and-such a section of the climb out of Colmar, or Gap, or Briançon.' Or a journalist might warn, 'Wise riders relax a little, maybe take shelter, on the *faux-plat* leading to that col, and that is where the *domestiques* must be at their leader's side.' Or the writer might say to the rider, 'The road suddenly turns as you leave Montrichard. High winds are there, almost always from the west. In the time trial stage of one Tour, in that very place – it is between Chatellerault and

Tours – I saw Stan Ockers lose many seconds because the wind struck him so forcibly, he missed his gear change and so the leading Belgian on that stage was Brankart, Jean Brankart!'

And so on. Journalists could give racing cyclists useful and sometimes precious information. So of course did the riders' team managers. But the journalists often knew more; and their complete accounts of a day's events on the road, together with interviews and comments, gave the *coureurs* an overall view of the race while they ate their first meal of the day, two hours before the start of the next stage. In such ways traditions were maintained and there was a decent relationship between the men of the peloton and those who described their adventures.

Some newspapermen aimed to cover the Tour de France for the whole of their working lives, and who can blame them? The Tour was so glamorous and loveable. For understandable reasons – the excitement, the company of the *coureurs*, the handouts, the twice-daily opportunities to sample the best of regional cuisine – a veteran reporter was not going to surrender his post to some upstart who had joined the same paper. It is a fact of life, is it not, that young journalists seldom understand *gastronomie*, or the need for reminiscence and reflection? Furthermore, only older and wiser journalists (or so I imagine some veteran remarking to his editor) are able to live with the riders, to sense their anxieties. And only a man of much experience can persuade racing cyclists that a photographer should sit with them in a hotel bedroom all evening – a lensman who might take all sorts of informal snaps.

The matter of photography was important, even crucial. Before the mid-1960s, which brought the rise of television and a new press coverage, only a few photographers covered the Tour de France from beginning to end. Most photographs came from stringers who happened to live in the stage towns. Action shots of the day's racing were only a part of their work. Pressmen introduced them to the cyclists and encouraged temporary friendships. The result is found in the thousands of photographs (still held in the archives of *Presse-Sports*, which is a subsidiary of *L'Equipe*) which first appeared in *Miroir-Sprint*. Today, we find them in the 'retro' sections that appear in all cycling magazines. Within hard covers, there is a selection published as *An Intimate Portrait of the Tour de France* (Paris, 1995), a book that is treasured by all cyclists.

Intimate indeed, these images, and incomparable. One does not have to be a cycling fan to realise that they are among the best of all sports photographs. Their intimacy is partly fraternal. Something about them tells us that they come from the land of *liberté, égalité, fraternité*. The tone is secular. Disasters and triumphs are of man's making. The *coureurs* are shown to belong to humble life. The photographs seem also to have been influenced by the camaraderie of French military service – just as some of the language of the old peloton was derived from terms used by the army.

These photographs could easily be set beside the contemporary and more official photography of Robert Capa, Robert Doisneau and Willi Ronis. There are similarities. But those men were individual artists. The point about the photography of the classic Tour de France is its collective identity. No photographer was ever credited or otherwise named. Differences of technique or competence were smoothed out in the Paris newspaper offices, and a light sepia wash was put over all images. This unified the page layout and also gave a sense of antiquity or timelessness, just as in the fine-art uses of sepia.

So here were the immortals of the Tour, a champion in pressed pyjamas (Bartali), a near-naked man lying on a bed and shaving his legs (Koblet), another soaking his feet in a bidet (Coppi), another being massaged (Anquetil), entertaining his mistress (Anquetil again), two men taking a bath together with a laughing chambermaid in attendance (Robic and Raoul Rémy); champions smoking, crying, eating, praying (Bartali again), brandishing a pump as a weapon (Kubler), raiding cafes and diving into fountains (all *domestiques*); and a sad man walking

309

along the Dunkerque station platform, bike in one hand, cardboard suitcase in the other, after a shattering abandonment in the 1957 Tour (Federico Bahamontes, 'the Eagle of Toledo', now facing a long, unhappy journey back to Spain).

*   *   *

Here, within cycling journalism, is the background to Fausto Coppi's later notoriety. Something went wrong with the intimacy between the press, the public and cycle sport. One witness, Salvatore Trence, a pressman of the 1950s, cried that 'I've followed races for over thirty years' and that, in Coppi's time, 'we sports columnists lived in common with the riders in the same inns; worked all day with them – they on their cycles, we in our cars'. The Tour de France was, Trence went on, 'like a moving village with only photographers and reporters strictly in the know'.

In the know about what topics? First, the terrain of the day's stage. Second, the form and morale of the riders. Third, their personal ambitions. Fourth, the tactics of their managers. All these things could easily be recounted in a newspaper. But journalists knew about other matters and had their suspicions about the secrets of the Tour. The first secret was the way that riders bought favours from each other. The second was their use of drugs. The third secret was the way that, if they had enough energy after a day's racing, cyclists were greedy for the women of any town.

Besides local girls, the Tour de France also had its camp followers, women who by one means or another followed the race from place to place. Some of them were settled girlfriends of riders, others were not. One or two were prostitutes. A Miss Belgium was often noted. And then there was Giulia Occhini Locatelli, who shocked the Italian nation when she became Fausto Coppi's mistress and lured him away from his wife and little daughter.

This Giulia was not a camp follower, nor even a cycling fan. She was mad with passion. The fan was her unfortunate husband, Dr Locatelli – a hard-working, somewhat dour person. Outside his work in medicine he had only one interest: cycling. He was a fervent supporter of Coppi. One day in 1948 he took his wife to see his hero ride. How he must have regretted that excursion! For Giulia Locatelli was immediately smitten. Gradually, then with increasing force, her adulation of the racing cyclist became hysterical.

For three or four years, sometimes accompanied by her husband but mainly alone, Giulia pursued Coppi as he went from race to race, shouting 'Fausto, Fausto, you are a god!', fighting her way through the crowds of *tifosi*, inventing more and more reasons – she was his wife, she was his sister, she was a nurse sent by his doctor – for gaining entry to the riders' quarters or hotel rooms. Coppi, of course, was never alone. He was surrounded by teammates, officials, journalists; and by his side was the awesome figure of the blind Cavanna. So Giulia was often bundled away. Doors were shut in her face, policemen escorted her from hotels where she had tried to fool the reception staff. Never, it seems, was she embarrassed.

Little by little, Giulia Locatelli came to be accepted by Coppi. He conversed with her, learnt her name and her husband's name. Sometimes he acknowledged her daily letters. But every kindness was a mistake.

Dr Locatelli must have known that his wife was unbalanced. Giulia may have been crazy even before her first sight of Fausto Coppi. In any case, the doctor was slow to deter his wife from her ruinous infatuation. Himself a hero worshipper, he was actually glad that Giulia had made Coppi's acquaintance; for as a result he could meet his hero, and then perhaps be able to say to his male acquaintances that the most celebrated man in Italy, *il campionissimo*, was his friend.

Useless to recount the machinations and betrayals of Coppi's affair. It took Giulia Locatelli four years to make Coppi her own.

Then there was no turning back. Her deranged love somehow transferred itself to Fausto. His adultery became public when newspapers noticed a strange woman at his side: 'La Dama Bianca', 'the Woman in White'. The name was taken from a light raincoat she had worn at the top of a mountain pass. How had this elegant person come to such a forsaken place and why was she waving and crying so loudly as Coppi pedalled past? A photographer thought it might make an interesting picture, and that was when the secret was revealed to all the world. Cycling journalists, when they had heard of Coppi's affair, had kept the sensational story from their colleagues on the news pages. Probably they were more shocked than anyone else.

I return to the testimony of Salvatore Trence, he who was so proud of the 'moving village' of riders, journalists and photographers. Years after Coppi's death in 1960 Trence described the awful silence when Fausto traduced one of the rituals of cycle sport.

In the folk religion of cycling, with its many reminiscences of Latin Christianity, no ceremony is more sacred than a team's communal evening meal. Their long table is laid with twelve places. No outsider sits with them. At the head of the table is the team's leader, gravely listening to his *domestiques* – in Italian his *gregarii* – as they recount their day on the road, and encouraging and advising them.

One night, however, Fausto Coppi was late and nowhere to be seen. When he eventually appeared in the dining room he had a woman with him. They sat together at a different table laid for two. His loyal team, Andrea Carrea first among them – then Loretto, Petrucci, Milano, Bini, Crippa, Piazza and the others – realised what was happening. They worshipped Coppi. Now they looked down at their plates, silent in shame.

That was in 1953, during the Giro d'Italia. Trence correctly said that the scandal was greater in Italy than in France. After the Giro all of Italy scrutinised another photograph. Coppi had travelled to Lugano and at last had won the world road championship. At the finish there was a crowd of 30,000 people, many of them Italians. It was a superb victory. And then the doctor's wife managed to appear on the podium as Coppi saluted his cheering followers.

All became chaos. Locatelli began legal proceedings against his wife. The Pope sent a personal message to Coppi, who threw the letter into the bin. The *campionissimo*'s picture was ripped from household and restaurant walls. Children were forbidden to speak his name, for he was a devil. Crowds gathered outside Coppi's house and the Locatellis' house. Police were called and were told that Locatelli had a gun and was going to a race to shoot Coppi as he crossed the finishing line.

The story was a glorious gift to a certain kind of journalism which fed on scandals in the lives of celebrities. For the first time, a cyclist received the same publicity as a film star. Coppi and his mistress – who soon appeared in public together, and in fashionable places – were followed by the first of the *paparazzi* photographers, who snatched pictures of the lovers and then ran. Here was a novel kind of camerawork, quite unlike the snaps by the men who were trusted by cyclists and who gave such dignified life to the pages of *Miroir-Sprint*.

XXXIII

Coppi with Jacques Anquetil, then 19 years old.

In modern fashionable life, the guilty person in a marital disaster often takes to the social stage. The innocent party goes into hiding. So it was with Fausto Coppi and his sweet wife Bruna. The young mother was left behind, forgotten. Coppi and his mistress were greeted at parties, receptions, photosessions with film stars, cocktail weekends at ski resorts. But Fausto was hardly at home in such places. Not with an effort of public relations, more with a revelation of another facet of his melancholia, Fausto let it be known that he was an unhappy victim of fate.

In this way another element was added to the Coppi myth. One part of Italy reviled him as an adulterer. Other Italians saw him as a simple, good man who had been trapped. Fausto, from the tiny hillside village of Castellania, was a prisoner within the falsities of high society. Many magazine articles were protective of Coppi, mainly, I suspect, because their authors disliked the Church. In his last competitive years Fausto was certainly sheltered by fellow professionals. They helped him through bad patches in road races and pedalled softly so that he would not be humilated on the track. Racing cyclists were often photographed with little Faustino, the *campionissimo*'s illegitimate son. The daughter of Coppi and Bruna was never seen.

Most of Coppi's final appearances were in exhibition races. They were often arranged by Raphael Geminiani. In December of 1959 Coppi and five French professionals flew to Ougadougou in the Haute Volta. The idea was that they would race against the locals, claim their fees, meet dignitaries and have a short safari. Most of them liked *la chasse*. All went according to plan, though the African mosquitoes were troublesome; Fausto saw a lioness with her cubs. He could not shoot anything so beautiful. The party returned to Europe. The next day both Geminiani and Coppi had malaria. Geminiani, in France, had the better medical attention whilst Coppi's Italian doctors could not even diagnose his illness. In a couple of days he was dead.

*　　*　　*

Coppi's legacy to cycling is as hard to define as the nature of his myth. Probably we are too content to think of him as an icon. No modern sportsman is more deserving of a biography but we will never have one: the materials are absent. Those who knew Fausto best are mostly gone, in their own graves, beyond the reach of ghost writers. There was a huge crowd at Coppi's burial. Mourners filled the fields of Castellania, for there was no room for them on the road to the church at the top of the hill. The coffin was borne by his old teammates and the crowd was mainly of the peasantry, among them dozens and dozens of racing cyclists. A white-faced, shaken Bartali, Louison Bobet, Fiorenzo Magni and so many more, including the young man who was Coppi's most successful follower, Jacques Anquetil.

Anquetil had been the junior member of the party that flew to Ougadougou. He was born in 1934, Coppi in 1919, so the relationship was almost like that between father and son. Yet Anquetil is rarely interpreted in this way, since his achievements were utterly individual. To connoisseurs, his name is synonymous with one race. Not the Tour de France, which he won five times, but the Grand Prix des Nations, which he won nine times in nine rides. Anquetil was victorious in many other events on the road and the track: he held the world Hour record; he took some Classics; and was triumphant both in the Giro d'Italia and the Vuelta a España. Nonetheless, we still associate him with time trialling and the Nations.

The Grand Prix des Nations was a quite late addition to the European calendar. Time trialling as a separate and personal skill was not much prized. The first time trial stage in the Tour de France was in 1934. Many more years passed before the Giro incorporated the discipline. The Grand Prix des Nations was born in 1932. It was the invention of Gaston Benac, who was the sports editor of *Paris-Soir*. Benac mapped a route that would start in Versailles, then loop round through Rambouillet and the Vallée de Chevreuse before a finish in central Paris. The distance was 140 kilometres, the terrain was mixed and there were difficult hills.

The race had an uncertain start but in a few years became the unofficial world championship of time trialling. Anquetil first rode the race in 1953. He was a teenager from Normandy and nobody had heard of him. He won the race with ease and the next morning was a sensation. The newspapers couldn't understand his awkward replies to their questions, nor his precise background. 'He is shy,' some people said, 'shy but with tremendous confidence,' said others. 'He wears clogs,' it was added, 'but that is sensible footwear in the mud,' it was answered, 'and his father takes his crop from the strawberry farm to a distant market in a large new truck. He pays the man who drives it. Ernest Anquetil has sent his son to technical college. So they are not peasants, this family in Quincampoix, though it is true that they are Normans and backward in many respects.'

In such ways (typical of Parisian interest in their regional countrymen) the boy was examined. But Jacques Anquetil could not be defined. He was already a master of bluff and concealment. Anquetil made his social background vague and gave misleading hints about his ambitions and way of life. Before an important race, still at the age of nineteen, he enjoyed a bottle of white wine with a plateful of shellfish. Anquetil's character was associated with champagne, fine foods and whisky (never the Calvados that had ruined his father's health). 'Diet, you say? No one will ever say a more dirty word than that under my roof.' The thin teenager was a dandy with almost ascetic looks. He was often photographed with wine and women. The lensmen didn't know that he threw away the champagne after the photos had been taken. He teased reporters: Anquetil claimed that he was allergic to grated carrots. This was a crack against Louison Bobet and other cyclists with careful eating habits. Jacques also told a group of journalists that he was allergic to water – and some of them believed him.

He liked to spend his evenings, evenings that lasted until dawn, playing bridge and poker, games of deceit and calculation. His favourite victory, he said, was not in the Tour de France but in a Rouen bridge tournament. Jacques Anquetil was contrary with all his team managers, until they learnt not to advise him. Only one person had his respect: Fausto Coppi. Just after his first win in the Grand Prix des Nations Anquetil invited himself to Coppi's home. The *campionissimo* was then living in a luxurious new villa in Novi Ligure. He warmly congratulated Jacques on his triumph in the Grand Prix des Nations, a race he himself had won in 1946 and 1947. Then the boy took his clothes off and lay on a table. The hands of the blind Cavanna went to their work. The ancient sorcerer was impressed. Never had he felt such a rib-cage, like a barrel on the frame of a sylph. Hardly ever had he counted such a slow heart rate. And the boy was not afraid of him. Most people were.

Here was the body of a future champion, but Cavanna could not tell what was in Jacques Anquetil's mind, nor in his eyes. Coppi had a clearer view. He saw that it was useless to tell Anquetil about diet or training, so Fausto advised careful financial management. 'Jacques, you must get an adviser, someone to take care of your finances and to help you to decide which contracts to accept and which to decline. In short, someone to help you through the jungles of professionalism . . .'

That jungle had become fiercer in the twenty years since Coppi had begun to race. The sport's governing bodies were scarcely able to regulate cycling activities. The Tour de France was run by a secretive and autocratic commercial organisation. There were more professionals, more agents, more teams, a quicker route from amateur cycling to the pressures of famous races. Top riders might be competing on 250 days of the year. They were surrounded by toadies and cheats as well as by mentors – former cyclists, with luck – who cared for them or profited from their racing. A number of people were minded to help young Jacques, but Coppi he could trust. François Pélissier was his manager. They did not like each other, but Pélissier was right to keep Anquetil away from the Tour de France until he reached physical maturity. Then there were Daniel Dousset, who was an agent, and the experienced journalist Pierre Chany. Anquetil neither received nor expected much loyalty from the *domestiques* he hired, but he did have a stalwart friend in André Darrigade, a fast-finishing roadman who was another Coppi *protégé*.

These men formed the first Anquetil family. Perhaps more important was Janine Boeda. Five years after Coppi left home for a future with Giulia Locatelli, Anquetil eloped with his own doctor's wife. Janine was a platinum blonde with the looks of a film star. Her style was in line with Anquetil's *svelte*, playboy appearance and she was older than Jacques by some years. One of her uses to him was that she was a trained nurse. She freed him from the mumbo-jumbo of the old *soigneurs*. Janine looked after Anquetil in a more modern and accomplished way. Her complicity in his use of drugs is not known.

Much else is obscure. In many ways Anquetil was a creature of the night: he reckoned his chances while other people slept. Five victories in the Tour de France ought to tell us something about him, for the Tour is a prolonged test of character. Anquetil is still a little mysterious. Of course he lived in the intensely private world of a time triallist but he was also simply too clever for other people. I say this on the evidence of a column he wrote – or more likely dictated – in *l'Equipe* during the 1970s. At the end of each stage of the Tour readers would telephone with questions about the day's racing. Anquetil's replies were supremely observant, and always right. No cycling journalism has ever equalled that column. It had a razor-like wisdom. Anquetil had been a professional for sixteen years. His experience was less impressive than the intelligence that cut through any kind of sentiment or ineffective memory. Anquetil had no belief at all in the 'romance' of the Tour de France. His column reflected the clinical way that he won stage races. The French fans never really took to him and said that he was cold and remote. Lovers of the Tour were not happy that he won their great race by time trialling ability rather than by dramatic breakaways in the high mountains. And it is true that Anquetil's victories were the result of calculation rather than panache.

On the other hand, the Tour as a whole was still a crazy epic romance that was won and lost by heroes. Anquetil's heroism was concealed by his talent, his reserved manner and lucid conversation. The coolness was apparent when he first won the Tour in 1957. As ever, there were magnificent sub-plots within the race. Tremendous heat caused the retirement of Charly Gaul. The other great climber, Federico Bahamontes, also abandoned. He'd fallen in the Alps and had had a collapse of the nerves, being a timorous descender. It was a Tour of retirements, and forty-three of the 125 *partants* had left the race by stage nine to Thonon-les-Bains. Here Anquetil won. But surely he had benefited from the early departure of Bahamontes and Gaul. The next day riders had to carry their bikes over avalanches above the Col du Galibier. Anquetil was now in yellow. In the Pyrenees he was continally harassed by the Spanish and Italians. The French national team surrounded him. Then, with three days to go, he dominated the time trial stage. At the Parc des Princes he was a clear winner. Jacques Anquetil was then twenty-three years old.

Anquetil won the Tour de France every year between 1961–4. In 1961 he announced that he would wear the yellow jersey from the first day to the last. This he did, aided by a time trial first stage and an exceptionally strong French national team. Anquetil's countrymen saw him safely back to Paris. In 1962, now riding for a trade team, Jacques once again used guile and politics. He bought his team's support, avoided confrontations in the mountain stages and dominated the final time trial. Then there was an unprecedented response at the Parc des Princes. Jacques Anquetil circled the track with the winner's bouquet under his arm; and all around the track he was booed and whistled.

Thus spoke the people of France, the *petit peuple*, those with little money, few aspirations and humble lives. They wanted a different sort of champion. Although it was impossible not to admire him, Anquetil had never been greatly loved. Now the French people wanted a conservatism that he could not provide. Was that feeling to do with politics, sport, or the fear that a national culture might soon disappear? No doubt a combination of these things. In any case a counterpart to Anquetil was easily found. He was Raymond Poulidor, who became a popular hero in *la France profonde*.

In so many rural farmhouse kitchens there were three icons on the walls: the Virgin Mary, a reproduction of Millet's *Angelus* and a photograph of Poulidor that had been cut from a newspaper. In this way the Limousin resembled Fausto Coppi. I suppose he was the last cyclist to be among the saints of a rural folk religion. He had such a place until his retirement in 1975, for French peasant life had not completely disappeared. Poulidor was never to win the Tour de France, and never wore yellow, but he was a threat to Anquetil, who therefore opposed him in ways that were malign. Poulidor was second in the Tour de France in 1964, 1965 and 1974 and he is still on his bike.

*   *   *

Not many cyclists, in France or in Britain, feel real antipathy towards Jacques Anquetil. He was supreme! And champions are symbols, while the rest of us deal with day-to-day people.

Anquetil ended his life as a gentleman-farmer in Normandy. He bought a house that had once belonged to Maupassant, then enlarged the estate until cancer took him away in 1987. Veterans of the Tour de France often die young, or before their time, which might be through exhaustion or because they had ruined their bodies through the use of drugs. Here's a reason why Anquetil has another role in history. He is, or was, a link between the *dopage* of the ancient Tour de France and the semi-defiant attitudes to drugs held by professionals of the present day.

Doping is endemic in professional cycle sport and will never disappear. Anquetil, unlike most cyclists, frankly said that he took drugs. He was influenced by the three Pélissier brothers, Henri, François and Charles, who were prominent racing men in the 1920s. They came from a rough Parisian family in the 16ᵉ, were all belligerent and were top-class riders. Henri, who won the Tour de France in 1923, was murdered by his mistress. The other brothers lived in a relatively tranquil fashion, apart from a fight or two. François (French road champion 1921, 1923 and 1924) is the one who most concerns us, for he was Anquetil's first manager.

In 1924 the three Pélissier brothers had retired from the Tour de France. They said that it was so hard that they had to take drugs in order to survive. They gave their story to a journalist who called them the '*Forçats de la Route*'. That is to say, they were convicts. They rode in competition, but really they were like the convicts who had been made to build the roads, men in chains. That was why they drugged themselves, and this has been an argument ever since. Many cyclists say that they themselves do not take drugs, though they understand why other people do so. Anquetil was never inclined to have conversations about drugs. He said that it was a personal matter, while often adding that 'one does not win the Tour de France on mineral water'.

XXXIV

The village hall,
centre of time-trialling civilisation.

For three years in the early 1960s and for a longer period in the 1970s I made a survey of the Oxford marsh, the vast slough of central England, whose flooded meadows and sedgy grassland continue to interest me.

The rivers that water and maintain the slough are principally the Cherwell and the Thames. Their confluence is at Oxford itself, where we may find a canal, many ponds and an underground stream. The traditional centre of Oxford is the crossroads known as Carfax. Here is the city's highest point, though Carfax is only 45 feet above sea level. In central Oxford one does not have a sense that Carfax is elevated. In the 1960s, if you walked down from that crossroads past Broadribb's bike shop and then into the district of slum housing known as St Ebbes, it was easy to imagine your surroundings as lower and wetter than anywhere else in the land.

Not far from Folly Bridge, where the high road to Abingdon crosses the lifeless flow of the Thames, is a Tudor building. At its ground level was a small general store, 'Alice's Shop'. It could still be recognised as the 'Old Sheep Shop', illustrated by John Tenniel in Lewis Carroll's watery book *Alice's Adventures in Wonderland*. Above the shop I had a flat, providing enough space for my library and a bike. I was on an Ephgrave at the time, a classic of fancy lugwork.

A narrow alley led from my flat in St Aldates into St Ebbes. Just past the Church Army Men's Welfare Hostel – where I spent a few nights at the end of my university career – was a pub called the Albion. Many regulars were indigent men who lived on the Church Army, and came to the pub with the hostel's administrator, 'the Captain'. Other customers at the Albion were college servants, railway workers and municipal employees, together with the relatives of Mr and Mrs Patrick, who ran the pub. We were friends for twenty years, then lost touch.

In 1963–4 I spent much of the day on the Ephgrave. At six in the evening, opening time, I went to the Albion. There was a coal fire in the back bar, and beside this fire a young man could sit for hours and read books, factual in nature always, history and biography, proper books that told you about people and the nature of the world. Poetry was my own business. Literary criticism had nothing to say to a person who had seen Fausto Coppi. I still read whatever books I like in pubs, after 50 miles or whatever I have done.

In the 1960s I could not find another undergraduate who was a racing cyclist. My racing career was ruined by higher education. I also lost the help of club life. With town and gown hostility still widespread, the two Oxford cycling clubs were not likely to welcome anyone from the University. My rides were solitary. I went from low-lying land to hills, from wet to dry, from misty to breezy, out of Oxford via the Windrush valley to the Cotswolds; or through the Vale of Thame to the Chilterns, or past Kingston Bagpuize and Wantage to the Berkshire Downs.

On occasion those rides included quite serious training. I didn't know anybody who trained 'scientifically' and there were no manuals to help one prepare. We just picked up ideas and adapted various routines for our own purposes. Mostly, extra training just meant more miles. But here's a climbing exercise for anyone who wants to escape from the Oxford marsh. The venue is Brill, a large village at the height of a sudden and quite steep hill. All the roads to Brill are climbs. There is a view towards the Vale of Thame in one direction, or towards the tall chimneys of Buckinghamshire brick manufacturing in the other.

This is the exercise. Depending on the severity of the gradient, choose a low climbing gear. Sprint from the bottom of the hill until you reach Brill. Freewheel down to the place where you started. Now sprint up again and freewheel down. Repeat ten times, if you can. It's a quick way to give yourself lots of suffering. With legs like jelly go to the useful public lavatories adjoining the playing field in Long Crendon. No showers, of course, but taps and a water fountain. Then 20 miles through the lanes back to Oxford.

This sort of exercise can be varied, especially if you have a training partner. A rider can vary his gearing. Or he can stop pedalling halfway up a climb so that an especial effort is needed to return to speed. Or a cyclist can simply race his partner up the hill, over and again. It depends where you live. Lucien van Impe – a wonderful climber and Tour de France winner – prepared by riding up the Mur de Grammont a few dozen times. That's at Geraardsbergen, near his home. Fausto Coppi had a high Alps training routine. He had eight teammates at the bottom of a col. They went off at one-minute intervals, Coppi being the last. He caught them all before the top.

Caught them and immediately dropped them. You don't want someone on your wheel. On a long climb the rider who sits behind you depresses your spirits, causing you to make mistakes. The very best cyclists practise psychological training in the high mountains. For instance, they try to develop a climber's most devastating tactic. They stare contemptuously at a rival, then change – with drama – to a bigger gear and sprint away, never once looking back. Major climbs in the Alps and Pyrenees might take half an hour from bottom to top, so there's plenty of time to try to develop techniques. The pain must be fearsome; and how do top professionals know when they have been overtraining in the mountains?

*   *   *

For obvious reasons, the kind of training I describe is not for time triallists. Oxford has never produced a roadman of the top flight (unless we count David Millar, who had a couple of teen-

326

age years in Worminghall). Nor do Oxford cyclists ride the track, since the city has never had a built track. Neither have I ever heard of any racing on grass in Oxford, where much of the green land is appropriated for university sports. But the region produces many fine time triallists. Apart from the remarkable Ian Dow (who in 1987 won the national twenty-four-hour championship with a ride of 500.09 miles) they favour the shorter distances. Surely this is because of the terrain around the city, the low flat marsh surrounded by hills. It is seldom windy and the minor roads are not too much disturbed by traffic, or used not to be.

On one of the low roads of the marsh, between Islip and Ambrosden, at some date in the mid-1970s, I was time trialling and on my way to the finish. All was progressing smoothly. My bike was a Hill Special, built by the Blackpool idealist and Clarion stalwart Adam Hill. Suddenly the bike and I were struck by a volley of stones. I did not know what was happening. Time trials are about concentration. I sat up, braked and saw a bunch of youths. Later I heard that they had stoned other riders.

Odd that one remembers a minor incident a quarter of a century later. Maybe it's the affront to the time-trialling experience that stays in the mind. I never felt at ease on the Ambrosden road, except at speed in about 85 inches. A picture of that country is known to everyone. Think of the chessboard land in *Through the Looking Glass*. That's it, Otmoor. Its one lane, often flooded, is the moor's northern boundary. Moor or marsh or bog, this sinister ground has never known the plough. Little wonder that the sullen and idle peasantry of the place rear children who throw stones at racing cyclists. Or their parents might have been dons.

Anyway, I return to my real subject, the kind of bike race you would find on Otmoor. There's a 10 course along the lane. In the old days the road was a distant leg in the South Bucks Road Club twelve-hour, a promotion now discontinued since it's hard to get enough marshals for a 12. The Otmoor 10s were purely local affairs, held on summer evenings with no fuss and no start sheet apart from the timekeeper's handwritten list of riders, the contents of which depended on who turned up. There would be twenty or thirty entries from the Oxford City RC and their deadly rivals the Oxonian CC, with maybe some visitors from the Banbury Star CC or the Didcot Phoenix CC. The event headquarters was the car park of the Swan pub at Islip. The start of the 10 was over the little bridge and a few yards along the lane that sets off for Charlton-on-Otmoor, Fencott and Murcott. At the turn 5 miles away some kind person acted as a marshal by standing in the middle of the road. You circled him or her and then retraced to the start, which was also the finish.

Here was English racing cycling at its basic level. There are similar events all over the country. They don't amount to much except that they are good, innocent and contribute to the real goal of cycling, which is happiness. I know what a difference there is between an Otmoor 10 and the kermesses that are the bedrock of cycling in Belgium and France. Belgium doesn't have a time-trialling tradition. Their races depend on a town and its marketplace. There is shouting and cheering outside cafes. An excited commentator has a public address system. There is prize money, betting, dirty tricks in the bunch and a continual scramble to be at the front. Both kinds of races, English or Belgian, can be loved, though from different parts of the heart.

*   *   *

Most cyclists are topographers by nature and remember the past as though the years were roads we ride every day. I learnt the lanes of the Oxford marsh so well as an undergraduate that I can still draw maps of them by memory. Oxford is a good place to study the history of British time trialling. The county has no grand destinations within its boundaries. So also with the adjoining Buckinghamshire. It is not a wild or remote part of the world. Villages have a contented air. Even quite small settlements have village halls, and these buildings are bound up with the routines of the English time trial. On summer Sunday mornings, when nobody else wants them, they are rented by cycling clubs for use as time trial HQs.

Do you know the great year of the modern village hall? I think it was 1953. Hundred of halls were built and opened in honour of Queen Elizabeth's coronation. The architects and builders must have been from local firms. I wonder whether they worked from some general pattern supplied by the government, for there is no such thing as an original village hall, just as there are no inventive council houses. All village halls look the same and smell the same, whether clad in pebble-dash, the black-and-white striations of mock Tudor or the green-painted ripples of corrugated iron. One enters a barn-like room with a serving hatch at one end communicating with the kitchen. Superior halls have a platform at their further end. There are always stacking chairs around the walls. A smaller room is used for committee meetings. Mundane announcements are on a noticeboard. There are lavatories but never any showers.

I know all this about these places because I am a cyclist. Curious to think that the unvarying nature of village halls, the length and breadth of the land, is best known to the fifteen or twenty thousand people who are time triallists. I suppose that the modesty of the halls has an affinity with our branch of cycle sport. Time trials also have a sameness, an anonymity, and they never take place in towns.

It is as though they wished to be unnoticed. Sunday morning, about 5.30 a.m. In dozens of separate village halls from Cornwall to Caithness time triallists change into racing gear. Then they get their numbers from the nice lady behind the trestle table, who belongs to the promoting club. You fix the numbers to your road jersey with pins taken from a big jar, often the sort of jar that once held sweets. A warm-up of a few miles before joining the queue at the start. No one gives you a clap, since bored girlfriends are sitting in cars, reading the newspaper if they have been able to buy one at the hour when we begin to race.

In the village hall is the result board. Every fifteen minutes a messenger comes back from the timekeeper. The results are written on the board until the last cyclist has finished. The maximum field is 120 riders. Therefore, if the event is a 25 and the average time is around an hour, the first man (always from the promoting club: he will sacrifice his ride if a marshal has failed to turn up) will be off at 6.01 a.m. and finish perhaps a little after 7; and, two hours later, the number 120 will stamp on his pedals and finish well before 10 a.m., for he is the top seed and probably the fastest competitor. The event is over, the village hall is swept and shut. It is still early on Sunday morning. In the rest of the world many folk are scarcely out of their beds.

Why do people trouble to compete in a sport that is so unglamorous, lonely, repetitive, that has no spectators, that requires one to get up before dawn, brings no reward and little esteem, and furthermore demands long hours of daily training?

There are different answers. I read one in a book about the aircraft industry in Bristol, contents otherwise forgotten. Its author claimed that his subjects rode time trials for their recreation because the sport reminded them of their daily work. In the hangars and toolsheds of their employment they performed neat and specific tasks, repetitively and efficiently. The same, reckoned this philosopher, with their recreation.

I think he was comparing the incomparable. There is nothing like the feeling of riding a bicycle at maximum speed, at dawn and alone. Concentration becomes meditation – or something else, almost beyond thought. It's unlike anything else in the world of physical effort. Cyclists ride time trials week after week because they love this experience. We are solipsistic, not particularly competitive but content with the thought of our own performances. Most British time triallists never win. They are happy to be a part of the field, their only target a 'personal best'. Champions don't feel this way, since champions are uncommon people.

XXXV

F. T. Bidlake.

One June Sunday morning in 1964 I rode up from St Aldates to have a look at the National 25-Mile Championship. It was being held on the Bicester course (event headquarters Wolvercote village hall) on the A421. No cyclist goes on that road today: it's too dangerous. In 1964 there were no safety problems, though time trialling had already begun to respond to traffic conditions and a number of cars accompanied the race.

A motor gave me a lift to the turn and we followed Trevor Bull of the Solihull for a few hundred yards. I remember his majestic cadence and until a few minutes ago also had the memory that Trevor was champion that year. Not so. A look at the book tells us that it was Bas Breedon of the Conisborough Ivanhoe CC with a 56.57. Record books are tantalising publications. They are the bare bones of some future history of time trialling, but their statistics can only arouse nostalgia and wistfulness in cyclists who know what the game used to be like.

The sport is dying, no question about that, but we can't say when it was at its peak. The rise and decline were simultaneous developments. Time trialling improved and got worse at one and the same period. This paradox belongs to the nature of the sport. Success is carefully measured by speed. As times became faster the race against the clock became artificial. Bicycles are now lighter and more specialised, roads are smoother, training is more intensive and cyclists follow the car. All new roads are designed for fast motoring so they also lend themselves to fast cycling.

Top time triallists – and many middling ones – prefer to ride on courses where they have the benefit of the airflow of passing vehicles. We have to admit that competitors are now given pace by cars and trucks. They are also killed by those vehicles. Most of us know someone who died when racing or training. Six time triallists were killed on British roads in 2003. Many more cyclists die than racing motorists. Minor roads are often more dangerous than dual carriageways. So I fear that the end is in sight and I know that fathers no longer encourage their sons to enter the sport.

*   *   *

The codification of the time trial began as long ago as 1894 and is agreed to have been the work of one man, Frederick Thomas Bidlake, who died in 1933 at the age of sixty-five (knocked down by a car on Barnet Hill) after decades of service to cycling. In his youth 'Biddy' had been a talented rider, winning records of all sorts on road and path. In his later years he came to have a lordly position within the cycling world, his wisdom accepted because of his record-breaking rides and his writing, for Bidlake was a contributor to *Cycling* almost from the birth of the magazine in 1891.

He also gained authority because he was a Londoner, therefore close to the centre of affairs, and because he was a bourgeois, a member of one of the 'collar-and-tie clubs', the North Road CC, based in Finchley and Barnet. It was on the Great North Road, as it leaves the London suburbs, that Bidlake and his club organised time trials.

Bidlake began as a competitor but middle age proved him to be one of nature's timekeepers. Photographs depict the gentleman from Barnet at the start and finish of North Road events wearing the neat and correct cycling clothes of flat shoes, long socks, plus-twos and a tight-fitting cap. We also note the waistcoat, bow tie and a large watch attached to Bidlake's jacket by a chain. In this garb – sporting but also official – he sent time triallists on their way.

That old timekeeper style went on until the mid-1970s, at least in some London clubs. We would line up for one of Bidlake's successors, who would look gravely at each rider and his bike, then read from his start sheet, 'Mr XXX, of the Middlesex Road Club . . . 5, 4, 3, 2, 1, off!'. A minute later, exactly, the official would look again at the start sheet and say, 'Mr XXX, of the Highgate club . . . 5, 4, 3, 2, 1, off!'

I think that such people had most power in Middlesex and Surrey and point out that the Clarion movement, with its radical and disorganised style, never found a place in the capital. I didn't like those timekeepers since of course I was a child of the League. One of them wouldn't let me start a race! Because I had pinned my number upside down! There is no such rule against upside-down numbers! I want my entry fee back if you don't let me start! I am not being hysterical!!! Other people were being pushed off while this went on. Eventually I recorded a slow time. All the same, there would have been 85 miles in my bank (30 to the start, 25 miles of effort, 30 back home), and I'd seen some clubmates.

*   *   *

Bidlake's invention of the time trial was fashioned by his fear of the police. In some of their divisions (Huntingdonshire, for instance, an important area for the North Road CC), authorities wanted a ban. It is true that some races lacked decorum. When Bidlake first became a champion, in 1891, cycle racing was all over the road. There was pacing. There was betting. A cycling competition was like a gypsy horse race, with all the atmosphere of a race devised in an ale-house. Bidlake won his first races in such circumstances, so he was convinced that he should become the foe of disorder.

In his view, British cycle racing needed to be reorganised.

335

Much or most competition should be on the track, 'the path', at places in which spectators would be welcomed and entertained. A purer form of sport would consist of road time trials, starting very early in the morning, with cyclists riding alone. Courses should be out-and-home, so that if wind and weather helped a rider to the turn he would be equally hindered on the way back. Competitors should start at one-minute intervals and they should be dressed in black, though their socks 'shall be white'. They were not allowed to wear shorts.

The formality of black tights and a black alpaca jacket persisted until the Second World War. Village humorists called out 'where's the funeral?' as cyclists went past. Time trialling was indeed a sober business. Bidlake devised his regulations before there was any danger from motor traffic, so I can only infer that he was a major pessimist. Here he is on the prospects for cycle sport:

> Wherever road racing now flourishes, clubs should take warning not to let it flourish too much, or it will kill itself. To be successful is suicidal, and the game can only be kept alive by not letting it become too lively.

This was long before my time. But, as I say, Bidlake's attitudes persisted. And we are still controlled by his innovations. Take the British Best All-Rounder competition. Bidlake was its founder. He maintained close relations with the magazine *Cycling*, since this weekly unified the interests of the country's disparate cycling clubs. When H. H. England (not a racing man) became the editor of *Cycling* in 1929 Bidlake took him up, invited him to become a member of the North Road CC and cultivated the idea of a nationwide ranking system.

The origin of the BBAR – which is still with us – lies in football. Although he was an enemy of professionalism in sport Bidlake was impressed by the Football League, which he thought had a firm grasp on the unruliness of soccer, particularly in the north. Bidlake was especially impressed by the League tables. Here was a system of awarding points, of which he approved. Here was a system of promotion and regulation, of which he also approved. And he liked the idea of a constant tabulation of all results by a hierarchical governing body.

How could similar tables be applied to cycling? Bidlake saw the answer in standardisation. If all time trials were of the same distances – 25, 50 or 100 miles – or were concentrated within a definite span of time – twelve hours or twenty-four hours – then the best times of all the country's racing cyclists could be recorded. A median average time for each rider could be calculated; and the winner, the 'best all-rounder', would be the person who, at the end of the season, had the fastest of these average times.

Harry England, in the *Cycling* office, was enchanted by Bidlake's idea, since all competitors would need to read *Cycling* every week to know what times other people were doing. In the early 1930s *Cycling* already had a circulation of around 95,000. Here was a way to consolidate and maybe extend its sales. And the supposedly independent magazine would have a hand in the management of a popular sport. Needless to point out that the winner of the British Best All-Rounder competition was not an all-rounder in a real sense of the term. The BBAR merely found the fastest person in specialised time trials. They were and are 50 miles, 100 miles and twelve hours. The 25-mile distance was tried and then abandoned, mainly because of its popularity. Too many calculations were called for, and the *Cycling* office might be overwhelmed with statistics.

The least popular BBAR distance was and is the 12. The half-day event calls for many hours of training and many miles of road. The strain of competing from six in the morning to six in the evening is formidable: many riders don't regain the edge of their best speed for six weeks after completing a 12. Also, the event is difficult for clubs to promote and marshal. Many of the few people who ride 12s do so only because they want a place in the final BBAR table. Most others ride 12s because of the challenge of the half-day event. Only half a dozen of maybe 100 riders have a chance of being in the placings. Everyone else looks for a personal best. I think the most praiseworthy competitors are those who make up the club teams. They are riding for their clubmates' handshakes.

*　　*　　*

For many years, but especially in the 1970s, the 25-mile distance had magical attractions and the 25 champion was a king among kings. Other, longer distances may have provided a sterner test, but the 25 had glamour. It was not always so. In the old days it was the distance that everyone rode. Tens were for boys and women. At a time when few cyclists owned cars, 25s were convenient. You could ride to the start, race, then ride home again. Most of your races were local. If you competed every weekend from Easter to the end of September you would probably ride three or four 50s in a season, two 100s and one 12. All your other time trials would be 25s. It was a bread-and-butter distance.

The prestige of the 25 increased after the early 1950s, when more and more riders went under the hour (in other words, rode the distance at more than 25 mph). There's a little confusion about the first man to go 'under'. Alo Donegan of the Portarlington Swifts CC recorded a 59.4 on the Navan Road course in 1934. The race was held under Irish rules, which allowed shorts and a singlet to be worn, and it was run in the evening rather than the early morning. *Cycling*'s report suggested that the Navan Road course was short; and anyway, since the record had been broken in distant Ireland, it seemed not to count. Donegan appeared in England a few times and also raced at Herne Hill – but on the whole his achievement was ignored.

Ralph Dougherty of the Rugby RCC was the first man to go under the hour on British roads. In 1939 he recorded 59.29 in the Solihull invitation race, an esteemed promotion. Then, in 1944, Cyril Cartwright of the Manchester Clarion achieved a 59.18. After the war fast 25s were part of the rebirth of cycle sport. In 1951 Bob Inman (Mercury RC) was the first man to do a 57. In 1953 Stanley Higginson (Halesowen A & CC) was the first to do a 56. Norman Sheil (Molyneaux CC) did a 55 in 1955. By that date about 400 people had achieved under-the-hour rides.

I look again at my lists of 25 champions and record breakers. Here's an intriguing rider, Stanley Higginson of the Halesowen. Just now I mentioned that he took the competition record in 1953. He was also national 25 champion in 1952, 1953 and 1954 and in those years won practically every 25 he entered.

A significant aspect of Stanley Higginson is found not within himself but in his brother. He was (and is) a twin, an identical twin but evidently not identical in all respects. I do not know whether his brother Bernard Higginson was born a few seconds before or after Stanley came to the timekeeper in the local hospital. Maybe those precious seconds afterwards, to judge from 25-mile results. For Bernard also became a racing cyclist who specialised in 25s. And, in race after race, he came second. Stanley came first, Bernard was just behind him, and the rest of the field was slower by far.

What we learn from the Higginsons about the physique and psychology of twins is a mystery. And we may go further into mysterious realms. A clubmate tells me there are more twins in the world than has ever been known, because they are bereaved twins, having lost their exact sibling at birth or in the womb. These are genuinely lonely people, my informant continues. Their loss, of which they consciously know nothing, prevents them from being normal social animals. They cannot fit in. They want to have a home but tend to wander. Is it not likely that many cyclists we have known are bereaved twins?

Here is a salient statistic. In some 300 time trials of a 25-mile length, during the years when the Higginsons were at the height of their prowess, Stanley was five or six seconds faster than Bernard more than 90 per cent of the time. Surely this shows how tight and specialised the 25-mile event had become. Non-cyclists will see my point. Twenty-five miles is not an enormous distance. Still, it is longer than most people would want to walk, or run, in a day. That doesn't matter if you're a cyclist: a racing bicycle brings the distance within grasp. Speed is a further matter. To ride 25 miles in less than an hour is a feat of strength and concentration. But racing cyclists do so, on open roads, and win or lose by a handful of seconds.

It is a sporting phenomenon. I mean that the modern 25-mile time trial is itself a phenomenon, especially at the highest levels of racing. Its nature would be less extraordinary if competitors began in a bunch or could combine on the way to the finish. But they don't, since they start at one-minute intervals. Time triallists are doing a very long solo sprint. With faster roads and more sophisticated bikes, that sprint has become longer and longer. The 25-mph speed is maintained over greater distances.

The first of the longer-distance champions to go under two hours for a 50 was George Fleming of the Belle Vue CC. In 1947 he returned to the timekeeper with a 1.59.14. Ray Booty from the Ericsson Wheelers did a 100 in 3.58.28 in 1956. Years later, in 1991, Glenn Longland of the Antelope RT extended the sprint – if we can still call it a sprint – to the twelve-hour record. He recorded 300.68 miles, the equivalent of twelve consecutive 25s ridden below the hour. All credit to Longland, though he could not have covered that distance at that speed in the days before motorway-like trunk roads and high-tech bicycle equipment.

XXXVI

Alf Engers, 25 mile champion.

Most people agree that time trial sport is dying, but I see that those same people are kicking hard as they lie on its deathbed. They are fit and they are numerous. In 2003, on English and Welsh roads, there were more than 160,000 separate rides in time trials. It's estimated that around 10,000 cyclists regularly take part in the sport. The figures don't show how many of those competitors are women, juniors or veterans (i.e., over 40 years of age). Other statistics tell us that about 8–10% are women. About the same percentage are juniors. And about 20–30% are seniors (i.e., below the age of 40). Therefore it's likely that, in any time trial field, most of the competitors who say good morning to the timekeeper are oldish or elderly.

Really and truly elderly, sometimes: pensioners, greybeards and grandfathers. The magic of the bicycle allows them to race, and to post reasonable or admirable times, when they are in their 70s. I like to see the old men ride so well. They are history in action. I also like their stories of days gone by, of each other's quirks, of the wonderful cyclists they once knew, or had glimpsed. 'He passed me once!' is a frequent exclamation.

Talk to old people about the last fifty years of the time trial game and you'll get information about anyone – for they are such retrospective gossips – and also discussion of favourite champions. There are quite a number of those favourites: Ray Booty, at his best in the 1950s; Beryl Burton, who reigned from the late '50s to the end of the '70s; Alf Engers, who rode at the same period as Burton; and Chris Boardman, who is not yet old enough (he was born in 1969) to take his place in legendary history. He is however a marvel of the record books.

These four were all of them exceptional. Ray Booty, we feel, is surely beyond compare. No one can summarise him, though as a man he is generally open in reminiscence. Whilst Boardman explains himself all the time, Booty doesn't answer a key question. It looks as if he threw his career away, as though careless of honours and fame. That must be the clue: Booty belonged to the end of the old time trialling life. He realised, just when he was at the height of his powers, that he was the child of an age that had suddenly passed.

Ray Booty could have done almost anything – he won the Empire Games road race and the Isle of Man International – but time trialling was his *forte* and 100 miles his best distance. He excelled when he rode at full pressure for four hours. The fatigue that comes after racing for twelve or twenty-four hours wasn't right for him. I suppose the shorter distances were too complicated. Anyway, Booty's immortality comes from his mastery of the 100-mile event. I don't know who brought him up in the cycling world. His home was in Nottingham. He was in the Ericsson Wheelers, a club now long defunct, and rode in the colours of the Army Cycling Union while on National Service. His two years in the army interrupted a long apprenticeship as an electrical engineer.

Ray Booty was an all-round cyclist who liked touring as well as competition. All holidays were spent on the bike and he rode to his races. Every weekend away from work was a jaunt. If he and his mates didn't have the money for digs, then they tossed a coin to see who would have to stuff a tent into his saddlebag. When Ray started breaking records, in 1954–5, the bike game was just as carefree as it was competitive. Everyone laughed with Ray and some of his clubmates went with him to jazz clubs on the night before a race. On Sunday mornings he used to drum up bacon and eggs for the riders he had just beaten. He was a winner with a big smile and lots of friends around his primus stove.

The ride we all remember was accomplished in the late

summer of 1956. It was in the Bath Road 100. A word first about this club and its course. The Bath RC (founded in 1886) had its home in outer west London. Like the North Road CC it claimed territory beyond the capital. The Bath RC looked towards Wiltshire and Berkshire, reached by the old A4. The club's prestigious event was its 100. The course began and ended at Pangbourne, on the western side of Reading. There was a northern leg to Shillingford. Then the route retraced before a much longer expedition to a turn not far from Savernake Forest. In those days Pangbourne Lane was hallowed ground for cyclists. Now the course is used no more; and the Bath Road Club's centenary dinner was held at the Crest Hotel in Hayes, normally used by Heathrow travellers. 'Where else could we go?' said one Bath Roader to me.

Ray Booty was a lanky young man, 6' 2" tall, with long and powerful legs. His big spectacles (which he wore both off and on the bike) gave him the appearance of a boffin. He had large feet and sometimes appeared awkward as he rode. I've heard that he looked more stylish when riding a tricycle. He seemed to enjoy everything in life, even the nasty conditions on the Bath Road when he began his 100. It was a cold morning with bad weather, the rain varying from drizzle to downpour. Such conditions gave no promise of a fast ride. But that Sunday morning in 1956 Booty flew round the course. Occasionally he took a slug of cold porridge from his feeding bottle, then returned to ultra-fast pedalling through the rain. Booty came back to Pangbourne Lane with a 3.58.28, a massive 11.34 minutes in front of the second-placed rider.

It was the first time that 100 miles had been ridden under four hours. The amazement of the crowd of clubfolk burst into rejoicing. Everyone wanted to shake Ray's hand. They still do. He has been the most popular champion we've known. Two years before, Roger Bannister had run a mile in less than four minutes, but you won't find a cyclist who doesn't say that Booty claimed the more glorious record. And neither will you find anyone outside cycling who has heard of the Nottingham apprentice from the Ericsson Wheelers.

Ray Booty has an especial place in our hearts because of his youth, his talents and innocently amateur attitudes. Whatever his victories, he always had the air of an artisan on holiday. His bike was tailored for him and also suited the rolling inclines and descents of the Bath Road. But Booty's 'iron' (that was the word we used) wasn't out of the ordinary. Nottingham boy that he was, Ray used a Raleigh track frame. It had mudguard clearance and mudguard eyes, so had been built for quotidian purposes as well as track racing. This was a 25-inch frame and its angles were 73" parallel. The saddle was raised about four inches above the seat cluster. The handlebar stem was about the same length. On his record ride Booty carried his porridge-filled feeding bottle, a pump and a spare tubular. His tubs were quite hefty, to judge from the photographs. They were fitted to wheels that had forty spokes at the back and thirty-six at the front. His gear was 84" fixed.

*   *   *

The instrument of a champion racing cyclist and also a bike for day-to-day use. Booty was riding it to work until the late 1980s, thirty years after his record. Will we ever see it in a museum? Would that museum's curator understand the deep meanings of the bicycle? This machine has a place in history because Booty's 100 was the last supreme feat of time trialling before racing bicycles became ultra-sophisticated and road traffic became dangerous. These were parallel developments: it's as though the whole world was gearing up for its suicide.

The first big change took only a few years. A decade after Booty's record, young riders thought that his attitude and equipment were as ancient as Stonehenge. On the other hand there were eager young cyclists who were proud to ride their father's bikes, if their fathers would agree to the loan. Tradition

345

and innovation clashed in different ways and in varying places. Some parts of the country, in particular East Anglia, were conservative. Elsewhere, especially in London and the home counties, there was an irreversible shift of mood. Fashions were more volatile than at any time since the early days of the League. And young people suddenly seemed so rich. Odd things remain in the mind, trivial but important at least to me. In 1965 I was at a race and, for the first time, saw a cyclist in his twenties take a new and shiny bike from the back seat of a new and shiny Mini. It seemed so modern, this way of going to a time trial. I wasn't old-fashioned by nature (or not then), but felt that something was going wrong.

The long-delayed change in British time trialling came with the use of variable gears. I cannot understand why racing men kept to a fixed wheel for so long. Surely Ray Booty could have gone even faster on the Bath Road if he had dashed down its long slopes in a gear twenty inches higher than his 84. Anyway, the fixed wheel was on the way out by the end of the 1950s. The pioneer of derailleur gears in British time trialling was John Woodburn. That was because he was a roadman (he had ridden the 'Peace Race', the hard Warsaw–Berlin–Prague) but mostly because he had studied French races against the clock.

Woodburn admired Jacques Anquetil and thought that he could learn from the clinical nature of his cycling. Anquetil's time trials were all won on a geared machine. His top was a 53×14, which means 102.2''. In 1953 he had pushed – indeed spun – this monster gear in the Grand Prix des Nations, as I've already described. Anquetil – though not caring about the matter – then showed how provincial was the standard of British time trialling. Now I have to mention a national humiliation. In that Grand Prix des Nations there were two English riders, Ken Joy and Bob Maitland. Anquetil beat them both by twenty minutes. Among his rewards was a Simca Chatelaine estate car and while he went to a celebration dinner in the Champs Elysées,

Joy and Maitland, stunned, got the train back to Calais and Dover.

Six or seven years later, around 1960, British time triallists began to use variable gears and searched for ever lighter, faster equipment. John Woodburn had gears on his bike when, riding for the Barnet CC, he won the 1961 national 25 championship (with a 56.1). From that date all the most prominent riders used not only gears but high ratios, perilously light sprints and tubulars, precipitous angles on frames; and in the passion for lightness many components – including the chainwheel and even the seat pin – were drilled. So the bicycle looked full of holes, like a colander. Such machines were useless for any other purpose than riding very fast, in a straight line, on a flat main road.

*   *   *

Alf Engers from Southgate in north London was the man most associated with that sort of bike. He was the national 25 champion in 1959 and then again in 1972–6. Engers joined and then left so many clubs that we can't say that he was allied to any one of them. He was a prima donna, the more so in his later career. Alf joined his new clubs not out of a change of loyalty but because he guessed that the new jersey would give a fillip to his efforts. He had been expelled from school ('misbehaving on every level') and had his first written warning from the hierarchy of the RTTC at the age of 16. Some people thought that he ought to be thrown out of cycle sport, but not me. It was thrilling to see Engers ride. Even to encounter him out training, on his favoured Barnet by-pass, made the heart leap with admiration. At speed – and he always trained on the drops, as far as I could see – Alf looked as though he had come from the stars, though Palmers Green was his real home and resting place.

His resting place in one specific way: Alf slept in an armchair, because of the nature of his job. He was a baker who made bagels in Whitechapel. On Saturdays he would finish work in the small hours, get back to Palmers Green, then have a couple of hours in the armchair before someone drove him to the start of a 25. He arrived in a racy-looking but obviously second-hand Jaguar. Over his racing kit Alf wore a big fur coat, all sheepskin and suede with fluffy lapels. He had a gold earring. There was the impression of an eccentric crook. We loved him, though he scarcely spoke to anyone.

The people who didn't love him were the officials of cycle sport. They loathed his arrogance and disregard for rules. And Engers returned their hatred. It must be admitted that he could have sometimes crossed the line. For instance, there was then a practice known as 'white-line riding'. The road before you turns towards the right. Seeking always his most direct route, our cyclist drifts towards the white line at the centre of the road. Then, as the road straightens, he returns to its left-hand side. A line of cars may have built up behind him. But, as they overtake, the rider benefits from their whoosh of air.

Engers had 25 years as a top cyclist. At the end of his career white-line riding and similar practices were common. There was much confusion about the rules of the sport. It is not against the law, for instance, for a fast cyclist to overtake a slow motorist. But in some circumstances this could be construed as 'taking pace'. Engers' earliest rides take us back to a time when motor cars did not dominate the roads. 'My technique and style was derived from the Higginson twins in the early 1950s. They sat absolutely still on the bike, they had their arms bent in the egg position and they rode in dead straight lines on the road. Of course, there wasn't any traffic about . . . I was twelve or thirteen years old then and by the time I started to race I was riding in straight lines, but of course the traffic was increasing . . .'

By the mid-1970s time trialling had become a dangerous sport. I doubt whether Engers' way of riding differed from the manner of lesser cyclists. Officials criticised him more frequently because he was such a visible and dramatic champion. He defied them and concentrated on a single aim. Engers wanted to be the first man to record a 25 time under 50 minutes. That means riding at more than 30 mph. In August 1978 he did it, on a course based on the A12 near Chelmsford – now banned, because it's a death trap. His time was 49.24. Alf had been riding amidst traffic, as was inevitable. Later, he said that he had been in a state of grace and that he had an out-of-body experience during the last miles of his ride. The officials had other views and for some time would not ratify his record. Thereafter, Alf Engers was only occasionally a cyclist. He turned to his other enthusiasm, fishing, and quite soon caught a 28½ lb carp. The big fish in his net seemed like another triumph over the Road Time Trials Council.

XXXVII

Beryl Burton on Nim Carline's rhubarb farm.

Coarse fishing and British cycling have some shared characteristics and are often practised by the same people, who appear to be quiet, perhaps reserved. Their pursuits occupy early Sunday mornings and the summer afternoons of a town's early-closing day. They are usually back home for dinner or tea. But do not imagine that anglers and bikies are normal citizens. Some are demented. Many of them are obsessed; and time trialling would not exist without the obsession that makes so many people test their legs, every week, for forty years or more, in races that they can never hope to win.

The cyclists who do win British time trials are also obsessive. Many of them do not retire until they fall from the tree. Beryl Burton, who was the supreme time triallist – male or female – was found dead on a Yorkshire road in 1996, still straddling her bike, feet in the toe-clips. She was 58. No vehicle was involved and Burton was in perfect health. She simply died. I think she left the world because of a lifetime of work. Many sports create or embrace extremists and Beryl Burton was an extremist in an obvious sense. She won everything, and for so long. Burton was the women's Best All Rounder champion every year for 25 years, won the 25 title 26 times, the 50 title 24 times and the 100 title 18 times. She was also an extremist in her attitude to work, human labour, paid or unpaid. Nothing could stop her from working, and this extremism ended in death.

Many and varied are the connections between cycling and manual work. We talk about people 'working' in any racing group. In continental cycle sport the *domestiques*, the servant class of a team, work for their leader. In some ways they were still peasants. Just as their families toiled for long hours in the fields, so the cyclist from any peasant family was fitted to hundreds of kilometres in the saddle. Only a handful of British cyclists come from an agricultural background (though there are many more, led by the farmer Sean Kelly, in Ireland). Instead, we have hundreds of cyclists from the old mining communities and an especial class – to which Burton belonged – of East Midlands and Yorkshire potato factors, tractor drivers and market gardeners.

A woman of Beryl Burton's character might have preferred to work at a coalface. Another kind of toil became her salvation when she was in her late teens. Beryl's husband, Charlie Burton, introduced her to the Morley Road Club. Morley is to the west of Leeds and in the late '50s and early '60s still had an independent character. The small town was on the edge of the 'rhubarb triangle': the area in west Yorkshire in which *Rheum rhabarbarum* is grown. Our plant, half-vegetable and half-fruit, likes a chilly climate, so in the Bradford–Batley–Bingley triangle it is grown as a special local crop.

A prominent member of the Morley Road Club was Nim (Yorkshire for Nehemiah?) Carline. He had a rhubarb farm in one of those northern places where council estates suddenly become moorland, as though the local council had lost the will to go further. Burton went to work for Carline at the age of nineteen. This was just after the birth of her daughter Denise. The infant was left with its father or grandparents while her mother laboured. Beryl later explained as follows:

> Even though Nim was a fellow club member, working for him was no cushy number – entirely the opposite. Nim had a business to run and there were no passengers. I worked alongside young men, lifting heavy boxes on and off vehicles, digging holes for the roots of whatever was being planted, ten at a time, and you had to be

finished by the time the lorry arrived with more. Carrying, lifting, bending, digging, all day long in all weathers until my back ached, my arms ached, my shoulders ached, my legs ached. I was determined not to let up but to match the others in everything . . .

These are the most eloquent sentences in Burton's autobiography. They say more about her than all the lists of championship victories. Carline had not finished with Beryl at the end of the market-gardening day:

At the end of the working day, most nights were spent out training, sometimes with Nim, who was as relentless on the bike as off it . . . He was such a hard taskmaster . . . I would wait in the house before a training run wishing that there was some way I could avoid it . . . in and out of the lavatory and perspiring . . . I had to match him side by side . . . tears in my eyes, but determined that I would not drop behind . . . It was the old determination not to be beaten, to keep going however fatigued I may have felt; the benefit of all this I have reaped in later years. It was not only crops I was planting but the seed of my future success.

Nim Carline specialised in the most fearsome of time trialling events, the 24. In a way, this is a simple race: you ride twice round the clock and then see what you've done. In many other ways a 24 is complex. The pressures of fatigue are so varied and demanding. An all-day rider has to know how and when to eat, how to get through the night, how to maintain or vary his pace. Such men look deep into their own abilities. The valiant cyclists who have managed to complete the event band themselves into the '24 Hour Fellowship'. There aren't many of them, and we listen to their stories with rare respect.

Carline's 24 technique was to be belligerent from the very beginning of the race. He started as though he were riding a 10. Just the sight of his 60-tooth chainwheel must have frightened others in the field. With a 5-up block it gave him a bottom gear of 90 and a top of 112. Every year, using these tremendous ratios, Carline powered away from the timekeeper on an August Saturday afternoon and finished at the same time on Sunday. He usually had 470–490 miles to his credit. Nim was the national 24 champion six times. In 1973, the year of his last victory, he was 45 years old.

Carline had first taken the championship (with 475 miles) in 1962. This was the period when the young Beryl Burton had begun to dig his fields and pluck rhubarb from the cold soil. Their relationship had many aspects. Nim, ten years older than Beryl, was at the same time her employer, mentor, father-figure; her inspiration, her club-mate and rival. But mainly Beryl needed him because he was a man. It was so easy for her to beat all the other women cyclists in the country, easy and routine. Her ambition told her that she had to beat the other sex.

On one occasion, in 1969, she caught and passed Carline in a 24. They had both begun the Mersey Roads CC event at a furious pace, in the rain. The course took the riders from the Wirral all the way along the north Wales coast road to Llandudno. Then they retraced before turning south from Cheshire into Shropshire, and back again. It must have been a strange moment for both Carline and Burton when, a little before midnight, she came up to him and then left him behind. They had then covered about 150 miles. Carline abandoned around the 300 mile mark. Burton also climbed off. The pain had been too much. So it had been a defeat for both of them. Burton never rode another 24. But, even in this failure, we may see her in the male stratosphere of cycle sport.

She regularly beat male cyclists. In 1967 Burton won the women's 12 championship with 277 miles. This distance also exceeded the men's record. And so it went on, season after season. There were some frightening aspects to her campaign to be the best and win everything. Burton had an immense greed for more and more victories, more and more miles. The ever-helpful Charlie Burton would drive her to races all over the country every weekend. Beryl would compete and get back in the family car. 100 miles from their Yorkshire home she stopped Charlie and rode the rest of the way. Then there was the cooking and the washing. She worked or trained at all hours and often did not speak to her husband and daughter. That was 'just my way'.

Many other cyclists thought her way of life inhuman. We know that it brought terrible strains to the Burton family. I suppose that there are champions in many sports who are beyond emotional reason. They have a temperament so narrow and intense that they cannot recognise other people if they have not defeated them. That was Burton's nature. Before a race, her demeanour alarmed such easy-going people as the present writer. Beryl's face was changeable. When she came to the starting line her features spoke of cruelty and domination. Later, after she had won, there was quite an amount of relaxation and charm.

Beryl Burton was at her best, socially speaking, at the dozens or hundreds of club dinners at which she was guest of honour. She was a strong believer in cycling club life. Many of our modest little societies benefited from her generous interest. But she would not be beaten. Her daughter Denise grew up to be a really good cyclist, then made the mistake of finishing a race in first place. It was quite a routine massed-start event. A break formed, and then mother and daughter were in the leading group. Denise won the sprint at the finish. Her incensed mother refused to shake her hand. A year later there was a reconciliation. We suppose, though, that the troubles between the two women cyclists went on for longer than twelve months.

XXXVIII

Chris Boardman training in
the laboratory.

Cyclists of the old school like homely myths. A favourite bit of folk lore concerns the father who is delighted when his son defeats him for the first time. Probably the boy has already been given his dad's training diaries, kept for so many years. No doubt he has borrowed those especially matured tubulars and is grateful for cash that pays for new equipment. And now the younger man of the family comes home first in the club 25. Father and son hug each other, laughing with pride. They will begin next season as a team in a two-up, just as in a *grand prix des gentlemen*. And so – except, alas, in the Burton family – another cycle of life would begin.

Chris Boardman, who became a national celebrity after he won an Olympic gold medal at Barcelona in 1992, had the right family background. His parents, Keith and Carol Boardman of the Birkenhead Victoria CC, were prominent Merseyside cyclists. Keith had begun racing in the mid-50s so was a near contemporary of Beryl Burton. He brought his son into the sport, encouraged him but gave him no special directions. The guidance came quite soon, and not from his father. Chris began time trialling in just the year when Burton stopped winning the top honours. In 1984, at the age of 15, he took the junior 25 championship with a 52.09.

An interesting contrast between Chris Boardman and Beryl Burton is in the way the two cyclists prepared for racing. Burton trained in ways that suited her habits, and she did not have a coach. Since she delighted in riding a bicycle Burton covered very many miles at any hour of the day: fast, but never in a gear above 70''. Boardman, on the other hand, turned to a coach immediately after his junior championship win in 1984. His mentor was Eddie Soens, a Liverpudlian former sergeant-major who had supervised many fast men since the 1940s. He was a motivator of a brusquely man-to-man sort. Soens died in 1986. Boardman then put himself under the tutelage of the sports scientist Peter Keen, who was a much younger man than Soens and had a modern approach. He tested – and trained – Boardman in laboratory conditions.

With Keen to guide him Boardman soon reached the heights. He was also helped by technology. The ultra-light, ultra-aerodynamic Lotus bicycle, with Chris in its saddle, was tested for hours at the Motor Institute Research Station. On this bike Boardman won the 1992 Olympic pursuit. After the Games his life suddenly changed. He had been a cabinet maker, was not always in work and worried about the bills for the small Wirral house where he lived with his wife and two children. Boardman came home from Barcelona in triumph and soon was paid £1,000 for an hour's work when he opened a new supermarket. It was obvious that he should become a professional cyclist.

Boardman, however, did not sign up as a full professional until the end of 1993. By that time he had the world record for the 'Hour': a solo 60-minute ride on the track. Keen, with the aid of computer programs, had been studying the Hour, with Boardman in mind, since 1990. His young amateur cyclist reported to Keen at his sports science laboratory, and the boffin (himself a former racing man) put all the numbers on a whiteboard. His student was quick to learn, but the prospect of the Hour was frightening. It is the ultimate time trialling test, and the pressure is mental as well as physical. You can't come second; you are the fastest man in the world, or nobody; you earn a fortune, or nothing. Wisely, Boardman also began to unburden himself to a sports psychologist. Their consultations are not recorded, but we do have Boardman's frank admissions:

To be absolutely honest, I actually don't like cycling. Cycling is just the medium that I have chosen. I am a natural competitor, and cycling is just the medium I have chosen for that. I don't ride a bike because I want to do well – I need to do well just to be normal. I don't think this is particularly healthy, but I think to be at the top in sport, especially this kind of sport, you have to be slightly mentally unbalanced . . .

*   *   *

In this interview Boardman was speaking of himself. Being a decent man, he was careful never to disparage a close rival who was indeed mentally unbalanced. The Scotsman Graeme Obree had taken the Hour record before Boardman. Obree's binge drinking, his fits of depression and suicide attempts were interwoven with amazing feats on the track. He appeared strange even to those who had no knowledge of his illnesses. Scientific training and dignified professionalism meant nothing to him. Before one record he stoked up with a meal of marmalade sandwiches, eaten at the trackside. Obree had a criminal record and a history of failure both in education and in his occasional employment in bike shops. But he was a good mechanic: Obree had built a bike for himself that incorporated parts from an old washing machine. Sometimes his handlebars were taken from a child's bike. That was because he had a most unorthodox position, hunched into himself, rather in the manner of a downhill skier. And on such a bicycle, at the track at Hamar in Norway, before a crowd of only a couple of dozen people, Obree covered 51.59 kilometres in 60 minutes. It was a new world record.

That was in July of 1993. Only six days later Boardman, riding the wooden indoor track at Bordeaux – and meticulously prepared in every way – rode 52.27 kilometres, a distance he and other riders have since bettered. Boardman is still the current record holder with 56.375 kms. He also holds the record for the 'Athlete's Hour'. This competition was introduced in 1996 because bicycles, and riders' positions on the bicycles, had become so *outré*. The 'Athlete's Hour' rules stipulate that the record must be attempted on a conventional bike with spoked wheels, dropped handlebars and round frame tubes.

Boardman's 'Athlete's Hour' record is 49.441 kms against his 'Absolute' distance of 56.375 kms, which shows how much can be gained by the use of space-age aerodynamic equipment. Nobody knows what the future of the Hour record might be. Boardman himself thinks that we are near the limit of human physical endeavour. If so, the 'Absolute' record will be exceeded with the help of technology. We have arrived at a crisis in cycle sport. If we look back now at the history of the Hour record we find, within half a century, a total cultural change, from the figure of Chronos on Fausto Coppi's alarm clock to the computers that record every stroke of Boardman's pedals and every beat of his heart. I begin my retrospective table with Obree's first record:

Graeme Obree	Hamar 1993	51.598
Francesco Moser	Mexico City 1984	51.151
Francesco Moser	Mexico City 1984	50.808
Eddy Merckx	Mexico City 1972	49.431
Ole Ritter	Mexico City 1968	48.653
Ferdinand Bracke	Rome 1967	48.093
Roger Rivière	Milan 1958	47.348
Roger Rivière	Milan 1957	46.923
Ercole Baldini	Milan 1956	46.393
Jacques Anquetil	Milan 1956	46.159
Fausto Coppi	Milan 1942	45.871

I don't list the other record breakers. The person who established the Hour record was Henri Desgrange, who in 1893 rode 35.325 kms at the Buffalo track in Paris. Now I make general and then specific comments on the post-war records. First, we may be absolutely sure that Boardman and Obree were free from drugs. However, we do know that some of the other riders admitted taking drugs. Second, the flurry of record attempts in the mid 1990s was the result of experiments in aerodynamics. Third, the choice of track obviously makes a difference to a record attempt. Fourth, and most important: the experience of the Hour is so horrible that we must salute the cyclists who have made the attempt. We also understand the reticence of champions – including Bernard Hinault, Greg Lemond and Lance Armstrong, all Tour de France winners and world champions – for whom the Hour has been too frightening a challenge.

Here are specific comments on the records:

Francesco Moser, 1984. He was a rider of the Classics who won Paris-Roubaix in three successive years (1978–80), was a world pursuit champion and a veteran of the six-day circuit. Moser made his Hour attempt in Mexico City because of its altitude. In the thin air you can go faster and use bigger gears. The track there was especially varnished for his attempt. Moser's bike was revolutionary. It had a carbon-fibre disk wheel at the back, which gave a flywheel effect, a smaller front wheel and low-profile frame and bars. Preparation for the record included 3,000 track kilometres and 2,000 kilometres in mountains around Mexico City. Moser climbed slowly, using his road bike's top gear. Then he used similar gears on the track. His first record was in $56 \times 15 = 100.8$; a few days later he rode in $57 \times 15 = 102.6$. The second ride was for the benefit of Italian fans who had flown to Mexico but had missed the first attempt.

Eddy Merckx, 1972. Merckx complained about Moser's 1984 equipment but in vain. The trend to high-tech bikes was irreversible and within a year bikes like Moser's were almost universal among top time triallists. In 1989 Greg Lemond won the Tour de France with tri-bars, now used by all riders against the clock, in the final time trial stage. Merckx's 1972 record was therefore the last on a conventional machine, apart from the 'Athlete's Hour'. Merckx went to Mexico only four days before his attempt. He had done little specific training for the Hour but had won 50 races that year, including the Giro d'Italia and the Tour de France. Unable to speak for half an hour after finishing his ride, he finally said 'never again' and later confessed that the Hour had taken more out of him than the three weeks of the French Tour.

Ole Ritter, 1968. This was the first attempt at high altitude. Ritter was a Danish-looking Dane who almost became an Italian. He lived in Italy and was prepared by Italian coaches. He made his final training rides with the Italian amateur track squad, who were in Mexico City for the Olympic Games.

Ferdinand Bracke, 1967. Bracke was the world pursuit champion in 1964 and 1969. His time trialling ability might have won him the 1968 Tour de France. Bracke was the first man to cover more than 48 kms for the Hour record, using the new Olympic track in Rome. In 1969 he failed to do better at altitude.

Roger Rivière, 1958 and 1957. As an ultra-talented new professional Rivière won Paris–Nice, the Dauphiné Liberé and the world professional pursuit championship in 1957, then at the end of the season tackled the Hour. As he was later quoted in *France-Dimanche*: 'I bettered the world hour record with the help of dope. I had to take stimulants for the heart and muscles. Five minutes before the start I had a big injection of amphetamine and solucamphor. During the attempt I had to take another five tablets because the injections would only work for forty minutes.' Rivière crashed when drugged in the 1960 Tour de France, never fully recovered, became addicted and died in 1976.

Ercole Baldini, 1956. The last amateur to take the professional Hour before Boardman in 1993. Baldini already held the amateur Hour record, with 44.870 kms. Earlier in 1956 he had won the Olympic road race.

Jacques Anquetil, 1956. This was after a failure in 1955, when he sat up with ten minutes to go. It was said that Anquetil loved Coppi too much to wish to break his record. Anquetil was better prepared the next year, but arrangements for the Hour were still haphazard at this period.

Fausto Coppi, 1942. As previously described. This had also been an ill-prepared record. Coppi could have improved on his distance during the years of his greatness but declined to make another attempt. The suffering might have shortened his career and his life. Note that Coppi believed that his many pursuits had tired him for road races; tired him not for a day or two but for months and years. To attempt an Hour record of around 50 kms means riding at pursuit pace (say, 4,000 metres in 4 mins 25 seconds), over and over again.

Chris Boardman and other recent Hour champions have had the benefit of expert coaches and concerned doctors. So they are more likely to survive without physical damage. You could say that the Hour record, after Anquetil beat Coppi's distance in 1956, entered a new and dangerous period which lasted about ten years. I personally think those ten years were the most malevolent in cycle sport, when cyclists had little idea about the drugs they were taking, did not know in what quantities they should inject themselves and had no one to guide them or help them to recover. With drugs in their bodies they became almost suicidal in their search for the Hour record, or the yellow jersey of the Tour de France; and this was the decade that formed the ambitions, and caused the death, of Tom Simpson.

XXXIX

Tom Simpson on the Ventoux.

I have mentioned J. B. Wadley's liking for British long-distance records and now point out that the writer's enthusiasm was shared by people whose thoughts were often elsewhere. Even young Leaguers with dark glasses and Italian road jerseys thought that place-to-place rides were a romantic test of sporting prowess. They admired record breakers even if they were on such an antiquated machine as a tandem trike.

Take a cyclist of a much later generation than Jock Wadley's, Tom Simpson. Wadley reports him as follows:

> I was about 16 at the time, and out with some of the lads on a Sunday run. We came across a dozen or so club chaps standing around an island near Ollerton. Thinking it might be a road race we stopped and asked what event it was. They said they were marshalling a record attempt by Crimes and Arnold on a tandem tricycle, and that they were due any minute now.
>
> We waited, expecting to see a pair of old codgers ambling along about 15 mph. Instead we saw two real athletes approaching at 25s on three wheels, taking the wide island on only two and leaning out like sidecar passengers, flattening out and tearing off down the road. That is one of my most thrilling memories of British cycling sport.

Most people under a certain age know of Tom Simpson only because of the way he died, on the thirteenth stage of the Tour de France in 1967. Older cyclists not only recollect his death, reported on television news at 9 p.m. that evening, but also collect information about our old and once familiar champion. I like the story about the A1 at Ollerton. Veterans know why we so often hang around at roundabouts to see other cyclists for twenty seconds. Simpson (born 1937) would have been an old man today, had he lived. And in old age I think he would always have celebrated the riders of his youth. They brought him up; and then they inspired him because he could beat them.

Albert Crimes and John Arnold – like Simpson himself – were extraordinary men who came from underprivileged families in the north of England. Crimes was from Cheshire. His club was the Crewe Clarion Wheelers. Arnold's home was just north of Manchester, and he was in the Middleton CC. Tom Simpson, on the occasion he describes, would have seen them on the Great North Road in 1953, the year when the two tricyclists had decided to make their combination.

Although he had been born in Haswell, Co. Durham, Tom Simpson's home was in Harworth, on the Nottinghamshire–Yorkshire border. The Simpsons were a mining family. They had moved to Harworth because the Durham coal seams were exhausted and there was no more work. Tom Simpson is often described as a Yorkshireman but, technically, he wasn't. I associate him with the Carlton country north of Nottingham, where the Dukeries and Sherwood Forest are almost side by side with pit villages. Chris Sidwells, who is Tom's nephew, believes that he had the further north-east in his character. In Co. Durham, he relates, there was a tradition of working-class comedians. Tom's father, when he was not at the colliery, ran a working men's club where aspiring comics were given their chance. I suppose that the father's night job encouraged the son's clownishness and helped him to be welcomed in the bars and cafes of east Flanders. These are also working men's clubs, but not so dismal and ingrown.

Jock Wadley's little tale about Crimes and Arnold points us to other characteristics of the sixteen-year-old Tom. There's the fascination with speed and daring, then a hint that he was watching a motorcycle race, even a car race. Very fast cars driven furiously were shortly to be Simpson's obsession. In this he resembles Reg Harris, who was an influence on Simpson's attitudes. They met at the Fallowfield track in 1956, just after Harris's retirement. Now that he was no longer racing, Harris gave the ultra-talented teenager lessons in trackcraft. Otherwise he would have kept his knowledge to himself.

Possibly Reg Harris's only direct pupil, Simpson never became a miner. He worked as an apprentice draughtsman until he turned professional in late 1958. His first bike was an ASP. Then he was able to borrow a Carlton, then to possess one, then to purchase continental equipment as he turned from the Harworth CC, his first club, towards the Scala Wheelers, whose members were much more inclined towards the BLRC.

The League showed Tom Simpson that his future lay far away from the Carlton country in which he had been raised. At the same time he was a typical though exceptional British cyclist. He didn't ride many road races in his amateur years. Simpson won local 25s but did not enter events of the longer time-trial distances. He became a young champion of that intense track event, the pursuit, which drains a rider in four minutes. As a trackman in this discipline Tom represented his country in the 1956 Olympic Games and the 1958 Commonwealth Games. He was also a hill-climb champion. That is significant. It means that Simpson knew how to use every bit of energy his body possessed before being helped from his bike by the 'catchers' at the finish line.

BLRC North Midlands Division Junior Hill-Climb Champion, 1954, when he was just sixteen, National Junior Hill-Climb Champion, 1955, BLRC Hill-Climb Champion, 1957. These triumphs foreshadow Simpson's death a decade later, as if his death were pre-ordained by the nature of his talent. Tom was very fast but not a pure sprinter. Unbeatable in a short-distance time trial, he had limited knowledge of tactical riding in a bunch. He invented his own intensive training and made other people help him. For instance, there was a two-up 100-mile ride up and down the Great North Road, every Saturday, with a suffering clubmate: bit and bit, one behind the other, over and through, no question of conversation, about four and a half hours of effort. Then Simpson's mate would go to bed. Tom would wash and have his tea before an evening's weight training in a local gym.

Tom Simpson hated moderation, which meant losing. The skinny kid, like his adult self, was utterly a winner and desolate in defeat. Nobody in the world was less equipped to be a *domestique*. He drove himself until he fell or broke down. Second places were the worst results in any competition, and no danger could moderate Simpson's will to be first. He crashed a lot – more than a professional should, for people in the bunch around you may also fall from their bikes when you do.

But Tom was reckless in any situation. He could be crazy with excitement when descending an Alpine pass in the rain, or gleeful with consumerism when he walked into an Alfa-Romeo saleroom. There was unbalanced greed for the things that money might buy: cars, furniture, suits, houses, but especially cars. When I brood on Tom's tastes he often reminds me of a modern footballer rather than a cyclist. His popularity was also rather modern, on the continent. The French and Belgians didn't mind his unfunny jokiness, the comic bowler hats, the demand that he should always be the centre of attention. They had never seen such a cyclist before.

People wanted to be with Tom. Women were thrilled. Men thought that they might not only be his friend but his brother or father. When he died it was like the bereavement of a very large family. British cycling is familial. That is why Simpson is remembered in a personal way and why there are still disputes about, for instance, who his friends were, who loved him best, who looked after him best; and it is the family of British cyclists who take part in the communal celebratory rides, the memorial road race held in Harworth every year, and make the thousands of expeditions to the memorial on Mont Ventoux. The marble block set in concrete is maintained in decent order by subscriptions from British clubfolk.

The cyclists who honour the departed Tom often know little about his career. I think that the origin of British pride in Simpson comes from his rise from modest surroundings to the height of European sport. This ascent might be called a leap. We first see Tom as a teenager riding the grass and cinder tracks of the north of England, winning local 25s, then starting a bright future in pursuiting. He's a Leaguer, an enthusiast, a young man of undoubted talent and charisma. But the Scala Wheelers, based in Rotherham, are not at the centre of the world. Tom is going to be a draughtsman, that typical cyclist's job; he is living with his mum and dad and thinking of ways to avoid National Service.

And then, he leapt. Simpson got a continental professional licence at the end of 1958, was recruited to the Rapha-Geminiani team and in 1959, his first full year as a pro, came fourth in the world road championship. Later in 1959 he took part in the Baracchi Trophy two-up time trial in north Italy. Among the other entries was Fausto Coppi, riding for nearly the last time. So Tom Simpson from Harworth had become world class and was in the same company as the great Italian *campionissimo* whose poster had been on the walls of the teenager's bedroom, back in Festival Avenue.

Apart from his natural ability and huge will, Simpson had other advantages when he made his leap. First of all he was indebted to his future wife Helen, whom he had met in Brittany in 1958 and would marry in January 1961. Secondly, Tom had the knack of getting advice from older cyclists, especially Brian Robinson, also in the Rapha-Geminiani team. Thirdly, Simpson had Ghent, where he and Helen made their home. Tourists probably know the Flemish city's medieval centre. Cross the railway tracks to the north-east and you will find another Ghent. Here Albert Beurick had his bar, Den Engel – a centre of cycling life. Beurick became Tom's protector, his second father. The loving cafe proprietor also became a father to Helen Simpson, so often alone while her husband pursued his life – and his death – as a racing cyclist.

* * *

Simpson raced on the European continent for eight years, always as Ghent's adopted son. His best wins had authority and panache. They always came in one-day classics: the Tour of Flanders in 1961, Bordeaux–Paris in 1963, Milan–San Remo in 1964, the world championship and also the Tour of Lombardy in 1965. Some failures were as memorable as the successes. In 1960 he did a 'suicide break' in Paris–Roubaix and was eventually caught only a couple of kilometres from the finish at the Roubaix velodrome. This was the first time that live television had followed 'L'Enfer du Nord', capturing a long solo breakaway that made him a hero throughout Europe. The immense publicity helped Tom to overcome his tears.

* * *

Tom Simpson should have concentrated on the classics and track racing. More specifically, he should have been a Belgian cyclist. He was accepted and liked by the country's top professionals, who were a combative group. His adopted city of Ghent gave him many a civic reception after his victories; his wife was busy in the quite large English community; he had interests in property in the Ghent suburbs and knew how to make Belgian money. Simpson could have become an even richer man by riding sixes. The world professional pursuit championship could have been his. There was also – though we are in the era of Anquetil and Merckx – the possibility of the Hour record. Tom's ambition would not allow him such targets; for the Tour de France was the biggest and hardest race of all, and that is why he wanted to win it.

Simpson rode the Tour seven times. This is what happened to him:

> 29th, 1960
> Abandoned stage 3, 1961
> 6th, 1962
> 14th, 1964
> Abandoned stage 20, 1965
> Abandoned stage 17, 1966
> Died stage 13, 1967.

This is not comparable with the standard set by the greatest racing cyclists. Tom's middling results and abandonments were the result of crashes, ill fortune or, mostly, insufficient strength. His body was built for one-day racing and his mind looked always for immediate opportunities. Magnificent though he was, Simpson did not have the physique or the temperament of a 'man of the Tour'. Let us match him against his contemporaries. In the years before 1967 he had ridden in the *grande boucle* against the following overall winners: Gastone Nencini, 1960; Jacques Anquetil, 1961; Jacques Anquetil, 1962; Jacques Anquetil, 1964; Felice Gimondi, 1965; and Lucien Aimar, 1966. Runners-up or potential winners in those years were, among others, Roger Rivière, Charly Gaul, Raymond Poulidor, Federico Bahamontes and Jan Janssen. All of them, apart perhaps from Rivière, were riders who could race for three weeks and never have a bad day: or, if they encountered a *jour sans*, then they had a strong team to see them through the bad patch.

Simpson's attempts to win the Tour de France must be seen in the context provided by such men – formidable opponents who had a lot of support. In 1967 Simpson had a team of British riders who were devoted to him. But six out of the team's ten members were riding their first Tour. Several abandoned during the first week. As the Tour approached the Alps

Simpson was aided by his close friend Vin Denson, Colin Lewis, Arthur Metcalfe and Barry Hoban. They were terrific riders, but Tom was mainly on his own.

So his strategy for the Tour was to ride with a mixture of caution – as everyone had recommended – and bravado, which was his own style. The plan was to attack on the Galibier stage, to attack again on the Ventoux stage and then to win the time trial. In this way, Simpson reckoned, he could ride into Paris wearing the yellow jersey.

He was in a satisfactory sixth place on General Classification as the Tour entered the Alps. Then the Galibier stage became a disaster. Simpson had been riding well but had lost strength as a result of stomach problems. He was vomiting and had diarrhoea. He came to a halt on the Galibier mountain, climbed off the bike, retched and spat, took down his shorts. At the end of the stage Harry Hall, the British team's mechanic, cleaned Tom's bike. It was 'covered in shit', he said. Vin Denson and the other members of the English party gave what help they could. 'I remember when we finished,' Denson recalled, 'we had to carry him up the stairs. He was ill and couldn't eat. I was telling him "have some soup, some broth"; he just said "I'm going to be sick" but the next morning he was as bright as a button.'

How ill was Tom Simpson and what killed him? We have some medical records and much anecdotal evidence. Memories vary. English books about Simpson do not quote the account of Lucien Aimar, who had won the Tour in the previous year and was a wise cyclist. I quote his recollections in the original French: 'Je savais par un équipier, Vin Denson, que Simpson était épuisé et que cela faisait douze jours qu'il ne s'alimentait plus que sous perfusion, parce qu'il ne pouvait plus avaler. C'est la faiblesse qui l'a tué.'

What was this *perfusion*? (The English word is 'perfusion' too.) It means moisture or liquid that is poured over something. Therefore it is the opposite of 'infusion', when something is covered or steeped in liquid. I do not understand how Simpson was being fed if he could not swallow (*avaler*), and do not know what was wrong with him. Most likely he took food in liquid form and was injected with vitamins and God knows what else. That kept him going. Was he being weighed? There was some sort of birdlike magic in his skeletal but immensely athletic body; and in addition there was the determination of mind that, as Denson says, made him 'bright as a button' on the morning after a collapse.

'Douze jours', says Lucien Aimar. He must mean the twelve days before the thirteenth stage, the climb over the Ventoux where Simpson died. The cyclist's body had not been functioning properly for nearly a fortnight. Tom was riding against illness as well as the heat, the mountains and his opponents. Among those rivals was Aimar, who liked Simpson. Towards the top of the Ventoux they were side by side. There was a bit of a battle, for they were in a race. But Aimar thought that Simpson was going wild in such conditions, in fearful heat and after 20 kilometres of climbing. He told Tom to take it easy, 'fais pas le con', and offered him water from his own feeding bottle. Then a point came when Simpson could no longer follow the Frenchman's wheel. Aimar heard a cry behind him but did not see Simpson fall.

Aimar did not know what was happening. Neither did the British party. Colin Lewis, Vin Denson and Arthur Metcalfe were well down the mountain. Alec Taylor, the team manager, and Harry Hall, the mechanic, were in a car behind Simpson, who was in sixth or seventh place as they approached the summit. Then Taylor and Hall saw him veering all over the road. Hall recounts:

> I was worried that he might go into the side or over the edge. Eventually, he ran into the side and fell against the bank. I got to him and said 'It's finished for you, Tom', and I undid his straps. He said, 'No, put me back on my bike. I must go on.' So I started to push him.

The toe-straps were still loose. Tom's last words were 'The straps, Harry! The straps!' He rode a couple of hundred metres, then fell off again. Taylor and Hall did what they could with their unconscious friend and hero. Doctor Dumas arrived. Then a helicopter flew down. It was too late. Tom was dead.

*   *   *

All thereafter was confusion, weeping and that blank loss of memory that sometimes accompanies shock and grief. Many riders could not afterwards remember what they said or did when the news of Tom's death came to the stage town of Carpentras. The peloton comforted the British riders as best they could. But after the tears and hugs, what else could they do? They wanted one of Tom's teammates to be given the next stage as a gesture, a token, a gift. Vin Denson was the nominee, but Vin scarcely knew what he was doing. Barry Hoban freewheeled over the finishing line. It scarcely mattered. The death on the Ventoux would have a long aftermath.

Without a doubt, professional cyclists in such an exhausting and terrible race as the Tour de France should have the constant care of properly qualified doctors. Instead, the riders' hotels were filled with the *soigneurs*, suppliers and quacks who trifled with the health of gullible young men at the limits of their strength. In 1967 it was soon learnt that ampoules of drugs had been found in Simpson's road jersey. Our guess is that Simpson should have had a doctor from the start of the race and that he would not have ridden himself to death if he had not taken amphetamines. On this subject, as always, the *coureurs* of the Tour de France are evasive. They bluster, they make up half-truths and they never blame each other.

XL

Father and son, the past and the future.

In 1967 the cycling community was much smaller than it had been in the mid-1950s, which now appears to have been the golden age of British cycling. We know what happened. In the 1960s cycling declined as other social forces defined the tone of the times. Motoring became a normal part of life and there was no prosperity in the cycle trade. No modern teenager would have dreamt of joining older cyclists on a club run and young people saw no point in exploring the lanes. Television had made the whole world an immediate spectacle. New attitudes to leisure and entertainment did not include the bike. Racing cycling – especially maybe after the victory of English football in the 1966 World Cup – seemed old-fashioned. And, in truth, cycling was a slightly antique way of approaching the world.

For all these reasons the 1960s produced fewer cyclists. The depression in club life was most acute in London. In the provinces the decline was mixed. The old ways went on in, for instance, rural and remote East Anglia (where, in the twenty-first century, many clubmen still ride a fixed wheel). There were variations in other parts of the country – countries, if we include Ireland, Scotland and Wales. It's said that a 'backwardness' in Irish cycling culture gave Sean Kelly and Stephen Roche to the world. People might argue that, in the 1970s, Scotland – Glasgow in particular – was 'backward' in this way. I do not know. But you would need to be a hard man of the old school to go up the road with the Glasgow Wheelers.

By the 1970s many cyclists had given up. A lovely fact is that so many of them later returned. There is no parallel in other sports. The cycling expression is that they had been 'out'. I have encountered dozens of people of this sort and am myself of their number. How rueful veteran racing cyclists are about the years when they were out, and how similar are their stories about wasted years, the depression of middle age, the increasingly bourgeois jobs, the houses and wives and children and bosses! People who were once out often mention smoking. 'Tim, do you remember when we put a shilling in a jam jar after a good ride, just to give thanks to the bike and to save up for tubulars?' I certainly did remember that practice. 'I knew I had to come back. I'd been out for thirteen years. First I gave up smoking and put all the cigarette money aside. Then I got a frame, then the other bits. I went off like a boy and thirty miles later collapsed with the bonk. Luckily there was a telephone nearby. The wife came to get me.'

People who have been out often reckon that they are reborn as youths. They are right. Youth is what they deserve. Old bikies are the avant garde of the elderly, living by the cycling motto 'We're all young on the bike'. They are quite dramatic old people, often argumentative, and early retirement has boosted their style. Look for them in the spring. The old cyclists' tea places have closed down, so now they congregate in those cafes in the larger garden centres. They wear bright cycling clothing with foreign advertisements in different styles of typography. Why are they so bronzed at Easter time? Because these veteran racing cyclists have spent the last two months on the roads of Majorca, where there is sunshine and the cost of living is about the same as in Lowestoft or London or Liverpool.

What a fine army of new anarchism might be recruited from these retired Leaguers. One bond is our common generation. We came into the bike game in the decade after 1945, left in the 1960s and began again in the 1970s and 1980s. There are hundreds and maybe thousands of us. We do as we will. No one dares oppose us. Our fortitude is nourished by dislike of officialdom, daily miles and shared memories. My own experience of being out is typical. First there were seven or eight

377

years of Golden Virginia and occasional, increasingly difficult excursions from central London (forty minutes before the traffic lights were left behind). Then my only bike was stolen. I went to parties every night and was as out as out could be.

My good fortune was that a charming deity looked after me and gave me a wink. She was and is the goddess of cycling, or maybe of communism of the Jean-and-Riri sort, or – who can say, apart from me? – the same divinity who is Fanny Hill's ghost and who once, disguised as a chambermaid, took Robert Blatchford into her attic bed at the Eagle in Wrentham and thus helped to mother the Clarion movement.

My protectress was amused by unorthodox interest in poetry. So she gave me an epiphany, one of four in my life. I was rubbing and sudding at the sink in St Alphonsus Road, Clapham, when I noticed the detergent packet's claims. All difficult stains could be overcome, even though they had been caused by

BLOOD, EGG, BLACKBERRY, GRASS

It had been rumoured since the early 1960s that poets made their daily living by writing advertising slogans. Maybe I had come across the work of such a person. In any case the four-word poem sent me wild with resolution. Why was I still pretending that I might have a career and take the chair at faculty meetings? Why wasn't I out there with the people who smirched their clothes with blood and blackberry? Unruly children, gypsies, poachers, amateur cooks – free people who laughed as they rolled over each other in summertime meadows. That was a world or a dream that had always attracted me. So on that day in Clapham I decided that I would be out no longer.

First I spent everything in the bank on a bike. Then I cautiously got the legs back into action. My routines resembled those of many cyclists in my part of south London. Half an hour on the rollers, three circuits of Richmond Park, expeditions to Shoreham or Box Hill, all leading to the challenge of the Catford CC Reliability Trial. This is small stuff, compared with racing, but when you're on the bike every day you feel different – wonderful! – and the prospect of a time trial can't be far away, and then the welcome to further testing, and the advanced study of village halls.

My folly was that I did not immediately go to Belgium. I could have learnt about Eddy Merckx, whose racing life was then (around 1976) coming to its end. He is a peerless example of the way that some Belgians are natural aristocrats, while remaining creatures of the suburbs. It amazes me that, to this day, so few British cyclists go to live in Ghent or other Belgian cities. We have been held in the grip of ancient England, the village hall our prison. In the 1970s and 1980s, on motorway-type roads around Oxford and Boroughbridge in Yorkshire, there were new champions and ever-faster times. But in club life little had changed. It was like returning to a school in which you had once been a pupil. The same elderly people were still running the sport's governing bodies. Drawings by Frank Patterson were the ornament of touring articles in *Cycling*. Reg Harris returned to competition, as a sort of *jeu d'esprit*, and in the national championships beat sprinters who were thirty years his junior.

That was in 1974. Harris had then been out for fourteen years. I was not sure whether cycling was a contemporary sport. Most of the competitors in time trials were veterans, i.e. over forty years of age. They still are, though now there is an even larger percentage of older riders. Many of them are those laughing desperadoes you find in garden centres. What stories they have to tell: 'Old Jack McClaren rode a trike until he died at the age of ninety. He was in the Kings Lynn CC. Jack was shot at dawn by a farmer when he was riding the North Road 24. The farmer thought he was a bird. That was when we first had road jerseys in club colours. Not a good idea to dress up as a pheasant. Anyway Jack wouldn't complain to the police, though an ambulance came . . .'

All old wheelmen like such stories, which is why there is – or was – such a cycling folklore. Our tradition of conversation combines rumour, memory and pedantry. Everyone has a collection of tales. Sometimes I wrote down things I'd heard, on the basis that cycling was about knowledge as well as good spirits. But it was impossible to be systematic: human relations come before writing. I thought that pilgrimages would be the best way to relive cycling history. A girl – from Balliol! – has telephoned to invite me to the Isle of Man. That would be easier than all my expeditions in the past years to mountain passes in the Pyrenees, and once again I could sail over to Irish roads.

The likelihood is that I will retrace old rides in the home counties. Recently I went to the junior road race championships, held that year (2000) on a course to the east of Stevenage, mostly on good B roads. The lads covered a 13-mile circuit seven times. My idea was to have a look at Bradley Wiggins, who was the favourite, and so was marked out of the race. Yanto Barker won in fine style. Nowadays he's doing well on the continent and so of course is Brad, who in 2003 became the world pursuit champion.

*   *   *

I was in a spot by the race's only *prime*, what they call a passing place, one of those sandy, gravelly or muddy bits of land carved from the sides of roads so that cars can get on with their business. At this point there were about twenty other spectators, mostly the laughing and proud parents of the riders, one or two of them with video cameras. The junior championship is always a happy family occasion. I was lying down in the passing place with nothing to read, just a few clouds to look at in the blue sky. No planes.

That August Sunday was like a pre-war day – or easy to imagine as pre-war because the ridge above Walkern, which is where we were, gives a view over a valley, watered by the River Beane, which possesses the Hertfordshire characteristic of seeming to be typical of rural old England and therefore of many places within old England, while offering no specific clue about where one might in actual fact be standing. Or lying, in my case. At that period I was prone to weeping fits. With so much distress in life there was some comfort in making a mental map of Hertfordshire and its skies.

A youth approached me as I lay in the passing place and showed concern. He asked if I had a son in the race. The nice boy offered me a drink from a feeding bottle filled from a huge container of some vitamin liquid. He was going to hand up bottles as the riders momentarily relaxed after the *prime*. The boy was down from Northumberland to support two clubmates who were in the championship. The next year, he thought, he would himself be strong enough to take part. We chatted about training and cyclists from his part of the world. He told me that his future would be in cycling. Rarely have I seen a young person look so eager and happy. It was wrong to enquire whether my new friend had any prospects in higher education: he had already left school. He wanted a new bike and could get the money because he would soon be starting a job. 'I'm going to be a postman!'

INDEX

Abrams, Sir Adolph 285
Addiscombe Cycling Club 294
Adkins, Eddie 28
Aimar, Lucien 66, 67, 371,
    372–3
Amstel Gold 164
Anquetil, Jacques 243, *314*
    character 317–21; Coppi,
    relationship with 207, 316,
    319, 321; diet 317–18;
    drug use 319, 323; gears
    346; Grand Prix des
    Nations 317–19, 346;
    Hour 363, 370; Isle of
    Man Week (1959) 23;
    journalism 319–20;
    Olympic Games (1952)
    245; photographs 309, 319;
    retirement 323; Tour de
    France 66, 232, 320–1,
    371; Tour of Lombardy
    167
Anslow, Chris 52
Archambaud, Maurice 72, 105,
    121–2, 160, 300
Argentin, Moreno 67
Armstrong, Lance 66, 361
Army Cycling Union 343
Arnold, John 285, 366

ASPs (All Spare Parts) 8, 93,
    367
Athletic Club de Boulogne-
    Billancourt 261
Atkins, Edith 292–3, 294
Atkins, John 293
Atkins, Ron 292, 293
Augendre, Jacques 299
Autodrome de Monthléry
    242
Azuréen 91, 103–9

Bahamontes, Federico 23, 231,
    232, 310, 320, 371
Baldassari, Jean 22
Baldini, Ercole 22, 363
Bannister, Roger 344
Baracchi Trophy (1959) 302–3,
    369
Barbotin, Pierre 203
Barker, Yanto 380
Barnet Cycling Club 23, 347
Bartali, Gino 166, *190*, 200
    advertising 256; attends
    Coppi's funeral 316; Coppi,
    contrasted with 191–8;
    Coppi, rivalry with 113,
    116–17, 118, 121, 122–3,
    124, 125, 126, 128, 222,

Bartali, Gino – *cont.*
300; photographs 309;
Tour de France 159,
205–6, 212, 213, 217,
219, 220, 223
Bartoli, Michèle 177–8, 179
Bastide, Roger 219
Bates Cycles 92, 147–8, 151
Bates, E. G. 'Basher' 92, 147
Bath Road Club 344
Beasley, John 200, 232
Beckett, Samuel 248–9, 260
Bedwell, Dave 241
Belgium 98, 120, 163, 164,
171, 174–9, 180, 182,
186, 193, 303, 304
Belle Vue Cycling Club 340
Benac, Gaston 317
Benacre Hall 42
Berigliano, Italo 298–9
Berlemont, Gaston 54, 55
Berlemont, Victor 54, 56
Bert, Raymond le 207, 221
Beurick, Albert 369–71
Beving, Paul 172
Bianchi 8, 92, 93, 122, 227
Bicester 334
Bidlake, Frederick Thomas
334–8
Bidot, Marcel 222
Binda, Alfredo 91
Birkenhead Victoria Cycling
Club 357
Birmingham CTC 8, 87
Bizzi, Olimpio 116, 121
Blackwell, H. 275
Blakelock, Eric 266

Blatchford, Robert *39*, 43–4,
46, 53, 82, 378
Blunden, Edmund 97–9
Boardman, Carol 357
Boardman, Chris 342, 343, *356*,
357–61, 363
Boardman, Keith 357
Bobet, Jean 197, 221–2, 231–2
Bobet, Louison *162*, 197, *199*,
201–4
attends Coppi's funeral 316;
Baracchi Trophy (1959)
303–4, 369; career crisis
224; character 206–10,
228; diet 207–9, 318;
finances 243–4; French
amateur road champion
(1946) 202, 203; Isle of
Man Week (1959) 19, 23,
24–5; mental strength
205–6; Paris–Roubaix
(1955) 300, 301–2;
Paris–Roubaix (1956) 184;
reputation 220–1; Tour de
France 66, 159, 184, 201;
Tour de France (1947)
203–4; Tour de France
(1948) 205–6; Tour De
France (1949) 206; Tour
de France (1950) 212, 213,
215, 217, 219, 220; Tour
de France (1952) 221;
Tour de France (1953)
222–5, 227, 228–30; Tour
de France (1954) 231;
Tour de France (1955)
231, 232, 233, 235–6,

237, 239, 242, 243–4;
training 206–10, 211;
world professional road
championship (1954) 202
Boeda, Janine 319
Booty, Ray 340, 342–7
Bordeaux–Paris 163, 370
Bracke, Ferdinand 362
Brambilla, Pierre 160, 161
Brankart, Jean 232, 233, 308
Breedon, Bas 333
Brighton–Glasgow (1945) 59
British League of Racing
Cyclists 38, 49–62, 63, 73,
79, 87, 89, 90, 94, 116,
245, 268, 346, 365, 367,
369, 377
British professional team 154–5
Brittain, Stan 245
Bruhat, Jean 254–5, 256, 257
Buckshee Wheelers 33–4,
99–100
Bull, Trevor 333
Burman, Albert 8–9
Burman, Gwen 9
Burman, Joan 9
Burton, Beryl 28, 294, 342,
350, 351–5, 357
Burton, Charlie 352, 355
Burton, Denise 352, 355
But et club 96
Butler, Claud 93, 153
Buzzati, Dino 123–4, 126–7

Calder Clarion Cycling Club 47
Campagnolo 93, 94, 279
Canonbury Bicycle Club 275

Capa, Robert 309
Carbutt, Paul 276, 277, 278–9,
280
Carline, Nim 352–4
Carlton Cycles 148, 149–50,
151–2, 153, 154, 367
Carrea, Andrea 312
Cartwright, Cyril 339
Casartelli, Fabio 166
Catford Cycling Club 75, 378
Cavanna, Biagio *110*, 114–15,
116, 121, 207, 311, 318
Championnat de Zurich 120
Chesterfield Spire Road Club 17
Chichester 40–2
Church Gresley Miners' Welfare
Sports Club 144–5
Civil Servants' Motoring
Association 11
Clague, Curwen 19, 22, 23, 24
Clague, Desmond 23
Clarion Cycling Clubs 17, 44–7,
76, 293, 327, 335, 378
Clarion, The 43, 44–5, 46, 53,
82
Clasica San Sebastian 163, 164,
303–4
classic races 164–72 *see also under*
individual event name
Clay Cross and Danesmoor
Miners' Welfare Association
144
Cofidis team 178
Commonwealth Games (1958)
367
Communist Party of Great
Britain 2–3, 265–6, 267

Conisborough Ivanhoe Cycling
Club 333
Coppi, Bruna 219, 311, 315
Coppi, Fausto 8, 68, *110*, *119*,
166, *191*, *259*, *314*, 325
aids Franco-Italian post-war
relations 299–300; alarm
clock 113, 134, 360;
Anquetil, relationship with
317, 318–19, 322; Baracchi
Trophy (1959) 303–4;
Bartali, contrasted with
191–8, 200; Bartali, rivalry
with 113, 116–17, 118,
121, 122–3, 124, 125,
126, 128, 222; body shape
113, 220; career record
128–9; character 207, 210,
219; collapses 218–20; dark
glasses 115–16; death
316–17; debut 116–17;
downfall, role of press in
306–13; early life 111–13;
extra-marital affair 310–13,
315; fans 220; Giro d'Italia
(1940) 117–18; Giro
d'Italia (1949) 128;
greatest achievements 128;
Hour 121–2, 363; injuries
212; Isle of Man Week
(1959) 19, 23, 25; last part
of career 243, 261–2, 263,
298–303; legacy 316;
osteoporosis 113;
Paris–Roubaix (1955) 301,
302–3; photographs 30,
96–7, 198, 309, 313–14,
316; pursuits 128; Reg
Harris, comparisons with
131, 133; Tour de France
(1947) 159; Tour de
France (1948) 161, 193–4;
Tour de France (1949)
128, 206; Tour de France
(1951) 217, 218, 219–20,
221; Tour de France
(1952) 128; Tour de
Lombardy 167; training
113–15, 207, 326; war
years 120–2; world road
championship (1953) 314
Corriere della sera 123–9
Coventry Cycling Club 282,
283, 284, 292
Coventry Road Club 292
Crewe Clarion Wheelers 366
Cricket Country (Blunden) 97–9
Crimes, Albert 285, 366
Criterium National 97
CTC Gazette 12, 81
cycling:
advertising 132, 256, 279;
amateur roots 23–4; art
81–6; coarse fishing and
351; collapse of industry
279; development of
professional 61; drugs and
68, 79, 198, 255, 321,
323, 361, 362, 363; fans
98, 220, 229–30; finances
of professional 243–4;
future of 380–1; golden
age 376–7; holidays 100;
journalism 86–7, 111–12,

304–5, 307–14, 320–1; Labour movement, links with 9–10; music and 127–8; nicknames 203, 216, 224; old-timer legend 77–8; 'out' of, reaction to being 376–8; pastoralism in 97–9; photographs 30, 96–7, 198, 290, 309–11, 313–14, 319, 334, 345; poetry and 72, 73–9, 81, 89–92, 127, 378; rolling-road mythology 76–9, 81; social class, politics and 3, 27–31, 44–6, 59–60, 352; training 113–15, 207, 208–10, 247, 268, 326–7, 353–5, 357–63; war veterans 100; women and 280, 282–90, 292–7; year 14–25

Cycling 9, 11–12, 53, 81, 84, 87, 334, 336, 337, 338, 379

Cycling is Such Fun! 87

Cyclists Touring Club 8–10, 32, 51, 81, 82, 87

cycling clubs, British 8–9, *26*, 32–3
    calendar 14–25; Clarion movement *see* Clarion Cycling Clubs; lectures 10–12; list of 33–8; magazines 76; *see also under individual club name*

cyclo-cross 9, 17, 160, 170, 180, 293

Daily Express 60

Daily News 86–7

Daily Worker 42–3

Darrigade, André 23, 24–5, 207, 233, 243, 319

Dauphiné Liberé 97, 362

Dawson, Mary 295

de Gaulle, Charles 201

Defillipis, Nino 299

Dejeante, Jean 249–53, 265, 378

Dejeante, Riri 249–53, 265, 378

Den Engel 369–70

Denham, Susie 294

Denson, Vin 372, 373, 374

Derksen, Ian 145, 261

Desgrange, Henri 72, 103, 158, 360–1

diet and supplements *see also* drugs 198, 207–9, 318–19
    'bonk bags', 79, 208; 'speed mixture' 79

Dinnington Colliery Institute 145

Doisneau, Robert 309

Donegan, Alo 338

Donovan, Dennis 139–40

Dougherty, Ralph 338–9

Dousset, Daniel 319

Dow, Ian 328

Drage, Joy 294

Dredge, Lillian 54, 287

Duckworth, Colin 248

Duffield, David 285

Dumas, Pierre 239, 375

Dunlop 132

Ealing Cycling Club 57–8
Ealing Paragon Cycling Club
    57–8
Earls Court Cycle Show 284
Edwards, Frank 28
Elliot, Shay 261
end-to-enders 275–80 *see also
    under individual event
    name*
Engers, Alf 23, 28, 348–9
England, H. H. 84, 336, 337
Ericsson Wheelers 340, 343,
    344

Fachtleitner, Edouard 159, 161
Fallowfield 145–6
Fignon, Laurent 160
First World War 46, 56, 85–6,
    99, 186, 191
Flèche Wallonne 164, 182–3,
    215
Fleming, George 340
Forestier, Jean *297*, 300, 301,
    302, 303
Frantz, Nicolas 232, 236
French amateur road
    championship:
(1946) 202, 203
(1953) 227
French national team 91,
    103–9, 159, 201, 203,
    207, 224, 322

Gaul, Charly *211*, 232–6, 237,
    243, 320, 371
Gazetta dello Sport 117, 306
gears, 93, 94, 234–5, 289, 346–7

Geminiani, Raphael 23, 160,
    212, 213, 217, 222, 224,
    225, *226*, 227–8, 231, 234,
    243, 256, 315, 316
Ghent-Wevelgem 164
Gimondi, Felice 180–1, 371
Giro d'Italia 97, 166, 306, 316,
    362
  (1936) 117; (1937) 117;
    (1938) 117; (1939) 118;
    (1940) 117–18; (1948)
    193; (1949) 123–8;
    (1950) 117; (1952)
    128, 221; (1953) 129,
    312–13; (1955) 301;
    (1958) 22; (1967) 180;
    (1987) 148; (1993) 166;
    (1998) 68
Glasgow Wheelers 376
Goddet, Jacques 103, 158,
    212–13, 214, 215, 238,
    256
Godeau, Roger *246*, 248–54,
    260, 261
Grand Prix de Cannes 241
Grand Prix des Champions 243
Grand Prix des Minimes 242
Grand Prix des Nations 97, 179,
    316
  (1932) 317; (1946) 318;
    (1947) 318; (1953) 317,
    318, 346
Grand Prix de Nice (1957) 245

Hall, Harry 61, 372–4
Harmon, C. A. 275
Harris, Joyce 295

Harris, Reg 78, *129*, 130–4, 135, 136, 138, 139–42, 144, 145–6, 154, 261, 367, 379
Harworth Cycling Club *13*, 367
Hassenforder, Roger 222–4
haystack nights 76–7
Hercules Cycles 245, 283, 284, 285, 287, 292
Herne Hill 17, 139, 140, 145, 298, 299, 338
Het Nieuwsblad 303
Het Volk 164, 304
Higgins, Fred 92
Higginson, Bernard 339
Higginson, Stanley 339, 348
Hill Special 327
Hill, Adam 327
Hill, Christopher 267
hill climbs 14–16, 22, 51–2 *see also under individual event name*
Hill, Fanny 266–8, 378
Hilton, John James 2
Hilton, Margaret *1*, 4–5, 265, 266
Hilton, Rodney *1*, 2–3, 4, 5
Hinault, Bernard 65, 157, 167, 177, 182, 184, 361
Hinds, Jim 23
Hoar, Tony 241, 242, 243
Hoban, Barry 47, 182, 372, 374
Hoban, Joe 47
Holdsworth, W. F. 93
Holland, Charlie 20, 72, 73
Huddersfield Road Club 244
Il Diario Vasco 303–4

Indurain, Miguel 66, 68
Inman, Bob 339
Intimate Portrait of the Tour de France, An 309
Isle of Man Week 14, 18–25, 50, 100, 272, 380
Isle of Man Examiner 19

Janssen, Jan 371
Jones, Stan 241
Jordan, Eileen 293–4
Joy, Ken 284, 285, 346
Joyous Cycling 87

Kafka, Franz 123–4, 126
Kain, Jimmy 56, 57, 58–9
Keen, Peter 358
Kelly, Sean 177, 352, 376
Kemp, Willy 243
Kentish Wheelers 284
Kingston Wheelers 140
Knetemann, Gerri 154
Koblet, Hugo 117, 120, 215–18, 220, 221, 222, 223, 231, 261, 310
Krebs, Fred 241
Kubler, Ferdinand 120, 121, 160, 213, 214, 215, 227–8, 231, 233, 239, 309
'Kuklos' (Wray, Fitzwater) 86

L'Auto 103
L'Equipe 103, 147, 214, 257, 299, 303, 319
L'Humanité 249, 257
Laidlaw, Ken 245

Lancashire Road Club 140
Land's End–John O'Groats 28, 276–8, 279, 280, 287, 289–90
Land's End–London 286
Laugh with Burman 9
Laurédi, Nello 224, 225
Lazarides, Apo 103–4, 159–60, 237
Lazarides, Lucien 237, 243
Le Parisien 103
Le Vélo 186
LeBlanc, Jean-Marie 55
Leducq, André 196
Leeson, John 89, 93–4
Legnano 113, 118
Lemond, Greg 66, 67, 361, 362
Les Sports 182
Lewis, Colin 372, 373
Liège–Bastogne–Liège 164, 171, 174–83
Liverpool–Edinburgh 286
Locatelli, Giulia Occhini 310–13, 319
London–Birmingham 280
London–York 279–80
Longland, Glenn 340
Lotus 358
Luxembourg-International team 232–3, 236–7, 241, 245

Madonna del Ghisallo 166
Maes, Sylvère 65, 159
Magne, Antonin 105, 107, 108, 210
Magni, Fiorenzo 121, 212, 213, 316

Mahe, François 222
Maitland, Bob 241–2, 346
Malléjac, Jean 222, 230–1, 238
Manchester Clarion 339
Manchester Wheelers 140
Manor Abbey stadium, Halesowen 146
Manx Cycling Festival 22–5, 50, 100
Martano, Gianni 107, 108
Maspes, Antonio 145, 261
Memoirs of a Woman of Pleasure (Cleland) 267
Mercian Cycles 153
Merckx, Eddy 66, 67, 99, 128, 163, 166, 167, *173*, 175, 177, 179–82, 361–2, 370, 379
Meridan memorial service 100–1
Mersey Roads Cycling Club 354
Metcalfe, Arthur 372, 373
Middleton Cycling Club 366
Midland Cycling and Athletic Club 20, 72
Midland League of Racing Cyclists 53
Milan–San Remo 91, 128, 141, 164–5, 168, 176, 180 (1907) 306; (1951) 215; (1955) 197; (1964) 370
Milk Race *see* Tour of Britain
Mirando, Joseph 219
Miroir-Sprint 55, 92, 96, 125, 249, 309, 313

Mitchell, Ken 241
Mockridge, Russell 200, 232, 238
Morley Road Club 352
Moser, Aldo 361
Moser, Francesco 166, 167, 361
Motor Institute Research Station 358
Mussolini, Benito 164–5

National Clarion Centenary 47
National Cyclists Union 20, 49–54, 56, 57, 60
Nencini, Gastone 371
Nolten, Jan 228, 230, 234, 235
North Midlands Division Junior Hill-Climb 367
North Road Cycling Club 334, 335, 344
North Road Hardriders 25 17

O'Donovan, Daniel 152–3
O'Donovan, Gerald 152, 154, 155
O'Donovan, Kevin 152
Obree, Graeme 359, 360, 361
Ockers, Stan 213, 215, 217, 308
Olympic Games 163, 358, 362
  (1948) 140, 141; (1952) 244–5; (1956) 367; (1964) 180; (1984) 294; (2000) 138
omnium 261–2
Orford, Dave 60, 61
Ouest team 160, 204, 222

Oxford 324–9
Oxford City Road Club 328
Oxonian Cycling Club 328

Pangbourne Lane 40
Pantani, Marco 68
Parc des Princes 230–1, 247, 260–3, 320
Paris–Brest–Paris 164
Paris–Nice 97, 103, 104, 180, 241
  (1955) 197; (1957) 362
Paris–Roubaix 164, 168, 184–9, 191
  (1950) 128, 301; (1951) 215; (1955) *297*, 300, 301
Paris–San Remo (1957) 245
Patterson, Frank 81–6, 258, 379
PCF (Parti communiste français) 252–3, 254, 257
Peeters, Ludo 183
Pélissier, Charles 105, 322
Pélissier, François 319, 322
Pélissier, Henri 322
Perez, Maurice 185, 186
Pevenage, Rudy 183
Picasso, Pablo 254–5, 257
Pingeon, Roger 66
Pius XII, Pope 166
Plattner, Oscar 145
Poole, Dick 276, 278, 280
Portarlington Swifts 338
Post, Peter 155
Poulidor, Raymond 321, 371
Price, Albert 52
Pusey, Bernard 241

Raas, Jan 154
'Ragged Staff' (Rex Coley) 87
Raleigh *see also* TI Raleigh 132,
    141, 142, 144, 154
Rann Trailer 92
Rapha-Geminiani team 369
Reynolds, Tessie 293
Riis, Bjarne 68
Rimmington, Susie 294–5
Ritter, Ole 362
Rivière, Roger 362, 371
Road Records Association 50
Road Time Trials Council 50,
    293–4, 349
Robic, Jean *156*, 160–1, 163,
    204, 212, 217, 221, 222,
    224, 228, 243, 310
Robinson, Brian 200, *240*, 241,
    242, 243, 244–5, 247,
    299, 369
Robinson, Desmond 244–5
Roche, Stephen 148, 149, 376
Rolland, Antonin 224, 231, 233
Ronde van Vlaanderen (Tour of
    Flanders) 164, 168–72,
    174, 175, 180, 303, 304
    (1905) 306; (1961) 370;
    (1969) 180, 181
Ronis, Willi 309
Rosslyn Ladies Cycling Club
    295–6
Rough Stuff Fellowship 87
RTTC 20, 53, 140, 347
Rugby RCC 338

Salford Park 146
Saracen Road Club 279

Scala Wheelers 367, 369
Schotte, Brik 193
Scodeller, Gilbert 301
Second World War 85, 99–100,
    103–4, 117, 120–2,
    135–6, 139, 202, 232,
    247–54, 336
Sheridan, Eileen 280, 282–90,
    292, 294
Sheridan, Ken 282, 283
Sheil, Norman 339
Simpson, Helen 369, 370
Simpson, Tom *13*, 19, 25, 27,
    61, 73, 74, 152, 167–8,
    237, 245, 363, 365–74
Skibby, Jesper 184
Soens, Eddie 358
Solihull Cycling Club 266
South Bucks Road Club 327–8
Southall, Frank 285, 286, 287,
    288, 289, 290
Southern Counties Cycling
    Union 17
Southern Ladies Road Club
    287
Southern Roads Cycling Club
    23
Sportwereld 303, 304
St Raphael-Geminiani team 256
Stablinski, Jean 186–7
Stallard, Percy *48*, 50–1, 53, 56,
    58, 59
Stancer, George Herbert 84
Stayaert, Karel 303
Steel, Ian 60, 241, 245
Sud-Ouest team 159
'suicide breaks' 178, 370

Sunday in Hell, A 188
Surrey League of Racing Cyclists 54
Sutton, Vic 245
Swerts, Roger 181

taking pace 348
tandems and tricycles 285
Tanners Hatch 40
Taylor, Alec 54, 373–4
Taylor, Jack 92
Teesside Road Club 295
Tesseire, Lucien 161
Thom, Bob 59
Thom, Jeannie 59
Thomas, Dylan 272
Thomson, George 268–72
Through the Looking Glass 327
time trials:
Anfield 24 Hours 14; Athletes
    Hour 360–1, 362; Bath
    Road 100 14, 40, 344–5,
    346; Best British All-
    Rounder (BBAR) 336–7,
    351; codification of 334–8;
    dangers of 348–9; decline
    of British 333–4, 342;
    falling asleep in 286,
    287–8, 290; 50-mile 351;
    first of the year 17; history
    of British 329–31; Hour
    22, 120–1, 316, 358, 358,
    359–62; Land's End–John
    O'Groats 28; National 25-
    mile Championship 333,
    347; 100 285–6, 351;
    Otmoor 10-mile 327–8;
Oxford 326–7; road deaths
    334, 349; set dates of 14;
    Solihull Invitation 25-mile
    14; 10-mile 328–9, 354;
    Tour de France 230, 231,
    318; training 326–7; tri
    bars and 362; 12 283, 329,
    354–5; 25-mile 9, 23, 28,
    333, 338–40, 351, 367; 24
    hour 353–4; 24 Hour
    Fellowship 353–4; village
    halls and 329–31, 379
TI Raleigh 155, 157
Tour de France 11, 28, 47, 62,
    98–9, 106, 111
  anti-clockwise 222; birth of
    65; British cyclists in 72–3,
    241–2, 244–5; camp
    followers 311–14; climbs
    234–5; directeur de la
    course 55, 210; doctors
    239, 372–4; drug use 8,
    79, 237, 239, 255, 321,
    323, 362, 363, 365–74;
    fitness required 191; French
    nationalism and post-war
    renaissance of 158–61;
    French national team 105,
    159, 201, 203, 207, 224,
    322; heat 237–9; hill
    climbs, introduction of 15,
    65; hypothermia 230;
    injuries and deaths 19, 61,
    74, 166, 364–74; maillot
    jaune (yellow jersey);
    management of 319–20;
    'man of the Tour', idea of

Tour de France – *cont*.
204–5, 215, 371; mental
strength and 204–5;
modern period 65;
modernisation 157;
mountain stages 65, 72,
159, 223–1, 236, 237–8,
239, 372, 373, 374; papers
associated with 257; Petit
Tour (1946) 103, 158;
photographs 96–7,
309–11, 313–14; post-
Tour criterium 242–4;
records 67; reflects the
emotions of Fourth
Republic 201; regional
squads 159, 160;
retirements 231, 237–8; as
the sport of rural France
160; team managers 309;
team selection 159; time
trial 230, 231, 318, 362;
trade teams 201; veterans
68; winners 65–9;
year by year: (1923) 323;
(1930) 196; (1931) 210;
(1932) 196; (1934) 105,
107–9, 158, 210, 318;
(1935) 109; (1937) 72–3;
(1938) 192, 196; (1939)
103, 159, 196; (1947) 103,
109, 157, 158–61, 163,
200, 203, 204; (1948) 161,
192, 193–4, 200, 205–6;
(1949) 161, 200, 206;
(1950) 22, 120, 200,
212–15; (1951) 200,
215–21, 222; (1952) 161,
200, 221; (1953) 65, 200,
201, 222–5, 227–31, 238;
(1954) 200, 201, 231, 238;
(1955) 59, 65, 73, 197,
200, 201, 231–9, 241,
245; (1956) 67; (1957) 65,
245, 310, 320; (1958) 245;
(1959) 245; (1960) 245,
362, 371; (1961) 245, 371;
(1962) 201, 371; (1964)
371; (1965) 371; (1966)
66, 371; (1967) 237,
364–74; (1968) 66; (1974)
99; (1975) 65; (1976) 163;
(1980) 67, 155, 157;
(1985) 65; (1987) 148;
(1989) 362; (1994) 166;
(1995) 166; (1996) 68;
(1998) 68
Tour of Britain:
(1951) 60; (1953) 28, 245
Tour of Calvados 241
Tour of Emilia 1941 121
Tour of Europe 1954 245
Tour of Flanders *see* Ronde van
Vlaanderen
Tour of Holland 241
Tour of Lombardy 128, 164,
165–8, 307
(1965) 370
Tour of Piedmont (1939)
116
Tour of Switzerland (1956)
245
Tour of the South-East
Provinces 241

Tour of Tuscany (1941) 121
Tour of Veneto (1941) 121
track racing 14, 147, 136–9,
    144–52, 261
sprint 135–42 *see also under*
    individual event name
Trence, Salvatore 310, 312–13
Turner, John 24–5
Twenty Years A-Growing
    (O'Sullivan) 270–1

Union cycliste internationale
    (UCI) 54
University of Birmingham
    270

Valetti, Giovanni 117
van Est, Wim 228, 233
van Impe, Lucien 163, 327
van Schil, Victor 181–2
Vandenbroucke, Frank 177–9
Vélodrome d'Hiver 247–8,
    260
Vel Vigorelli 22, 121, 122,
    134, 140, 145, 220,
    300
'Veterans Song, The' 89–92
Victor Berlemont Memorial
    Road Race 54
Vienne, Theodore 185, 186
Vietto, René *102*, 104–6,
    107–9, 111, 157, 158,
    161, 203–4
Viking Cycles 59, 278–9
Vlaeminck, Eric de 180
Vlaeminck, Roger de 171–2,
    177, 180–1

Vliet, Arie van 145, 261
Vuelta a España 97, 316
    (1956) 245; (1968) 180

Wadley, J. B. 299, 365
Wagtmans, Wout 228
Waiting for Godot (Beckett)
    248, 249
Walkowiak, Roger 67
Warwickshire Road Club 8,
    266
Warsaw–Berlin–Prague (1952)
    59, 60
'Wayfarer' (Walter McGregor
    Robinson) 87
Weekend Ardennais 182
West Croydon Wheelers 287
What is Socialism (Hyndman/
    Morris) 44
white-line riding 348
Wiggins, Bradley 380
Wild Wales (Borrow) 273
Wilkinson, Andy 28
Wilson, David 93
Wilson, Marguerite 287, 288,
    292–3
Wilson's Cycles 93–4, 96
Wolverhampton RCC 51–2
Wolverhampton Wheelers 52,
    59
Wood, Bevis 241
Woodburn, John 346–7
work miles 29
world amateur road
    championships 50, 141
world amateur sprint
    championships 154

world professional pursuit
    championship 362,
    370
world professional road race
    championship 22, 67, 163,
    166
    (1953) 129, 314; (1954) 202,
    231; (1987) 148
world professional track
    championships 147

Wrentham Hall 41–2, 43
Wright, Orville 149
Wright, Wilbur 149

Yates, Sean 28
York Rally 18
Youth Hostels Association 101

Zoetemelk, Joop 67, 154–5, 157
Zurich Grand Prix 164